On a personal level, *Walking in The Deep End* touched me so deeply. To read about the many traumatic, heart-wrenching events that have been a part of the fabric of your life, and then to read about you emerging triumphantly in the end is so inspiring. I can't begin to tell you the number of times the different people from your life have crept into my mind. . . . I'm so immensely grateful that you broke the pattern set forth by your family and wrote this book. It holds so many life lessons, epitomized not by you telling the reader, but by example through the awareness you've gained as you've lived the very rich life that is yours. . . . It's so exciting to see a yet-undiscovered author as talented as you emerge. . . . You are so incredibly gifted, with an authentic voice and distinct writing style. The way you are able to write so purposefully and so succinctly, yet so poetically at the same time is—to say the very least—quite impressive.

– Elizabeth Day

Walking in the Deep End

Susan Parker

Silver Threads

San Diego, California

Walking in the Deep End, by Susan Parker

For information, contact:

Silver Threads
3930 Valley Centre Drive, PMB 102
San Diego, California 92130
858-794-1597

Silverthreads is an imprint of Silvercat Publishing™

This is a work of non-fiction. The events and experiences are all true and have been faithfully rendered as I have remembered them to the best of my ability. I experienced everything that I present in this telling, but I have taken minimal liberties to keep the narrative as focused as possible, combining or condensing conversations and some events to best reflect their mood and spirit—rather than a word-for-word documentation. However, my recollections are often painfully sharp, and I have stayed true to this essence. The settings and situations are real although I have changed some names and identifying details of individuals to protect their privacy.

ISBN: 978-0-893067-09-7
LCCN: 2009933432

printed in the United States of America

Acknowledgements

It's impossible to properly thank all who supported me in the writing of this book. Consider this an abbreviation of the many who've listened and coached, believed and hoped.

It begins with my children who bring me great joy and keep me laughing. My love and gratitude for you are overwhelming.

For my sister, mom and step-dad whom I love dearly.

To the memory of my father, grandparents, aunts, uncle and cousin; and to the memory of my friends, Debbie Chips, Daniel Romero and Kathie Rostas.

For Jodi Baron, the best and most forgiving friend anyone could have.

For Julie Naughton, MJ Smith, and Alina Zakrocki. You gave me the courage and support to go on in those days of turmoil and re-discovery.

For Laura Brabander, Cheryl Brown, Maggie Cannon, Laura Giordano, Stefanie Griffith, Pam Kutner, Donna Murphy, Gail McClurg, Pat Neal, Tim Regan, Annette Robinson, Laurie Robinson, Nancy Schlenger, Jo Taper, Carol Tirbaso and Sally Tristan, for your love and support in the long days between all of the many re-writes of this book.

For my "family" in Spain, including: Dolores, Larry and Chickie Lukecart; Carmen Marcelo; Maria Luisa Marroquí; Virginia and Clara Pascual; and Rosario, Magüi, Adolfo, and Fito Romero. You gave me life and a second home.

For Brian Sorge, your loving support and friendship mean so much.

For Leslie Hector, one of the most supportive and generous people I've ever known.

For Grace Moore, for being one of the biggest hearts on the planet.

For DaRhonda Williams, for telling me to write this book and challenging me to *Stand*.

For Diane Butler, Candace Chellew-Hodge, Mark Clements, Elizabeth Day, Crystal Dunn, Tony Diaz, Miriam Frank, Wayne Irwin, Angela Martin, Cristina Martinez, Rosanna Moreno, Earl Pike, Paty Popovich, Rob Raasch, Ali Russell, Angie Underwood, John Westfield, and Carol Wyatt for your talent, insights and help in making this book a reality.

For those whom I have loved and who have loved me, including my ex-husband who continues to be my friend.

For "Charlotte" who shared so much and unburied me with her questions and kindness.

For so many others who've offered an encouraging word and more.

Lastly, for those at Silver Threads who made this book a reality, including, my brilliant editor, who has become my dear friend, Peggy Lang, who never stopped believing in me as she pushed, challenged and instructed me to keep writing and re-writing. For Bob Goodman, who took a chance on this book and on me. To all of you and more, who *cared*. I stand in awe and gratitude.

Part One

The Deep End

One

Daddy Duty

WHENEVER I LET MYSELF REMEMBER that Sunday before my eleventh birthday, I see my father's hands. They fidgeted with his tie, then his hat. He was about to run; I could feel it. The churchgoers at St. Timothy's had probably never seen anyone bolt for the door during Mass, though many probably wanted to do just that. Dad and I stood in the back of the auditorium that served as a weekend church. Mom sat in the third row with my six-year-old sister, Ann. They had found the last of the folding chairs, while I'd stayed with Dad as he parked the car. I didn't envy them being so close to the front—it was too hard to daydream up there.

Squirmy in the uncomfortable dress Mom insisted I wear, I tried hard to focus on the *Lord-Be-With-You* part. Concentrating was difficult, not only because this was the weekend of my eleventh birthday and I was dreaming of presents and celebrating with my visiting grandmother, but I also had to keep my eye on my father, home from the hospital on one of the visits they allowed every other weekend. The Northern Virginia Mental Health Institute. *A mental hospital.* No one told me exactly what he'd done three months earlier to be taken there in such a rush, but even as an almost-eleven-year-old, I'd known he wasn't acting right and that something needed to be done. I did know about *some* things. In the months leading up to his stay in the hospital I'd watched and listened.

The fact that the grown-ups were *not* talking about the way my dad had grown increasingly distant had made me pause in the hall, alert whenever Mom talked on the phone or tried to reason with

Dad. I wanted to understand how this new version of my father had replaced the one who told corny jokes and offered me pocket change for baseball cards and candy. His vacant eyes left me wondering whether he still cared about his family—or about me.

That Sunday, I turned the thin, wrinkled pages of my Misselette, but I watched him. His right leg was shaking to a rhythm faster than my heartbeat. Even though Father Joe hurried through the Mass, it was still too long for Dad. He made huffing noises and cleared his throat constantly as he rocked back and forth, glancing at the exit, his watch, and then the exit again. People glared at us. I looked away, embarrassed, only to see an older kid in sixth grade snickering at me, a bully named Harold. I begged God to keep Dad from doing something really weird.

"Do you want to sit in the car with me and wait?" I whispered to him.

He didn't reply, but turned and then followed me, sighing as though walking was so *very* hard to do. As we slipped past our fellow parishioners, Harold tried to trip me, but I swerved aside in time, and then continued on out the door of the drab brick building that tomorrow would go back to being London Towne Elementary School. It fit right in with the houses that sat like boxes on identical square lots in our new neighborhood in the Virginia suburbs of Washington D.C., which I still couldn't think of as home.

Home to me was a two-story, wood-and-brick house in a tree-lined Cleveland neighborhood, where playing ball with the gang was no big deal even for a girl. Mom had said Dad would be so much happier at his job in Washington D.C., however, so I didn't kick and scream about the move. I would have agreed to just about anything that could make Dad turn back into his old self, but he hadn't improved at all in his new surroundings. He was much worse, and I felt lied to. It was a sickening feeling, as if the earth beneath our house were turning to mud.

Discovering what was really true about my Dad would be entirely up to me, and I became hyper-vigilant. I took my "daddy duty" seriously. What if he did the same thing his sister did, my Aunt Mary Ellen? At almost eleven, I seemed to be the only one considering this horrifying thought.

After exiting the auditorium, I stepped over crumbling pavement in the parking lot, trying to avoid the puddles from a rain that wouldn't let up. I watched Dad more than where I was stepping, and my shoes got wet. *Darn it.* He seemed stiff when he walked, arms hanging straight at his sides. When we finally reached our four-year-old, aqua-blue boat of a car, a '68 Chevy Biscayne, my jacket was soaked. I opened the passenger door and slid along the blue, vinyl front-bench seat while Dad folded his tall frame into the car behind the wheel. We both shut our doors and sat in silence, staring at the rainy windshield. The cold seat still smelled of my mother's sweet perfume.

We waited. Not just for Mom and Ann to return to the car. We both knew something bad was going to happen.

It was hard to think about him at that place where they kept the people no one knew what to do with, the crazy people. Sometimes I pretended he was traveling on business, so his home visits seemed more normal.

We sat there. I fidgeted almost as much as he did. I looked down at my fingernails edged with a thin line of dirt from yesterday's ball game, a game in which the neighborhood boys only grudgingly allowed me to play. Dad's hands kept up a constant motion, fiddling with his glasses, scratching his head, smoothing down his pants for the second and third times. I tapped idly on the aqua-blue dashboard and stared at a raindrop that traveled in a squiggly line down the side of the window. Dad stared straight ahead. I squinted at the clock. That red second hand silently ticked the moments away in tiny increments. I thought about my birthday again, hoping I'd get money to buy some new collectible cards from the latest catalog.

"Boy, I sure hope the Indians get some pitching this year, don't you?" I asked.

"Uh-huh."

"Yeah, 'cuz Gaylord Perry can't be expected to carry the whole staff, ya know?"

"Yeah, that's true."

As we sat there, I remained passionate in my loyalty to the Cleveland Indians—Washington didn't even have a team at the time—and chattered on about them and my card collection. Baseball cards were better than Kennedy half-dollars. I thought about the shiny pictures of Buddy Bell and Charlie Spikes and recited from memory the statistics printed on the rough, cardboard flip side. Dad's eyes told me my jabbering barely registered. His body followed his muddled mind to a location that might as well be underwater. He just stared straight ahead at nothing I could see. I knew where he was: down in the deep end—the one grown-ups always said people had gone off of.

"Do you want me to put on the radio?"

As he shook his head, I noticed that his left leg hadn't stopped bouncing up and down.

"I'm really looking forward to dinner with Grandma, aren't you?" I said to break the silence and stop the screaming in my head.

No answer.

"She makes the best chicken and dumplings in the world." I drew a smiley-face with my fingertip on the moisture of the car window, wishing I could blink my eyes like Samantha on *Bewitched* and return to happier days in Ohio.

"Dad, you wanna play Tic-Tac-Toe? Look here, I can draw it on the window."

More silence. Having covered baseball, Grandma's food, and drawing, I ran out of things to talk about and went back to daydreaming. Finally, Ann and Mom emerged from church.

"There they are," I told him, relieved to know Mom would soon spell me off. A break from Daddy duty and a possible return to thoughts of my birthday, if only for a few minutes. While Mom's presence would help temporarily, I knew nothing could fully distract me from the dark cloud engulfing Dad. My weekend birthday plans were veering out of control the way my bicycle did when the front tire got caught in the space between the grass and the pavement; the bike steering me instead of me steering it.

Without a word, Dad started the engine, put the car in gear, and drove toward Mom and Ann. I watched them push against the driving rain, hand in hand, as they stepped over puddles and put their shoulders to the wind.

I jumped out of the car and hopped into the back, making sure to help my sweet sister climb in.

"Thanks for the ride, handsome," Mom said as she climbed into the front seat. She reached over and brushed his cheek with the back of her hand. Dad made a sound that was more like a throat clearing than a reply.

Her flirtation startled me because it was new; I hadn't remembered ever seeing any public displays of affection from either of them. Maybe Mom gave it a try, hoping it would help her pretend things weren't so bad, the reality of the situation buried under a veneer of platitudes and compliments. She could keep living in her parallel universe where the new job and the move were great ideas on her part.

Dad hit the accelerator before we were settled into our seats, and my sister and I lurched forward. The ride smoothed out until the next intersection, a stop sign we would have ploughed through if Mom hadn't told Dad to stop... *Stop!*

Was I the only one who thought it was odd for a mental patient to be driving us all over town?

We drove through the rain along a country road dotted with orange construction barrels, riding along without any of the usual mindless chatter that was supposed to make us forget that Dad was visiting us from the PsychwardLooneyBinMentalCasePlace. Mom reminded Dad that we needed to go to the pharmacy for his sleeping pills. We traveled on for five minutes until we neared another red brick complex of boxes, a shopping plaza where People's Drugstore was located. People? What people? It was such an odd name to me.

Stores in suburban D.C. didn't have real people behind the counters the way Cleveland stores did. In Cleveland, Mr. Fitch ran Fitch's

Drug Store. We had Alesci's Food, Rini's Grocery, Lenny's Deli, and Bill's Barbershop. I felt safer and more connected there. People seemed glad to know each other and to be proud of where they came from. I missed it terribly. All the Cleveland jokes ever unleashed— Cleveland, the mistake by the lake—couldn't erase the beauty and expanse of Lake Erie, the tenth largest in the world. As Dad poked along through Washington traffic, I pictured Erie in the dead of winter, its waters frozen into solid chunks of ice, layers of moist, white snow crunching under my boots, my tongue out to catch the swirling snowflakes. I remembered the trees along the still shore, sprinkled with a white lace; thinking about my hometown took my spirit to a place where I'd much rather be.

Washington felt strange in so many ways, yet I was grateful for the gift of anonymity that Food Giant and Kid's Cuts gave us that year. My dad acted so strangely and lost so much weight that his six-foot, two-inch frame didn't seem so tall anymore, as if his body weight had been replaced by the weight of the world.

I was anxious to get home to my grandma and presents, irritated that we had to stop at the pharmacy for his medicine. Dad maneuvered the car into the parking lot of People's and mom directed him to a spot close to the entrance. He exhaled as he put the car in park and cut the engine.

"Can I buy candy?" Ann asked.

"Not today, Sweetie." Mom answered as she opened her door and told Dad to open his. All four of us trudged through the parking lot and into the store, following Mom to the back. When we arrived at the pharmacy window, I glanced over at Dad. He didn't say a word but stared straight ahead with his hands at his sides.

Mom asked me to watch Ann and then turned to Dad. "Dick, why don't you go ahead and take a seat?" Mom said to him. I hated it when she called him "Dick." Why couldn't she call him Rich or Richard or Melvin, for that matter? Anything, but D-I-C-K! Didn't people her age know what that meant?

He slumped into the waiting chair like an irritable kid. Almost immediately, his right knee shook and his left foot danced a complementary shuffle.

At least he has on matching socks today.

Mom directed her attention to the pharmacist and asked for Dad's prescription. He replied after checking on our order. "Ma'am, I'm sorry to have to tell ya'll this, but the delivery truck didn't make it in on Friday. All I can give you is half of his prescription. If you can come back tomorrow afternoon, I'm sure we'll have the rest by then."

"Fine." Prescription paid for, Mom said, "C'mon kids, let's go."

As we headed for the door, Dad's hair was sticking up from all the scratching and fidgeting he had done during the wait. I hoped no one from school would see us as we walked through the parking lot toward our car. Dad mumbled to himself as he arrived at the driver side door. I looked around to see if anyone was watching. Nobody was, thank goodness. *Why can't Mom drive?* We got in the car and waited as Dad fumbled to put the key in the ignition. *Why can't our family just be normal?*

Dad muttered nearly the whole way home, "What could I have done? I should have known she was so upset. Why did she do it?"

I remembered hearing him say the same thing the previous night while he paced the floors of his bedroom. The pacing had been going on nearly the whole time we'd been living in Centreville. At first, I wasn't sure why he couldn't sleep, and I worked up the courage to ask Mom about it weeks earlier. She explained that he was nervous about his new job and feeling guilty about things that had happened to his family. Okay, uh-huh...but then I couldn't understand why he no longer seemed to care about me the way I cared about him. *Step on a crack, break your mother's back.* I never stepped on even one, in case that would somehow hurt either Mom or Dad in some way. Not only that, I tried to think of just the right words to say to God in my prayers so He'd swoop in and help us. So far, God was as invisible as ever, and it was up to me to keep an eye on Dad.

My father was forty-one. On some level, I knew our family's secrets had driven him to act this way. I had yet to learn all the stories about his family, but I knew the nice way everyone talked had nothing to do with a terrible *something* that took him down—something that started inside the mind and that neither God nor the doctors at the mental hospital could yet fix.

Two

Bathwater

GRANDMA MARIE WAITED IN OUR home while we continued on our never-ending stop-lurch-crawl from St. Timothy's, to People's, and back home. Grandma was Lutheran, not Catholic, so rather than attend Mass, she'd sing a hymn and make my birthday supper. *Lucky her.*

I pictured her sipping coffee while punching dough, hacking chicken parts, beating egg whites, and committing other acts of kitchen violence—a sturdy matron, humming among the pots and pans, creating heavenly smells and flavors in my honor. Grandma always looked on the bright side of things; doing anything else was a waste of time, she'd said. Whenever she entered a room she was in search of the good conversation, the story, and the laugh. Mischief flashed in her blue-green eyes, and she greeted everyone warmly. Although it was 1972, she still wore her white hair in a style from the 1940s. Her tall frame allowed the athletic ease of a younger person. She'd played softball and had been a good bowler; now in her sixties, she said she still felt good enough to perform the Dance of the Seven Veils. Whatever that was, I didn't want to know.

Normally, I was grateful for her cheer, but I was beginning to see that her positive strength had another side to it. When she arrived the day before, Dad didn't cater to her like he usually did. Worse, he became agitated and staggered away from the dinner table when she made sunny comments about our home. In the past, he'd seemed happy to see her. As long as I could remember, it seemed he believed pleasing her was a million times more important than other priorities.

Once, back in Cleveland, we'd all gone to an Italian restaurant with Grandma, Dad's older sister Aunt Nora, and Nora's five kids. We made the twenty-minute drive in three separate cars, settled in, and ordered our drinks. Only then did Grandma decide pizza wasn't what she wanted, the was chair uncomfortable, and the place was unclean. She let Dad know, and before we could sip our sodas, he rounded us out of our chairs and into the car for a trip to Miller's—her favorite—where Grandma was sure we'd all be happier and more comfortable.

In subtle ways, I got the message that Grandma Marie was in charge. The Queen Bee. She was pleasant enough about it; maybe that's why in the past Dad didn't seem to mind tending to her every whim or why his siblings always made sure Grandma was seated in the most comfortable chair and served supper before anyone else.

Grandma once told me she'd learned to hide her fears, believing that people "smelled fear and pounced." She wasn't about to be anyone's victim, and she always let you know what she thought about everything. We all knew she hated Aunt Nora's husband, Uncle Roy, a big, burly man who grunted and demanded things "like a Neanderthal who thinks he's an emperor." More than once, she told me about Roy asking her to run his bathwater the night she came over to help Nora with her first newborn.

"I told his sorry self that it'd be a *cold day in hell before I ever ran him a bath*! Then I told him I liked my toast lightly buttered, thank you very much. You should have seen the look on his face!" She slapped her knee and laughed at the memory of her defiance.

Her first husband, James, my dad's father and my grandpa, had been the only person who could rattle her. He did more than rattle the whole family. He gambled and drank incessantly. He also slept with a loaded pistol under his pillow. Staggering home from a "date with the ponies," he'd complain about the jockey and the various conspiracies that kept him losing. "I'll kill him; I tell you, I saw the bony bastard rounding the final turn, holding that horse back. He thinks I don't know what he did? Where's my damn gun? I tell ya, he needs to get his due so he never sticks it to me like this again."

Grandma soothed him with soft words. "I know, dear, just settle down and get some rest and we'll talk in the morning." Her resolve was firm as she led him off to bed. Then she slipped the gun from under the pillow and put it in the night stand drawer. By morning, his anger had dissipated, and his overnight alchemy had cooked up new optimism about his luck at the track. He was penniless by the time he'd had enough of the short horse racing season in Cleveland and determined to make his fortunes at the tracks in Florida. In the summer of 1938, he mounted his motorcycle, promised to return with riches for Grandma and his two daughters and his seven-year-old son—my dad—and roared off toward the south. They didn't hear from my grandfather again for thirty years. No one dealt with the feelings of the children, and Dad never discussed growing up fatherless.

At least that gun was out of the house. Grandma searched for ways to feed her children and pay the bills. She mended clothes, cleaned houses, and cut hair. Eventually she landed a job as a live-in maid with a wealthy family who asked her to move in because they liked her light-heartedness and thought her daughters would be good company for their own daughter. Grandma worried that having an eight-year-old son might hurt her chances, so she didn't mention my dad. Only his sisters, Nora and Mary Ellen, were deemed assets worthy of inclusion.

Grandma sent my dad to live with his paternal grandmother— the mother of the drunken gambler who deserted his family—and picked him up on Sunday afternoons for visits at the park. She promised him it wouldn't be for long. But that wasn't true.

While children are expected to accept the logic of adults, on some deeper level, they absorb the reality of adult actions. His mother had no problem keeping his sisters, but he must have gotten the message that he was somewhat expendable. What hurt and fear did he learn to hide away then? He probably tried his hardest to please Grandma Marie on her short visits so that she'd love him and remember her promise. He dared not have a tantrum or act out. He could never be himself or be at ease. His only option was to be perfect. Always.

No one talked to him about his fears and feelings. No one talked to Nora and Mary Ellen about how they felt about their mother giving their brother away to someone else.

Two and a half years later, Grandma found a new job as a daytime maid for another well-to-do family and finally sent for my father. She didn't apologize to him for the separation, nor did she allow anyone to spend a whole lot of time asking about it.

Dad and his sisters had no way of knowing that by the time Grandma had found her second job and sent for my father, she'd been having an affair with her employer, the man whose floors she swept and beds she made. *Gerry*. She kept it secret, even when she became pregnant in the early months of 1947. Rather than face their families, she and Gerry decided to hide the child growing inside her beneath excuses and her baggy clothes.

The world didn't recognize Uncle Art on his birthday because Grandma never announced his birth. No celebrations, no new blue crocheted outfits or warm wishes. Just a hidden existence, thanks to parents who told no one he'd been conceived. There would be no great celebration in his family, only hurried plans and hushed voices as Grandma and Gerry immediately sent him away to be raised by a woman they'd hired who lived in the country. When he was old enough for school, they sent him to a military academy in Indiana. Amazingly, no one in the family had any idea of his existence for *thirteen years*.

Even after Gerry divorced his wife and married Grandma, they still chose to keep Art's birth a secret. When I first heard the story from my mother, I was about ten. I was shocked that Grandma was capable of such a thing. Maybe Gerry had convinced her that a secret was safer than the truth, that his ex-wife would challenge the divorce settlement and they'd lose everything. Whatever the reason, the truth was submerged into Grandma's river of secrets. Some twenty-five years later, when I was about to turn eleven, it threatened to overflow into our suburban Washington home.

After what seemed like forever, our drive finally ended. I opened the door before we came to a full stop, tearing inside to see Grandma. I could hardly contain myself and nearly ripped open my presents right then and there. Grandma calmed me down. "Now, just hold on. Supper isn't quite ready, so why don't you go change your clothes and come back downstairs to visit?"

I ran up to my room, spent a few minutes going through my baseball cards, carefully selected only the best ones to show Grandma, then changed into a pair of tan corduroys and a brown sweater. A quick check in the mirror to smooth down my hair. I passed my parent's bedroom and heard only the murmur of their conversation. Mom was on duty now, and I was free to talk with Grandma—who was actually interested in my baseball cards.

Within the hour, we sat down to supper. Grandma seemed pleased that I relished her cooking. At first, Mom was especially animated in that way that I knew meant she was trying to downplay her sadness. She clinked her silverware on her white china plate, stopped and smiled on cue, and went back to her clinking. As the meal progressed, she didn't say much, probably glad to have another adult relieve her of talking with Ann and me. Grandma asked us about school and our new friends. Ann started talking and soon she was dancing some new steps she'd choreographed just for Grandma. And my father? He stared at his meal like it was mere scenery.

When we'd had our fill of chicken and dumplings, Grandma brought my birthday cake into the dining room. Mom lit eleven candles. So far, so good. Dad was still okay, and I knew he'd return to the safety of the hospital early the next morning.

Mom, Grandma and Ann sang the HappyBirthdaySong. Dad joined in near the end, when he half whispered, half sang "Dear Susan" before he went back to the world in his head.

Although Dad wasn't hungry for dessert, the rest of us devoured chocolate cake and ice cream. Food always helped everything feel better for me—especially if chocolate was involved. Ann laughed when I accidentally brushed frosting on the tip of my nose. I wiped it off and giggled, forgetting my worries for a short few moments. Afterwards, I ripped into a stack of presents and was pleased to find plenty of cash and baseball cards. *Not bad, not bad at all.*

Grandma told a funny story, but Dad coughed, got up, and staggered a circle from the dining room, through the kitchen, and back again. Grandma ignored him as though he were a misbehaving two-year-old. Dad huffed loudly and then scratched his forearm. His eyes darted around the room. He looked irritated. *Did he even LIKE his mother anymore?*

I hoped that Grandma and my mother would talk about making sure Dad didn't hurt himself, but adults had this way of beating around the bush. They said simple enough things, but hidden meanings made them react in ways I could *not* understand.

"You know, Jean," Grandma said to my mother, "Arthur is doing very well. He's begun a new job here in Washington."

Mom nodded. "That's good to hear."

"Yes, and I'm planning to go see him and celebrate an early Christmas with him when I leave here."

Uncle Art was living in Washington? I wondered why we hadn't invited him to my birthday party. Dad didn't say a word; instead, he turned and circled back around into the kitchen, as if the sound of Art's name was more than he could bear.

❧

I'd always wondered about the funny look on his face at the mention of his half-brother, my Uncle Art. There was so much that I didn't know then that weighed on the events of that night. Though I didn't learn about them until later in life when I needed to understand my family, this particular history proved especially mind-boggling. I wanted to learn more about the secrecy around Art's birth and probed family history. "How did Dad find out about him?" I asked Mom.

"It was odd," she said thoughtfully. "Back in 1960, your dad and I were at Grandma's house just a few months before our wedding. Aunt Mary Ellen and Aunt Nora were there too. We were sitting at the kitchen table, and your dad was in the living room watching TV, I think. Out of the blue, your grandma asks me if 'Art' is going to be in the wedding party. 'Art?' I say. 'Who's that?' Then she looked at me like she was telling me her address and said, 'He's your fiancé's brother.'"

This stunned me. "Well, how does a person . . .? How could she just not ever mention . . .?"

"Yeah, isn't that somethin'?" Mom continued, "I was in shock, and so were Mary Ellen and Nora. Eventually they started questioning her, but at first, you could have heard a pin drop."

Mom said my father had walked in during the conversation that day. He acted as if he'd overheard someone saying that the neighbor's dog had puppies rather than he'd had a thirteen-year-old brother hidden away until that moment. Mom didn't know what to do except go along with Grandma's nonchalant attitude. Everyone played along with Grandma's world of The Unquestioned. My parents made plans for Art to be in the wedding party, as if his hidden existence had been *no big deal*. Grandma probably thought she'd handled the situation admirably. No need to fuss over things.

If Dad and my aunts didn't fuss, however, others did. The rumors spread through the neighborhood that Mary Ellen, not Grandma, was Art's real mother. When Art was brought out of hiding, Mary Ellen was thirty years old and unmarried. People realized she would have been seventeen when Art was born. The gossip-fueled commotion caught her completely off-guard. The rumor humiliated Grandma's own daughter, yet Grandma took not a single step out of her way to set the record straight.

"People believe what they want to believe," she said. And in typical Grandma Fashion, that settled that.

Only it didn't settle anything at all. Mary Ellen had fumed and soured. Growing up, I'd sensed that something important inside Aunt Mary Ellen had gotten lost at some point. Grandma's default betrayal offered a possible explanation. And Uncle Art? If being abandoned for two and a half years scarred my father, how traumatic must this whole mess have been for thirteen-year-old Art, the "shame child" hidden from the rest of the world?

Mom went on about the first time she met Art at the wedding rehearsal. "I drove my parents to St. Felicitas—your dad and the rest of the wedding party planned to meet us there. The bridesmaids showed up on time, and your Dad did too. Most of his friends were late because they were coming from the other side of town. Grandma Marie, the last one there, brought Art with her and introduced him as *her youngest son, Arthur.*" Mom gazed off, as if seeing a mental replay of that day. "I just said *hello,* shook his hand, he congratulated me. That was it."

"What did he look like?" I asked.

"He was handsome, with sandy hair and blue eyes."

A picture of Uncle Art holding me when I was a baby hung in a hallway somewhere. My dark, curly hair was sticking out of a silly-looking sunbonnet. Uncle Art cradled me awkwardly as we both reclined on a lounge chair in a backyard I didn't recognize. He looked about fourteen or fifteen, handsome—as Mom had said—with slicked back hair and expensive-looking clothes for a teenager. I thought of my uncle as the unfinished sentence of the family.

"Well, you know Art, he...well...I dunno...."

❧

My family's unacknowledged conspiracy of keeping up appearances created a massive dam of omissions, memory loss, dismissive shrugs, and lies that had taken generations to build. Eventually the truth would ooze out, drowning some and isolating others on islands of guilt and shame—this toxic overflow that was my bathwater.

Three

Aunt Mary Ellen

I WAS BEGINNING TO THINK my dad would get through this weekend without anything terrible happening. Ann and I helped Mom and Grandma clean up the kitchen while Dad took a nap in his brown, leatherette *Lazy Boy* in the adjoining family room. Mom whispered something to Grandma about how he liked to sleep during the day and pace at night. She was no doubt hoping the sleeping pills might help solve that problem. Grandma nodded, as if pacing and pills were the most normal of things.

I wiped down the kitchen table and watched Dad's skinny chest heave up and down, his ribs protruding through his knit golf shirt. I was sure dad's depressive descent had everything to do with an event I knew more about than anyone guessed. Another Big Family Secret that had happened four years earlier and affected everyone profoundly, but stayed hidden under still more *SHUSH-ing*. Dad's sister Mary Ellen had survived something awful.

It happened during the evening hours one Wednesday in 1968. Mary Ellen walked to her car after viewing an exhibition at the Cleveland Museum of Art. A middle-aged black man approached her saying he needed a ride back home to his kids, because he was worried about them, especially since they were alone, their mother having died earlier in the year.

Mary Ellen trusted him. She was a compassionate and thinking person who knew better than others in her family; people were people, no matter what their skin color—of this she was sure. I still remember my aunt's adamant defense of the poor and the oppressed. She seemed independent and headstrong. Before that night.

Maybe a click went off in her brain when he climbed into her car, muttering something about the luck of it all. He thanked her as they reached his street corner, right by the park.

Before she knew what was happening, he dragged her out of her car toward the woods. He wrenched the crook of his arm around her neck and bent her left hand behind her back. I could only imagine the agony when he pushed her into the ground and held her. She later talked about the smell of the earth mixed with the faint odor of alcohol on his breath.

When he finished with her, he told her she was the dumbest bitch he'd ever met. "I hope your momma doesn't have any more stupid daughters, 'cuz if she does, they'll probably fall for the same shit you just did."

Since they so often avoided even the most mildly uncomfortable topics, I knew that anyone in the family reacting to this devastation would probably have done little more than give Mary Ellen a critical look for helping a "Negro" or, at best, a *there-there* pat. The word *rape* was probably never mentioned, the trauma never discussed. Two years later, she still suffered from the memories and the silence, old feelings buried under words of outrage never spoken. My dad was, no doubt, as silent as everyone else when it happened, but by the time we lived in Centreville, he mumbled about Mary Ellen, her attack and what happened afterwards, these thoughts all part of the murky mess of regret his mind navigated obsessively.

Mary Ellen's "nerves" prevented her from holding down a job, so she moved in with Grandma Marie, then a widow after Gerry's death. Grandma thought it might provide the opportunity to help Mary Ellen see the brighter side of things. I had no idea about the full extent of all this until a few years later, but I knew everyone was very guarded around Aunt Mary Ellen. No one wanted to upset her in any way. Far from shielding me from reality, the secrecy around the event powerfully locked the details—the few I did know about—into my mind.

Mom did say that Mary Ellen had never even been close to getting married, as if this hinted at an underlying explanation. Through the years, I noticed that my Aunt Mary Ellen seemed angry, her good humor a thin veneer hiding her pain. The last time I'd seen her was about six months before our move to Washington and about a year prior to Grandma's visit for my birthday. She'd come to our house in Cleveland for Sunday supper. I was finishing up a football game when Mom called me home to say she'd arrived. When I walked through the front door, Ann was already perched on her lap and beaming. My aunt and I greeted one another, and she quickly went back to Ann and their coloring plans.

I was tired of carrying the mantel of the firstborn and was relieved when Aunt Mary Ellen seemed so much more interested in Ann. My aunt knew what it felt like to be the younger sister, how hard it was to try to rekindle the excitement a firstborn enjoys. Maybe that was why she seemed to defend Ann any time we fought. That didn't bother me. I loved my little sister and felt satisfied knowing Aunt Mary Ellen loved her too.

"See how I put two smaller snowmen next to the big one?" Ann asked her.

Mary Ellen looked bored, then caught herself, feigned interest, and patted Ann's back. During a roast beef and mashed potato dinner, she seemed tired and awkwardly distracted as she ate. No one guessed how much torment she continued to feel even three years after the rape. No one asked, and in that family, no one volunteered to talk about it. Talking about things made them real, so there would be no talking. She slipped away without dessert soon after the meal. I don't remember any good-bye, but I heard Mom tell Dad that Mary Ellen seemed sad. She seemed listless and disconnected. I knew something about her then that I knew better than to say to anyone—my aunt didn't care about her life anymore.

After she left that night, Dad, Ann, and I helped Mom with the dishes, Then Dad and I sat in the kitchen nook to draw and paint together, as was our practice on the weekends. He seemed chipper and must have thought his sister was only slightly more withdrawn than usual. I was almost ten and my concern for my aunt had melted away in anticipation of our art session; I couldn't wait to get started. The nook was barely large enough to hold our table and chairs, but it was our sanctuary. I sat down and breathed the smell of the pastels so neatly placed in the white box full of all that color.

Dad leaned over my shoulder. "What ya plannin' to draw, sweets?"

"I dunno, maybe a few horses grazing in the field or a dog lying by the fireplace."

"Well, let me know when you need some help. I'm gonna get started on a sketch for a landscape oil." He seemed as happy as I was to be there. This was my real Daddy.

Twenty minutes later, I asked for help with my quarter horse. He was patient and never made it seem like I was an interruption. "See here, how you can sketch in an oval, like so..." He pointed at the paper, giving detailed suggestions.

He cracked open one of his *Famous Artist* textbooks filled with sketches, paintings, and drawings from artists we discussed and analyzed. I lovingly touched the binding and listened to him tell me about his days at the New York Art Students League, where he once studied under famous artists like Charles Alston, Frank Mason, and Frank J. Reilly.

I saw examples of ways to create fluid lines and movement in my work. If I could have, I would have sat there for days, just drawing with Dad. Art connected us. It plugged us into places where words didn't work and made us happy in a way that seemed natural. I was sure nothing could take that away from us.

"I wish I could draw like Picasso or Dalí," I said. I was only in the fourth grade, but he made me feel so grown-up. "Maybe one day we can go to Spain and see their real paintings."

"Don't forget Velazquez, Goya, and Murillo; Picasso and Dalí are exceptional," he said, "and let's not forget the more traditional artists."

"Like Andrew Wyeth?" I knew he was Dad's favorite.

"Look what he can do with a simple wooden chair and sunlight streaming through a window."

We went on like that for almost two hours, talking about Realism and then Post-Impressionistic artists like Cezanne, Van Gogh, and Gauguin, interspersing discussions about the New York Art Students League and all that he'd learned there. Every now and then, I glanced at his sketch, watching it take shape as he whistled and brushed the charcoal in quick strokes over the canvas. I had no idea that such a moment could be so fragile.

It was nearly bedtime when Ann joined us, digging her fingers into globs of yellow, red, and blue finger-paint that Mom set up for her so she could feel included. Mom didn't have any interest in drawing or painting, but she admired our work and told us how much she looked forward to displaying it on the refrigerator. Mom didn't always encourage Dad's creations though.

Later that week, I came home from school to find Dad home from work early, dressed in jeans and a T-shirt, wearing his painter's apron. Deep in thought, he stared at the wall, holding his palette primed with earth tones.

"Hiya, Sweets, how was your day?" he asked as he dabbed his brush into a swirl of brown.

❧

"Good." I put my books down on the dining room table. "What're ya painting?" Moving closer, I realized he had painted directly onto the dining room wall. *Uh-oh.*

"I'm painting a landscape mural. Like it?"

Removing my coat, I took a closer look. "Yeah, it's nice. Does Mom know?"

"Not yet. I thought I'd surprise her. I think she'll like it, don't you?" he asked.

"Yeah, yeah, I think so." I didn't have the heart to tell him I thought she would hate it. The house was her domain—decorating, a passion of hers.

An hour later, during my homework and Ann's TV time, Mom walked through the door.

"Hi family! It's so g—" She stopped mid-sentence.

Dad looked pleased. "Like it? I thought I'd surprise you!"

"Oh my! Why did you paint directly on the wall? Oh my! Do I like it? Well, if you want my honest answer, no! No, I don't. I mean the painting is nice and all, but I don't want that on the dining room wall! It doesn't go with anything in the house really."

His shoulders slumped. "Well, I like it," he said.

I thought it did go. Then again, maybe she was right. Maybe it was too elegant for the Midwestern, suburban-catalog, early-American look we had going on.

Three days later, they were still arguing about the mural. When I came home from school that day, Mom and Ann were out running errands. Dad came home soon after me, greeted me with a kiss, put down his briefcase, sighed, and went upstairs. He returned in his painting clothes and walked slowly toward the kitchen and down to the basement. In a few minutes, he returned with a silver tray of paint and a paint roller. I glanced around and noticed his art brushes and palette, alone in the corner of the room. He took one last look at the mural, dipped the roller into the tray and rolled a coat of Sherwin-Williams' *Best* over the serene country scene.

⚜

A few weeks later, on a dreary December Saturday, Mary Ellen accompanied Grandma to the West 25th Street market to buy fresh meat and produce. My grandmother must have felt nervous; she always did with Mary Ellen. Talking to my aunt required a mental thesaurus of words that wouldn't offend. Worse yet, if Grandma responded with the wrong facial expression or comment after one of

Mary Ellen's stories or opinions, the possibility of any further conversations that day came to an ice-cold end.

Grandma and Mary Ellen drove down Lorain Avenue with only a smattering of comments about mundane things.

Grandma tried her best. "I'm making chicken paprikash and dumplings. I need to see if we can't find us a freshly plucked chicken along with some vegetables."

Nothing.

"Would you like me to make German chocolate cake for dessert?"

"Sure."

Mary Ellen opened her black handbag and reached for her compact, looking at the lines around her eye. As was her habit, she smoothed down her gray-flecked hair near her temples.

At West 150th Street, their white Chrysler sedan cautiously eased onto I-71 and headed toward downtown. As they exited onto West 25th, Mary Ellen interrupted the silence.

"Stop the car."

⚜

"What does it matter? Just please stop."

Feeling once again that she just could never get it right with Mary Ellen, Grandma agreed. "Okay, dear, just let me make sure there are no cars behind me."

My grandmother checked her rearview mirror and pulled over, leaving the motor running. Mary Ellen placed her purse on the floor and pulled the door latch open.

"Where are you going? The market is at least a mile from here."

"Nowhere."

Mary Ellen calmly swung both feet outside to the pavement. Without a word, she closed the door.

"You don't need any more exercise," Grandma said. "You need to get back into the car so there'll be enough time to cook the paprikash."

Mary Ellen ignored Grandma and walked intently toward the bridge railing.

Did she feel a surge of relief? In later years, I would understand this feeling all too well.

My aunt swung around and, staring through the windshield at her mother, smiled, mouthing the words, *Bye, Mom.*

Grandma screamed as Mary Ellen sailed off the bridge toward the highway below.

At Mary Ellen's funeral, I huddled together with my parents and sister against the strong Ohio wind that blew over the cemetery, looking at the black lacquer finish of her casket that was in the hole that had been dug in the frozen black soil. I wanted to sob at the small, awkward reception at Messiah Lutheran, but overwhelmed with an adult solemnity that felt inauthentic somehow, I watched and listened instead. Mourners made small talk and ate egg-salad sandwiches on crust-less bread while our family pretended that Aunt Mary Ellen had died from something as common as an infectious disease.

꿈

After her death at age forty-one, I found a brief newspaper article and read it over and over. I was horrified although the suicide hadn't completely surprised me. I had known that my aunt was just *done* with this thing called life. Although I didn't understand everything about *why,* I remembered the tired look on her face the last time we spoke.

I tried not to imagine what that face must have looked like splattered on the interstate, her kind exterior mixed with her angry core.

My father uttered not a word during the reception. Even weeks later, he sat in a chair with his head in his hands, still refusing to share his grief. Christmas was grim that year, and we never spoke of my aunt after that. Mary Ellen became "the person who never was," while life for the rest of us careened on.

Mary Ellen took her life and with it, much of my father's interest in art. I don't recall ever sitting with him in the kitchen nook for art sessions after that. Her death changed him. He looked different, spoke differently, and read different books. His "thinking overload" turned his silence into an alarm in my head. The only thing that seemed to matter to my Dad was alleviating the pain and guilt he felt as a result of Mary Ellen's death. I began to study my father as he tried to make sense of it all, instinctively sensing that what lay ahead could harm us both.

Over the next year, Dad's depression intensified. Someone besides his nearly eleven-year-old daughter should have considered whether or not he might do the same thing as his beloved sister, but until that happened, I would remain vigilant.

Four

King of the Mountain

DAD CONTINUED TO SNOOZE IN his chair, and I sat on the floor nearby, working on the "birthday" puzzle my mom's sister, Aunt Joy, had sent me. I was still feeling relieved that nothing bad had happened. Soon Mom would cart Dad back to the hospital. I wished Mary Beth could be here to help with this puzzle. We'd invited my new best friend for supper, but she had to attend some sort of church function. Probably better for her not to see Dad like this anyway.

I looked at Dad and wondered if he ever worried about where his sister was spending eternity. Holly Adams, the skinny girl with braids who had sat next to me in my fourth grade CCD class at St. Clare's—the church we attended at the time of Mary Ellen's death— had an opinion about everything, including what happened to people who committed suicide. *People who kill themselves go straight to hell.* Yes, that was right, based on what Holly said, both Jimi Hendrix and Janis Joplin were now singing in hell. So...was Aunt Mary Ellen in heaven or not? Holly had stated her belief about suicide and damnation with absolute certainty.

After such a pronouncement, I stared at her like she was nuts. All I cared about that day was being able to escape St. Clare's and play some football.

I remember Holly flitting from suicide and eternal damnation to something far more important as we sat in our CCD class. "Hey, you goin' to Judi Newmark's costume party?" she whispered, risking a swat with the ruler from Sister Edna. "I'm going to be a princess, or maybe wear a blonde wig and go as a life-size Barbie doll."

I stared at my note pad, hoping Sister Edna's hearing aid battery was on the fritz. I hated princesses that needed to be rescued and Barbie's boring life. I wanted adventure and fun and the competition that allowed me to know where I stood in the world. Holly was a skinny know-it-all who had decided I was her friend because, when the bullies pestered her at our school, I literally walked her through the halls for a week, poking anyone who messed with her or telling them to "stick it" and leave her alone. They finally did.

Just that morning at school, a boy named Michael Ruth had grabbed my basketball and laughed while he and another kid drew me into an involuntary game of keep-away. I pushed the first boy and then pinned Michael to the ground as a ring of students circled round. My fourth grade teacher was Miss Miller, and she shouted out the window of our classroom.

"Susan! You stop it right this instant!"

I hesitated. "Hit him! Hit him! Hit him!" shouted the crowd. I looked over at my teacher and then punched Michael three times above the belt. I knew the code.

I bent down nose to nose. "Don't ever take my basketball again,"

Sitting in CCD class, I smiled at how powerful I felt. I knew I was supposed to feel guilty, but I didn't. I also knew that Michael would now respect me on the court. He'd been so embarrassed that he denied I'd hurt him, so I didn't get into too much trouble, but I didn't need Sister Edna on my case on top of the school's report to my folks.

Holly interrupted my mental movie. "So what're ya gonna be?""

"Not sure—maybe Batman. Maybe Zorro."

Long pause. "Oh." She didn't have anything else to say after that, and that was perfect. I was miffed at her for making me wonder if my aunt was in hell listening to the sounds of Janis and Jimi. I just couldn't accept injustice, not from bullies and not from God. I decided that Holly's and Sister Edna's version of God and the after-life was just that—their version, because how could a loving God send people to burn for eternity just because they were too miserable or scared to go on living in a place that was sometimes miserable and scary?

Back then, I thought Sister Edna and Holly were stupid and uncaring for thinking my Aunt Mary Ellen was perpetually charred. I now think a better description is *brainwashed*, the same kind of brainwashing that would intensify in my life. Adults in my world often pretended that the bad things in life weren't happening. Increasingly, they put Bible band-aids on issues and problems that even a child could see were not going to go away until everyone faced the truth.

I think my father did make an attempt to find the truth—at first. After Mary Ellen's death, he turned to self-help books. I remember reading the back flap of *Psycho-Cybernetics*, the shiny red and white hardcover written by a plastic surgeon who was inspired to treat *"inner scars"* rather than just "outer scars."

Another book he read was called *I'm OK, You're OK*. Both seemed pretty upbeat to me, and I watched him, hoping for positive changes. After a few weeks of this new genre, I thought his mood seemed lighter. He even seemed to regain some of his interest in art, although he didn't invite me to join him at the kitchen table. Instead, he set up shop in the basement where he worked on a vibrant watercolor illustration of two cartoon-like rabbits on a hill. He said it was for a children's book he'd dubbed *Yabbit the Rabbit,* a story about an excuse-making bunny and his friends.

I was proud of his project, which captured a playfulness that I'd never seen in his work before. Was it a confidence that came from being *"OK"*?

When he finished *Yabbit the Rabbit*, he sent it out to various publishers who rejected it but sent back compliments about the artwork. He ignored the positive comments and focused only on the rejection. I soon noticed another small paperback on his desk called *None of These Diseases*. Because he had grown so distant again, I thought I'd better snoop and see what this book was telling him.

One Saturday morning, I slipped into my parents' bedroom, picked up *None of These Diseases,* and felt its ragged corners as I read fragments here and there. Nearly every word was underlined, as if Dad was really trying to teach himself something. *What's this?* Could it really be saying that we wouldn't have any illnesses if we just stopped all our worrying? God Himself was telling us not to worry when relatives walked off bridges?

My heart raced. I sat down on his bed, book in hand, the wind knocked out of me. It scared me to think the bad stuff that happened was really our own fault—that if we got sick, well, it must be because we didn't have enough faith and trust in God.

Mom called me downstairs for breakfast. I returned the book to its place on the table next to his bed and headed downstairs, angry. How dare this writer blame Dad? I wanted to pick a fight with the author, or maybe even with God.

Dad looked right through me at the breakfast table, a drop of milk traveled down his chin. Ann hummed a song from *Sesame Street*, and I pushed golden Cap'N Crunch cereal nuggets in with my spoon. I'd always thought Dad knew almost everything there was to know in the world, but somehow he thought that yucky book held answers he didn't have. God could fix everything *if* we could somehow have enough faith in Him. So if we didn't have that kind of faith, we were just plain out of luck. And poor Mary Ellen, well, she must not have trusted God either because He sure didn't help her.

So did that mean that God wouldn't help Dad—a man who was already trying *so hard* to be perfect—until his faith was perfect? Dad just wanted to feel okay, and now he had to be perfect, not just for his family, but for God too? I hated that. And where did that leave me? I knew I'd never get even close to anything like perfect.

A few weeks later, Dad was offered a promotion, which would mean moving from the government job he held in Cleveland to the Washington D.C. headquarters. Mom hoped it would be just what was needed. Leave Cleveland. Leave family and friends behind so that Dad could make a nice, fresh start with strangers. For some people, this approach might have worked. Mom told me about our moving plans one cold Sunday night. We would be leaving at the end of the school year. She was hopeful, but I was devastated. I just bit my lip though, because I wanted my Dad to get happy again. I believed it when Mom said this would do the trick.

The following morning, a six-inch-thick layer of snow had fallen like a white cloak over the sludge of my worry. The move was a long way off. The snow was here today. Excitedly, I stepped into my snowsuit and hurried to school as fast as a kid can in boots, snowsuit, scarf, and mittens. I was hoping to arrive before anyone else. The snowplow always formed a huge mountain of snow in our schoolyard. I knew that other students brave enough to play *King of the Mountain* would be hurrying to school too.

I didn't even wait for Jimmy Dittoe to join me on the mile walk to school. I needed to get there, and I wasn't about to wait for anyone, not even my best friend. I rounded the final corner and made a short skip with glee. *No one's there!* I did my best SnowSuitWaddleGallop and arrived, heaving with exhaustion, at the glistening heap of snow.

I took one last look around to see if anyone else was coming. *Nope.* I threw off my mittens, knowing it was a trade-off I'd have to make. I needed my fingers free to dig into the icy snow. I bent toward the hill and started the climb. Two steps up with my hands, two up with my feet. I stopped and grabbed some snow and rolled a snowball in case someone came. I looked to my left and took one step closer to the summit when I felt a pull on the hem of my snowsuit, followed by the primal scream of Mark Ewing. I knew it was him because of his high-pitched voice. I kicked my leg and tried to shake him, but he held on as my left hand dug into the side of the hill. I readied the snowball in my right hand, and I saw in his face the misplaced joy of someone who actually thought they were going to beat me to the top.

I threw a side arm shot and hit him square in the forehead. He screamed and let go. I knew his outcry was less from pain than from knowing I had him beat. Mark rolled down the hill, and I climbed one level higher. I was nearly there. I looked out and saw Michael Ruth and Pat Dittoe, Jimmy's younger brother, heading my way. There was no time to make more ammunition—I needed to get to the top of the hill. I made a final lunge and pulled myself up onto the peak just as they reached the bottom.

I was standing now, my hands stretched out, ready and waiting. My enemies would charge, one at a time, like the rules say. My fingers were numb from the cold, but I didn't care. I'd made it. I could do anything. *I was King of the Mountain*. My empire might be difficult to maintain, but I relished the challenge.

Pat came at me. He dodged and weaved like he was running up a steep football field. His fancy moves only caused him to slip and fall, and he slid to the bottom, cursing his plastic boots and dumb luck.

Next up was Michael, out for revenge. I readied myself, and he charged like a polar bear. I let him place a paw at the summit, then I shoved him hard. He tumbled down the hill and knocked over a new kid I didn't recognize. Michael made a second attempt, and I handled him easily with a short shove that sent him flying down the snowy mountain like a green plastic miniature army man. By this time, the schoolyard had filled up with kids. The girls watched, and the boys kicked at the snow, pondering a charge. Soon, they started coming, and I tossed them aside, one by one, until the bell rang. Thankfully, Big Mike Verek was late that day and never showed up to challenge me.

At dinner, I tried to tell Mom and Dad about my uninterrupted reign.

"Mom, Dad, you shoulda seen me before school today. We played King of the Mountain before the bell rang and I—"

"What's that honey?" Mom asked as she spooned corn onto her plate. "Ann, do you want any corn? I'm sorry," she said, "go on."

"We play this game, but only if there's been a lot of snow. The snowplows push the snow and make these—"

"Ann, please stop kicking the table—sorry, go ahead," said Dad, giving me a wink.

With this small encouragement, I added, "Anyway, we just try to stay on the 'mountain' of snow, and the rule is that only one person can come and attack you at a time."

"Attack? What do you mean, attack?" Mom asked.

"You know—they run at me and try to push me off the mountain."

"Oh," my parents said in near unison while Ann kicked the table one more time and caught Mom's glare.

"Can I have more milk, please?" asked Ann.

"That sounds nice," Dad said as Mom got up to refill Ann's glass.

"Well, I mean, it's not really *nice*. But it is fun. And *I* was the King of the Mountain, 'cuz no one could push me off." I waited for their accolades, especially from Dad, but he was already deep in thought..

"Can I have another bread 'n' butter, please?" asked Ann.

"Sure, honey." Mom got up from the table again.

Finally from Mom, "Oh, well, that's good sweetie. I'm glad you had fun. Say, it's been almost two months since Christmas, and you still haven't written Aunt Anna that thank-you note."

"Sorry, I'll do it tonight." I wished they could have understood what my glory reign had felt like. Aunt Anna always bought me ugly clothes like the latest dress with red and white polka dots and frilly, laced stuff I'd never, ever wear. I knew I should have sent the thank-you note, but why did Mom have to bring that up right then?

Events like that morning's were important to me, and even if they didn't register as important to my family, I would always look back on them with pride and a grin of satisfaction—the innocent times when being a tomboy was different but acceptable. I hated to leave my little world where I'd been King of the Mountain and had Saturday adventures with Jimmy Dittoe. Were tomboys okay in Virginia? And what about Dad? We were moving to a totally different community with what felt like a totally different man inside my dad's skin.

In April of 1972, five months after my reign as King of the Hill, we took Dad to the airport so he could begin his new job in Washington. On the way home from the airport, Mom dropped off Ann at her friend Jackie's house and then had something to tell me. My father had burned *Yabbit the Rabbit* and all but one of its beautiful illustrations.

I couldn't believe it. She said something about how he thought he painted them in some sort of sacrilege because he had done them after reading *I'm Ok, You're OK,* which he now felt was All Wrong. Did that mean he wasn't "OK" anymore? *Okay* was normal, and *Normal* was EXACTLY how I wanted him to be. Other kids might have thought *normal* was boring, but to me, it meant art sessions, family dinners, and Dad's encouragement. I was pretty sure that book-burning wasn't normal.

Where and how did he do it? I imagined him assembling the story and its original watercolor illustrations, old newspaper, and matches. Did he tear his bright pictures into pieces first? Did he light them one-by-one in the fireplace? Or maybe a bonfire somewhere in the yard? Once the news sank in, I needed to know more and tried asking Mom about it.

"But, Mom... I don't see why—"

She signaled and turned onto our street. "What is it?" She exhaled her words, and I could almost feel her tiredness permeate the air and enter my lungs. My questions would only wear her down more.

"What is it, honey?" Her tone let me know she hoped my question wasn't too hard.

"Nothing, never mind." I looked out the window at the world I was losing.

Five

"Many a Conflict, Many a Doubt"

DAD WAS ALL ALONE IN Washington while Mom held down the fort in Cleveland and Ann and I finished the school year—fourth grade for me and preschool for her. He was still settling into his new job when he came home one weekend in May to help us get things ready for the move. Things seemed to go well at first.

"Hi, Sweets, I brought you something from DC."

I ran to him, and he hugged me hard, then held out a small bag. I reached in to find a yellow antique car that was about three times the size of a *Hot Wheel*, but it was more detailed and solid like a *Matchbox*. I hugged him again and felt the scratch of his stubbly cheek as I kissed him and inhaled the cheap smell of English Leather.

That night, we ate spaghetti and meatballs and talked about how we would soon get to see the Lincoln Memorial and the Washington Monument. Mom was upbeat about the move, but Dad seemed quieter than usual. I still thought things were fine, though, as I twirled the noodles onto my fork and slurped in the sauce that had been cooking all day. Ann giggled at the sound, grinning an orange, tomato-saucy smile that nearly made me laugh my chocolate milk out my nose. It's one of the few clear memories I have of her back then. I was focusing so much on my parents and the other adults and their craziness that my memories of interactingwith her are a blur.

&

After dinner, Mom and I challenged Dad and Ann to a match of ping-pong. Our German shepherd, Duchess, darted back and forth alongside the table like a ball girl at Flushing Meadows, barking when my mom and I whooped in victory.

We all celebrated with ice cream in front of our black and white TV set, catching an episode of *The Mary Tyler Moore Show*. I sat on the green shag carpet, captivated as Mare tossed her hat. I loved the turn of her mouth when she was about to cry, and the "Oh, Mr. Graaaant." I wanted to be able, like her, to take a nothing day and make it all seem worthwhile. Dad didn't laugh—not even once. I think that's when my worrying began in earnest.

The next morning, I awoke to the sound of the lawnmower buzzing in the backyard. By the time I joined Dad in our driveway, he was weeding the rock garden around the bright yellow tulips. I summoned my super powers—a favorite fantasy—to help him.

I became *Fiberglass Man*, battling villains along the way with fiberglass that streamed from my wrists like Spiderman's webs—wrappng criminals in an impenetrable prison. Heroic problem-solving felt natural to me. I loved that idea so much that it gained a powerful footing somewhere in my young mind. *Susan to the rescue!* I crept to the backyard in Fiberglass Man style to see if Dad needed the help of my powers to attack the weeds.

"What'd you say?" he said after I had asked him twice. Then he made excuses about rain. I scanned for rain clouds and saw only the eternal Cleveland milk sky and then offered to help pack moving boxes that in six short weeks would be loaded on the moving truck. He was ready to take a nap, however. His bare left ankle protruded from the edge of his too-short pants. How could he have forgotten to put on one of his socks? Dirt caked on his Converse shoes. He didn't notice or care. He seemed to be underwater or in a well. I couldn't reach him. It scared me to think that I didn't have access to my father and that the mundane things of life, the things he always took care of, were now overwhelming him. He couldn't even put on two socks, for God sakes! The flower beds would go unweeded, and the boxes would remain unpacked.

I walked around the side of the white clapboard garage, past the colorful snapdragons, seeking a reliable distraction for my troubled mind. My Mattel Bronco *Vroom* bike tempted me. I'd outgrown it, but I still loved its motocross looks. I used to store my candy money and baseball cards in its special compartment. Its peeling, fake chrome shock absorbers and exhaust pipes presented sharp edges that had cut me and sent me to the hospital for stitches two days in a row. The injuries and accompanying questions from the hospital staff led my parents to believe it was time for a new bicycle. Dad had gotten a kick out of buying me a new red, twenty-six-inch, three-speed Columbia girl's bike. He'd smiled and put his arm around my shoulder. "We'll take it," he told the shopkeeper at Friedrich's Bike Shop. Dad always wanted to provide me with more than just the basics, and I adored him for it.

Today, Dad wasn't smiling at all. I booted the three-speed's kickstand and steered it out of the garage, hopping on and pedaling as fast as I could. Would I ever get my real Dad back?

We'd soon be moving to Washington D.C. where the stranger who had replaced my father now lived. The life I'd lived up until that moment was evaporating. Just as the Bronco *Vroom* bike could no longer carry me through my daily adventures, my carefree childhood could no longer mute my concern for my father and worry about finding my place in a new neighborhood and school. It hit me that there would be no more riding with Jimmy Dittoe to Rini's Stop-N-Shop store for ten-cent Hershey bars or Topp's baseball cards. I loved ripping open a new pack in search of a Pete Rose, Roberto Clemente, or Hank Aaron before we got home. There would be no more cardboard outposts in Jimmy's backyard, built from salvaging carpet scraps for refrigerator-box living rooms and washing-machine-box dining rooms. No magic words upon completion: "Let's go get a pizza." We'd never ride to Giuseppe's again and plunk down our quarters and dimes to pay for the greasy $1.05 sausage pizza, Jimmy balancing its plain, white box on his handlebars as we rode to our fort to gobble it down.

Those times of glorious normality had a certain kind of freedom that might not be available to me after we moved. In Cleveland, I'd had no time or patience for pinafores or polka dots. I wore skirts to school because I had to—and *never* without shorts underneath. After all, how could you kick a homer if you had to worry about your underwear showing? Mattel and Parker Brothers earned my business with *Hot Wheels, Johnny West,* and *GI Joe.* No one worried that I was definitely *not* interested in *Ken, Barbie,* their friends, possessions, or offspring. (Did they have offspring?)

I was proud to be different and thought many of the girls I knew were silly, wimpy, boring, powerless creatures. I felt heroic as I flew through the neighborhood streets on my bike. Everything felt like an option to me; all manner of dreams were possible in the world of my Cleveland childhood. I knew somehow that nothing would be the same when we moved.

❧

Dreading change and fearing the powerlessness of totally new surroundings, I turned inward. My spiritual dilemmas first came into sharp focus on the day when relatives joined us for a last Sunday get-together at our house before we left for D.C. Mom argued with Aunt Nora about religion and the general state of the world, feeling that things were not as bad as her sister-in-law contended. Nora was Dad's older sister, the one who married Roy, the imperial Neanderthal. Before our move, my mother's staunch Catholicism guided her but didn't exactly pull her cart. While my cousins and I played a game of rummy in our pleasant, screened-in porch, I listened to the adults talking in the adjoining living room. Mom and Aunt Nora were arguing about a graduate.

"There was nothing wrong with *The Graduate*. It's a good movie, a slice of life," Mom said.

"Well, I don't agree. I think it's just one more example of Hollywood's negative influence on our culture," Aunt Nora countered.

I strained to hear more. Okay, so it was a movie they were speaking about. Then Aunt Nora said something about Pat Boone and his book, *Born Again*. Mom said something else about being Catholic, that it was the true WAY. Aunt Nora countered that *Jesus* was the Way, the Truth, and the Life.

I was inclined to agree with Aunt Nora on that last point. Our Cleveland neighbors had invited us to attend the Billy Graham Crusade at the Municipal Stadium. Mom and I went. Reverend Graham's words invoked a spiritual presence I hadn't experienced before, one that felt deep, personal, and real.

He said that God loved me and knew I wasn't perfect and that I didn't need to be. His explanations made sense to me. *Why couldn't the priests and nuns ever say that?* Jesus loved me and thought I was okay. This was so much better than the message in that scary book of Dad's, *None of These Diseases*, that only a perfect faith would earn God's help.

"Just As I Am," said the song the nice man from the Crusade had led us in singing. Two of the verses soothed my deepest fears.

Just as I am, though tossed about
With many a conflict, many a doubt...

I had felt moved to go forward for the altar call and started to leave my seat, but Mom stopped me.

"No, honey, that's something we Catholics *don't do*."

Right. What was I thinking? I knew what we Catholics did—we felt guilty and did it better than anyone. Had I sinned—or not? Was I okay? Or was God angry and about to strike? Maybe He was upset about something I wasn't aware of. I hadn't heard Father Fitzgerald at St. Clare's tell me that I could come *just as I was*. In fact, Father Fitzgerald had screamed at my CCD class when we were in the second grade because one of the kids had dropped the Host—a Communion wafer.

"You're all unworthy! Every last one of you!"

Were we really? Was that why things were going badly for our family? I lost focus on the card game I had been playing with my cousins in the porch. I didn't win, but I decided to place all my hopes on the idea that God did love us and planned to rescue us from the mess we found ourselves in.

❧

Moving boxes and plastic wrap littered the living room of our Ohio home.

"Hon, can you give me a hand with this box?" Mom grunted, straining with the box, and then wiped her brow. "Need to put it in the screened-in porch for now."

On the count of three, we both reached down and hoisted the box of pots and pans and headed through the dining and living rooms over to the porch on the side of the house. "Anything else I can do?"

"I need a few of those small, empty boxes from the basement. Do you mind?"

Down in the basement, I noticed a stack of Dad's paintings and drawings leaning against the wall next to the empty boxes. I bent down, combed through and found my favorite one, a pastel drawing of a chestnut foal standing in a field of flowers and butterflies. I carefully cradled it in my right arm and grabbed two small empty boxes with my left. In the kitchen I dropped the boxes beside Mom, pointed to the picture, and asked "When did Dad draw this?"

She stopped wrapping china. "Well, you know, it was really sweet. He gave it to me after our first date. I couldn't believe it! I was only nineteen. Met him at a dance."

"Was he in college?"

"Yeah, he'd gone back to school at Kent and was finishing up his business degree. He graduated about a year and a half after we met, and then we got married in September of that year—1960."

I tried to picture them as a happy bride and groom as I helped her arrange and wrap china so everything would fit. My hands were blackened from the newsprint, and Mom had a smudge on her cheek. I followed her then to the basement, the place where secrets were buried, a place that might contain answers to my incessant questions and satisfy my need to snoop. My eavesdropping never told me enough. While Mom looked through a stack of old books, I rummaged through a carton of photographs and memorabilia, scanning pictures of Dad's past, hoping to understand who he'd been and why he was fading away.

I pestered Mom to show me old yearbooks and asked dozens of questions. Dad's yearbook from his senior year, 1949, showed an optimistic young man. He'd worked at a grocery store the first year after graduation, but he couldn't save enough money for college or art school, so he joined the navy. A five-by-seven, black-and-white photo showed Dad with his shipmates during the Korean War. Mom told me that saving money was almost impossible then.

"Why?"

"Well, because he sent most of his navy paychecks home to Grandma Marie." She hesitated as though she thought she should be careful. Her tone told me there was something unfair about this. "Are you going to pack or yak, Miss Nosy?" She was trying to block my curiosity.

Only in later years would the implications hit me. Would my father have sacrificed his future and sent all that money home if he'd known about Gerry, the lover who bought her clothes and candy? *And a son?* When Dad finished his tour with the navy, he returned to his job at the local grocery market and enrolled in classes at Fenn College. Two years later, he tried again to pursue his dreams by enrolling in the Cleveland Institute of Art.

I picked up a cache of his drawings: detailed cross-sections of airplanes, pencil sketches of nudes, and historical personalities like Abraham Lincoln. In our long art discussions, he'd told me that his teachers encouraged him to continue his studies, and in 1957, he set off to study at the New York Art Students League. At the time I thought his drawings were masterpieces. They weren't, but I knew they'd earned him a chance to study at the Sorbonne in Paris. I thought of the way he'd said, "Sorbonne." A look of reverent excitement had come over his face, as if an inner switch had lit a bulb inside him. It must have excited him as nothing else had.

I ran upstairs to the kitchen. "Mom, why didn't Dad go to the Sorbonne?"

Mom was sorting cleaning products under the sink. "Grandma Marie said she needed him. So he gave it up and came back to Cleveland to finish his business degree on the G.I. Bill. Now you go finish up down there, please."

I went back downstairs, but I found Dad's Kent State yearbook near the bottom of an already packed box. In it was a note from Aunt Nora to my Dad commenting on his last semester spent living in his car and eating cold beans out of the can. On weekends, he stocked up on Grandma Marie's cooking.

❀

With maturity, I realized Dad probably never thought about sacrificing the Sorbonne opportunity until that day in 1960 when Grandma made her matter-of-fact proclamation about the existence of her hidden son, Art. How long did it take him to fully realize that while he dutifully sent her money from his meager paychecks and turned down the chance to study overseas, she had a rich man at her beck and call?

Dad had built his entire life around Grandma's deceptions. If she had just admitted her illicit affair and the child it produced, how vastly different might things have turned out? I found a shot of a bald, old man with no teeth I recognized as "Grandpa Joe." He had shown up sometime in the late sixties, needing a place to stay. No one had seen or heard from him in the thirty years since he left for Florida to earn his "fortune" at the racetrack. Dad didn't tell him to go to hell, never yelled at him for deserting them, never expressed sadness or any emotion at all. He simply found a rest home for his biological father, and we were told the old wreck was our grandfather. I remember him as the ancient, weird guy we had to go visit from time to time.

I can only guess that after all Dad had been through, his outrage became unmanageable. It wasn't in his temperament to take his pain out on others or drown it in a whiskey bottle; he was a gentle artist who internalized his emotion and turned it on himself. At the time, I didn't fully understand these things, but I *did* know he walked around with millions of unsaid words that were going to come out— one way or the other.

Six

Centreville

We joined dad in Centreville, arriving with Mom in her 1972 lime green Chevy Vega the same day as the moving truck. Mom was a cloud of activity and orders, Dad was as slow-moving as Grandpa Joe. Ann and I helped Mom unpack boxes in the kitchen while Dad worked in the adjoining family room, his face as expressionless as if shot full of Novocaine. Our arrival barely seemed to register. As the weeks passed, Mom worked at maintaining life as usual. She introduced herself to the neighbors, planted bright petunias and marigolds, and made sure we participated in neighborhood potluck dinners.

Mary Beth Bowen lived on our street. She and her family had moved into the neighborhood from San Diego the previous summer. She was going into the fifth grade and was tall like me, but with her long, blonde hair and blue-green eyes, she looked just the way I thought someone from Southern California should look. The first day we played together, we talked about the subjects we hated at school and the songs and TV shows we liked. We both loved *Rocket Man* by a new singer named Elton John. Hesitantly, I confessed that I really liked the Jackson Five too. Mary Beth revealed that she sometimes watched their cartoon show, which was a good sign, because I did the same but would never have admitted it first.

A week after we moved in, Mary Beth and I rode the seesaw in her backyard and chatted away. Where had the afternoon gone? I looked up at the early evening sky, thinking, *I may have actually found a friend!*

"Look at how big and round the sun is." I was so happy, I turned poetic. "Looks like a big, orange ball of fire."

"What? That's the moon, silly," she said.

I checked. Yes, it certainly was. *How could I be so stupid?* I cringed. She'd no longer want to spend time with me and might even tell others how lame I was. I might as well kiss off friendships, because sooner or later I was going to embarrass myself with some stupid comment or action that made no sense to the rest of the human race or that revealed my father's craziness.

But, the next day, the doorbell rang, and Mary Beth stood grinning on my porch. We raced up to my room to listen to the radio. She told me about the new boy that she met at the park. We saw each other all the time after that. She was fun to be with even though she wasn't interested in sports. I think she hoped that by some process of osmosis she would one day understand what all the fuss over athletics was about. Mary Beth told her brother Russ about my baseball card collection, and he bolted over to my house to see it.

"How many ya got?" Russ wanted to know.

"About 8000 singles and another 2000 or so doubles," I replied.

"Dang, girl! You're lucky!"

We jawed about Pete Rose's headfirst slides, Roberto Clemente's bat, and Gaylord Perry's alleged spitballs. Russ reverently held the cards and began studying their statistics harder than the Bible or any of his schoolbooks. I gave him some of my doubles to help him get his own collection going, and soon he was an expert on ERA's, batting averages, and the latest trades.

So far, so good. But what if they found out about Dad?

Right from the start, Mrs. Bowen was one of my favorite people in Washington. Her accent was Southern, like her husband's, but soft and warm as the cinnamon rolls my mom used to make before my dad's depression overran her life. The first weekend we met, Mrs. Bowen took Russ, Mary Beth, and me to Bull Run Park to swim in the gigantic, cloverleaf pool. Yankees and Rebels fought the first major land battle right there along Bull Run Creek in our town of

Centreville on the very spot where we now played, two children of the South and one of the North, so free of care.

The following day, Russ invited me to play ball. By the time I got to his house, there were about ten boys tossing baseballs in his front yard. I felt a bit intimidated but walked up the drive and said "hey" to Russ.

"What's SHE doing here?" said a kid I didn't recognize.

"She's prob'ly better than all of you!" Russ said.

"It ain't possible," said a tall, blonde kid.

"Aw, c'mon, man!" responded Clay Doubleday, an actual descendant of the game's founder. "Let's play some ball and find out!"

The game wasn't even close. Russ doubled, and I hit the game-winning home run. From then on, no one questioned my presence, including me. Being a tomboy was still okay. Holding my own at school was another matter, however. The Susan-to-the-Rescue side of me couldn't muster the same confidence and went into hiding.

Halitosis Hal, a kid named Harold who always tried to trip me and insult me, sometimes waited for me after school. One day, I was riding my bike home from the playing field, alone because Russ and Mary Beth had gone on ahead of me. When I stopped to wait for a car to pass before crossing the street, there he was, across the street, sitting on his bike, glaring at me.

"Four Eyes, good to see you!" Hal grinned at me. "I'm here to give you your ass kicking!" I wasn't happy about the fact that this was the first year I needed to wear my glasses for more than just reading the blackboard. Normally, I would have taken him on, but *this* was a different world and I was a *different me*.

I made a quick decision to ride my bike straight at him and turn at the last second to throw him off balance. My maneuver surprised him enough to give me some time, but I did what I had never done before—I ran scared. I pedaled like a crazy woman until I got to my driveway. He chased me the whole way, but never caught up to me. As I got to the garage, he laughed.

"There's always next time, Four Eyes! I'll be waiting for you!"

I panted hard as I watched his bike turn the corner. I needed to try to calm myself in the garage before going into the house. I started to cry, but stopped. *What good would it do?* For a second, I thought about telling my mom about the bullying. But if I couldn't even speak to her about Dad, how could I dare add my little problems to her worries? Her unspoken fears about our present and future filled the house almost as powerfully as Dad's behavior. Thanks to the neighborhood women, it was tempered by the fact that she'd learned that Jesus was more than a plaster icon on a cross. Wednesday was now the day my mother lived for, the day she received an infusion of Bible buzz and friendship from Mrs. Bowen and others who'd invited her to a Stonecroft Bible study. Rather quickly, Mom's vocabulary morphed to include phrases like, "Praise the Lord" and "God willing." Soon she was professing to be a Born-Again Christian.

In the wake of this year's problems, Mom had come around to Aunt Nora's way of thinking. After joining Mrs. Bowen's prayer group, Mom inundated the family with Bible quotes, blessings and assurances of God's love that came by way of Assembly of God Tongues, Lutheran Grace, Baptist Fire, Episcopal Logic, and Methodist Works—denominations represented by the women in her group.

At the center of it all was The Bible—the Ultimate Authority on Everything. To think otherwise was blasphemous, since it was, after all, *The Word of God.* Mom focused on positive verses like: *"I can do all things through Christ who strengthens me,"* and, *"For God has not given us a spirit of fear, but of power and love and a sound mind."* As strange as all the religious fervor seemed to me, those verses helped me sometimes and reminded me that I had felt God's presence with me *long* before Mom started recognizing Him in The Book.

The Centreville neighborhood ladies had encouraged Mom to take her family to church socials and prayer groups, so we tagged along. Dad even started reading the Bible. I wanted to say, *Remember? I wanted to follow Jesus when we attended the Billy Graham Crusade.* But I was grateful that my parents' new friends were helpful, even if they did confuse me with their odd vocabularies that didn't feel natural. I wanted it all to feel *real*, and that part of it just didn't. *I'm sorry, Jesus, but I don't want to talk like the other "Believers." I want to be* just as I am. *I hope you were serious about that part.* I prayed that Dad would believe he could go to God *just as he was* and find peace.

In the meantime, it was hard to maintain a "God's-taking-care-of-us" attitude in light of Dad's startling decline.

❧

No amount of praying could divert my fears about Dad's pervasive depression or change all his new gray hair back to the jet-black hair of a year ago. His blank stares and the shocking weight loss that diminished his once strong frame panicked me, and my chest would tighten—a symptom that happened more and more often. My family seemed to believe that if we didn't talk about the problems, if we acted as though life was as normal as could be, well then, it really wasn't that bad.

Within three months or our arrival, Mom's dinner ritual had come to include heartfelt and specific prayers that she set out along with the food on the table.

> Dear Lord, we thank you for this food and most importantly for who you are, the Redeemer, and we thank you for watching over us.

Mom's eyes were closed, Dad's were completely vacant. I looked over at Ann, her little hands folded in earnest, eyes shut tightly. *Is God really taking care of us?*

"I talked to Father Joe, and do you know what he told me when I told him that I found comfort in the Bible?" She didn't wait for my reply. "He said that *I* wasn't to read the Bible—that it was strictly for the *priests* to read and interpret for us! Can you believe that?!"

Mom was pretty much *only* reading the Bible at that point. I wondered why she talked about so many things I didn't need to hear and withheld so many that I did. I was about to be late for school, but she kept on.

"He really doesn't understand the Good News of the Gospel at all. And no thanks to him, we're getting plenty of love and support from others who do! Your father's going to be healed! He's starting to read the Bible and he's getting much better now that there are so many prayers going out for him."

Healed? He was sick? It seemed more like overwhelmed and sad to me. If this was "sick," I sure hoped I couldn't catch it. This was definitely *not* what Mom told me would happen. Things were supposed to be better here in Virginia. I left all of my friends for *this*? In Cleveland, I had Mom's mother, whom we called "Gramma," and my Aunt Joy—Mom's sister—my cousins, and a whole school of friends. No bully dared chase me home, either.

I wanted to scream and throw my fried chicken and mashed potatoes across the room, but I didn't because I was afraid it would make Mom and Ann cry. *Dad was getting better?* He was sitting across from me like a zombie. I wanted to scream at him. *Why are you doing this to us?* I didn't know what effect it might have on him—probably none.

⚘

During our first few months in Centreville, I watched Mom as she did everything she could to make things better, trying to fix our lives without fixing anything at all.

"Dick, honey, let's make sure you brush your hair," Mom said, as she exited the downstairs bathroom and headed toward the foyer where Dad and I were waiting. "C'mon now, we're going to the Schneider's house for a cookout. You need to straighten up and look nice."

I glanced at Ann, who was sitting on the steps trying to tie her shoelaces. Her blonde hair fell forward on her face as she leaned over her chubby, kindergarten legs and exhaled in frustration. Her eyebrows furrowed and she stomped her right foot.

"I can't do it!" Ann cried.

"Let me help you, honey." Mom leaned over to get the knot out as Dad stared off into space.

She had to do everything because Dad was no longer the parent he had been. He didn't listen to stories anymore about friends at school or the good grade I received on my science project. Surely he couldn't be expected to actually lean over and tie someone else's shoes. He rarely tied his own.

Mom must have thought that he should get over this nonsense and get back to being a good parent. I couldn't tell if she was angry, but she did seem tired. She stood up and put the tip of her right forefinger in her mouth and bit down, like she did when things were really bothering her. Her elevated and pleasant tone had tried to cover it, but it wasn't working.

What's wrong with him? I wondered. Did Mom wonder too?

The barbecue was boring. Mom felt good when she was around her new friends, but I felt sick with worry the whole time. Socializing with people I hardly knew made things worse. What if someone talked to Dad and he just stared at them? Would he soon start getting looks and whispers? Would I? *And there's his daughter... Poor kid... Honey, go on over and play with her... Because I said so.*

As I sat in the living room, drinking my soda, daydreaming and listening to the adults, the freckled-faced son of our host approached me.

"You wanna play kickball with me and my friends at the park? It's just down the street."

I couldn't even remember his name. "I don't feel like it. Thanks, though."

The boy shrugged and turned to walk away.

Mom had overheard the exchange.

"Honey, why don't you want to play? Go on, have some fun."

I wanted to shout at her that I needed to curl up into a ball and cry, but I knew it would make us both feel worse.

"Wait up," I called out the front door. The boy stopped and waited. I caught up with him and we walked without conversation. When we approached the park, I said, "Listen, I think I'll just watch, okay?"

He gave me a SuitYourself look and shrugged.

On the way home, Mom asked about the game. I lied and told her it was fun. Inside the house, I felt like crashing my fist through the wall, but like Dad, I was learning to simply stuff my feelings. Lying in bed that night, I couldn't sleep. Why couldn't Dad snap out of it and take care of me again? Would he ever get back to normal? I wanted to go back to what we used to do, to sit at the *same* table in the *same* house and work on the *same* drawing techniques. I was watching him sink into deeper and deeper waters, while I helplessly ran up and down the riverbank, wondering why I couldn't save him and why we weren't enough to make him happy.

Seven

Halitosis Hal

Dear God, you are Holy and All Powerful. I love you and want to serve you. I will not be afraid because You are with me.

I wrote out this prayer on three-by-five note cards while lying on the family room floor. I'd gotten bored with my puzzle, but before I sketched our German Shepherd, Duchess, I figured I'd better nudge God again, because I was starting to feel afraid in this strange, new life.

I was careful to hide the note card within my sketch pad. The last time I wrote down a prayer, things hadn't turned out so well. It had been two weeks earlier and I'd been in a hurry to get outside for a recess that was never long enough. I could escape all my problems through sports. Although few people knew my name in class, they seemed to remember me on the sports fields, calling me out early as teams were set. I loved the feeling of scoring a goal on the soccer field or catching the winning touchdown. I wasn't fast, but I found a way, sometimes willing both my body and the ball toward the goal. Unfortunately, there were always more plays to run than time to play. After recess, we lined up to go inside. Halitosis Hal, the class bully I had run from earlier earlier, was right in front of me, tormenting another girl.

"Hey, Ugly!" he said. "Nice pants. Where'd you get those? Salvation Army?"

The girl said nothing. She wasn't ugly, but Hal and all of his friends called her *Ugly* so often, I couldn't remember her real name. I wished I had the strength to put a stop to it. The old me would have felt so infuriated at his meanness, there would have been no question about trying to stop it. But my King-of-the-Mountain days were long gone. The new me had lost all confidence in my ability to change anything at all. Instead, I pretended to tie my shoelace in order to fade into the background and put some distance between Hal and me. A minute later, as I walked into the classroom, I was horrified to see Hal holding my "prayer cards."

"Hey, will ya look at this! Who's the religious nut who wrote all this crap?"

The cards must have fallen out of my pocket. Hal laughed and read them out loud in a mocking tone. I couldn't move. "What ya lookin' at, Four Eyes? Are these yours?"

"Of course not. Now move out of my way."

"No problem," he said, stepping aside and tripping me at the last moment.

Feeling both relieved and ashamed, I stumbled back to my desk, wanting nothing more than to run home and hide. *Jesus, I'm so sorry.* I had denied my love for God faster than you could say "Saint Peter."

⁘

Back in the family room, I looked up at Dad. He was starting to stir. He grunted and then sat up quickly, blinked and said, "Oh, um, yeah, hello."

Oh boy. Halitosis Hal was a big enough problem as it was, but if he knew how strange my father was acting, he'd have a field day. I hated the fact that Hal lived only one street over. I worried that he might learn of Dad's problems and tell kids at school. Friends were hard enough to come by in this new school and neighborhood. I wished I could see Mary Beth and Russ more, but they were always doing stuff with church. And they had other friends. The fact that Dad was no longer able to connect with me hurt the most. I was so lonely.

My only hope was something I remembered from the Bible. Jesus had said that He would *never* leave us or forsake us, and that he would be with us, "Even unto the end of the earth." I held onto the hope that He would step in and take away the sick feeling in my gut and let me get back to being the fearless kid I had been. *Maybe with Jesus' help, I can even stand up to Hal. I'm sick of him and I don't care how big he is, I need to stop this once and for all.* I knew running away would never accomplish what a good punch to his nose would do. Imagining that made me feel good and remember the person I had been—the Fiberglass Man superhero who could defend the weak. Now I'd be lucky if I could defend myself.

The day after Hal made fun of my prayer cards, I decided to wait for him the way he usually waited for me and the other poor souls he'd chosen to torment. I planned to pummel him on behalf of all the kids he'd tormented. Feeling like a Christian soldier moving onward, I watched the idiot swagger down the hall toward the east exit of the building, his ever-present sneer plastered on his face. He tripped a short kid and laughed, and then his fat-ass friends patted him on the back like he'd scored a touchdown. Their laughing stopped suddenly when a kiss-ass named Lee pointed to the girl they called *Ugly.*

"Hey, Ugly."

She ignored him.

"Hey, Ugly!" he yelled. "What you say we take a walk to the bus stop together? Hmm? Maybe you can invite me over to that shack you call your home? I can meet your Pappy and help with them thar chickens ya got. Or maybe we can have a little *date* in your barn. Huh, Ugly?"

The girl backed away from him, and Hal's friends surrounded her. I saw Hal move closer, backing her into his slob of a friend. She could probably feel his breath on her neck. I could almost feel it myself. Any day of the week of any year in Ohio, I would have had the guts to push them aside and take my chances. But not today. Not here. I had lost my nerve and backed away, ashamed of my weakness. Hoping she would be all right, I turned and walked home.

In that moment, I realized I was never going to confront Hal. Something inside me had changed. My fears had taken away my spine. Even though the girl seemed okay the next day at school, I felt sick inside and wished I had done something to help her.

Not long after my non-confrontation with Halitosis-Idiot-Hal, I decided to try to forget the fact that I was an absolute chicken at school. Like some sort of barnacle, I clung to the things I loved, like sports and art. When I received word that I'd won an award for a watercolor landscape I'd completed in art class, I was thrilled. The teacher told me she was going to recommend me for entrance into a special school for the artistically gifted. Okay, so I wasn't tough, but I was "gifted."

I couldn't wait to make the announcement at home and hurried to show Mom. As I ran inside, I shouted, "Mom, my watercolor won first place!"

Rather than responding to my good news, she called me into the family room. *Something was up.*

I stepped down from the linoleum floor of the kitchen to the carpeted and cozy room and leaned my painting against the wall.

Mom was alone on the couch and motioned me over. "Hi, honey, have a seat here on the couch. Would you like something to drink?"

"Where's Ann?"

"She's playing at a friend's house."

"Oh." I wanted my sister there to share the weight of whatever I was going to hear.

Mom looked tired, exhausted because by then, the days had filled with trips taking Dad to the psychiatrist, housework, and worry. The nights were a constant struggle for sleep, as his nocturnal march wore a path in the carpet of their bedroom next to mine. I also kept late-night vigils, listening, but I had grown tired of the nighttime drama. Eavesdropping on his mutterings and Mom's occasional pleas or attempts at sympathy or reason hadn't provided as many insights as overhearing my mother's recent phone conversations with her friends. I heard her crying a lot, and although she had tried to maintain an *everything's-gonna-be-all-right* attitude, my father had worn her down.

She folded her hands in a let's-get-on-with-this gesture. "Did you know that Poppy had a history of mental illness and even numerous 'breakdowns' too?"

Breakdown. *Oh. That explains it. I get it now.* Everything that had happened since we moved was wrapped up inside that word. *But what is it?* Poppy was her father, my grandfather, and this was news to me. It scared me. Was this breakdown thing catching?

I couldn't grasp what it meant to have a "breakdown," but I could see that my dad was definitely *not* stable at that point. I sat there, saying nothing.

"You know, one of the reasons I married your father was because he seemed so stable, so different than my father. So you just never know. Still, I believe your father will get better…like Poppy did."

Right. Me too. *He'll get better.* I really wanted to help her, help Dad, change things, but I was ten. All I could think of was, *Can I go now?*

"So, honey, since your dad hasn't been himself lately. Well, we've decided he needs to see the doctors more often, so we've taken him to a hospital where they're going to help make him better."

I couldn't really think of who "we" would be, and I knew she meant a *mental* hospital, but I didn't ask and just nodded.

"Do you have any questions about it?"

Questions? I don't understand one single thing about all this! My dad, who I love more than life, *is in a loony bin!*

I didn't say a word. I got up and stood by the sliding glass patio door and thought about all the other families housed in our neighborhood. *Why was this happening to us?* It didn't seem like anyone else had parents who were "mental cases." *Even stupid Hal probably had parents that didn't go to a mental hospital!* I wanted to run away, but where and to whom?

I pressed my nose on the glass door and grabbed the curtain and started to cry. The smell of Windex had always been a comforting reminder of Mom's care and concern for our family. I caught a whiff of it then. I wanted to be mad at her, but she didn't deserve this. I wanted to be mad at Dad—when he was around—but the angry stare of a ten-year-old might push him over the edge. How close to the edge was he? Why was this decision made *now*? Had something changed?

Yes.

৯৪

I found out years later what precipitated his stay at the hospital. While Ann and I were at school that day, Dad called Mom from work to make an announcement. He'd decided to *jump* off the HUD building downtown. Mom, of course, was terrified and was caught completely off guard. She immediately called Mrs. Bowen, and together they rushed to the city, running in circles when they arrived, not knowing what to do. They finally ran to a bank of pay phones, contacted Dad's boss, and looked up the nearest mental hospital in the Yellow Pages.

Minutes later, an emergency crew found him on top of the roof. They coaxed him away from the ledge and took him away in a straight jacket to the Northern Virginia Mental Health Institute.

Eight

The 700 Club

WHILE DAD WAS IN THE hospital, Mom turned to prayer. Not just before sleep or at meal times. She was after serious prayer. The move hadn't helped Dad, and may have even been what made him worse, and the hospital wasn't making any progress. So she tuned in to a new television talk show hosted by a man named Pat Robertson. *The 700 Club* gave my mom a television prayer partner to go along with all of the neighborhood ones. Every now and then I listened to the folksy man and what he had to say.

"Ladies and gentleman, God is doing mighty and wonderful things." Mr. Robertson spoke with an earnestness that was hard to ignore.

I kicked off my slippers and brought my pillow and blanket to the floor of the family room so I could get a closer view of the TV set.

"We're asking you to join us as partners of *The 700 Club* and help us bring this ministry to people all over the world."

The camera closed in on his friendly face, and he continued, "Please pray with us as we listen to what God is saying...Dear Lord, we stand here as a people who are seeking your ways—not our ways, Jesus, but your ways. Lord, we know there are people out there in the viewing audience who are crying out for help. They need a miracle today...and God, we claim those miracles...."

He stopped for a moment, looked earnestly into the camera, the expression on his face was dead serious. He was getting a "Word of Knowledge." Then he bowed his head and closed his eyes.

"...Yes...there's someone in the viewing audience RIGHT NOW who is suffering from back pain. You've had this pain for a long time and it is in the lower back...Yes...Thank you, Lord, I think her name is Julie or Julia...Yes, you are being healed RIGHT NOW! Praise the Lord!"

Mr. Robertson kept his head down and continued with more *knowledge*.

"There is a lady, yes...a young woman, who has been praying for a new job so she can take care of her children...Yes, Lord, thank you...*right now*, God is sending you a job! Glory to God!"

He went on this way for a several more minutes. By now I was sitting straight up and waiting for the "knowledge" I wanted to hear—the one about the scared fifth-grader in Centreville, Virginia, who needed her father to be healed from his nervous breakdown.

Mom went into the other room to talk to Aunt Joy on the phone, so I turned off the television and tried to keep any tears from falling, thinking that maybe I shouldn't be so disappointed. Maybe it took longer than just one time for the "knowledge" message to get from God to him and then to me. I tuned in every day that week.

It never came.

❦

The first time we pulled into the parking lot of the Northern Virginia Mental Health Hospital, Mom gave our name to the parking attendant. He checked his roster of patients and let us through.

"Now kids, there's nothing to worry about. This is a nice and clean place, and they're taking good care of your father."

I stared ahead and detached the cord inside that connected my senses to my heart. Ann was singing another one of her babyish songs from *Sesame Street*. The move had upset her world as well. Her big blue eyes looked disinterested, and she kicked the seat until we parked the car.

As we got out of Mom's Vega, she did a quick check of our hair and clothes to make sure we looked presentable. She took in a deep breath and whimpered. Was Mom crying? Yes. I saw her wipe away a tear. That scary pain hit inside my chest, as if my heart was in the grasp of a tightly clenched fist. I was pretty sure it would go away, like it always did, but it still made me stop and take a deep breath. Although I felt bad for Mom, I also felt a twinge of anger. *How good do we really need to look?* I put my Johnny West doll and his horse, Thunderbolt, on the floor near my feet; then at the last minute, I decided to bring them both in for moral support.

We walked up to the entrance huddled together like three scared laboratory rodents, passed through the door, and stopped at the nurses' station to sign in. "Girls, I'm going to show you where the waiting area is. Wait for me there while I go see your father and talk to his doctors. Then, when he's ready, Dad will come here to see you."

Okay, this is good. At least we don't have to see him in some kind of weird padded room. The waiting room was actually sort of cozy, more like a small library, I thought. You could choose a book from one of the many bookshelves and nestle into a comfortable couch or chair for a quiet read. I headed over to a record player on a small desk and looked through the stack of albums.

"Would you like to listen to one of the records?" said an older lady who apparently worked there. "You can put on any one of these that you like... See?"

I put on a James Taylor record:

> ... I've seen lonely times when I could not find a friend,
> But I always thought that I'd see you again...

"Honey, your dad is here to see you," Mom said, interrupting "Sweet Baby James."

I looked up and saw my father standing there, thin and pale, looking like one of those cardboard cutout, point-of-sale displays at the grocery store. It was him, but not him. All our prayers and pretending would not make this feel okay to me.

"Sweetie, why don't you give Ann a hug, she's excited to see you."

He reached over and hugged Ann the way Nixon hugged small children on the campaign trail. When there was nothing more to say or pretend, we said our good-byes and headed toward the nurses' station to check out. Walking through the surrealistic halls, I felt like I was in a movie I'd never want to see. In the car, Mom wiped away her tears. I tried not to cry, but near the end of the trip I couldn't hold it back anymore, and I choked out the question we all wanted an answer to.

"Why does this have to happen to us?" I asked her.

"Behind the door of every home, something's going on—something difficult, that we don't know about. *This* is what's happening to us, but every family has something. No one escapes trouble forever."

Mom had moments of wisdom and honesty that allowed us to share the experience rather than shut me out with fake smiles. I felt guilty for wishing Dad's trouble was something else—something more *normal*. It occurred to me that Pat Robertson never received words of *knowledge* about people in mental wards who needed miracles to keep their brains working right.

Gary? Or, no, it's Christine. Yes, Christine, your mind is being unscrambled as we speak. *Praise Jesus!* Sorry, Gary. Sorry, Mr. Richard Parker. Keep those checks coming! Be sure to pray for a blessing, and maybe I'll soon get a really clear connection through to the Big Guy.

The next day, I had difficulty concentrating in class and looked around at my classmates, huffing at how ignorant they all seemed. The day dragged on forever until I shuffled through the door at home and hugged Duchess, who whined in sympathy and licked my face.

Mom was talking on the phone and waved to me as I walked into the kitchen. The phone cord was wrapped around her left hand and she was leaning against the wall, not making any attempt to lower her voice. I heard her say something about electric shock treatments.

Three weeks later, when we made the long trek back to the hospital, I worried that the tips of his fingers and toes would be burnt. *Would his hair be singed?*

The drive over was much like the first. *I'm a Rocket Man*, I sang along, rocketing out of my body to that place in my head where no one would find me.

When we got to the waiting room, I wasted no time looking through the stack of albums. A Three Dog Night album caught my eye because it had a song called *Easy to Be Hard* that reminded me of Hal and all the other bullies I had known.

> How can people be so heartless?
> How can people be so cruel?

In a different way, the song also reminded me of our neighbors back in Ohio who first introduced me to Three Dog Night. And things were *normal*.

How could my life have changed this fast?

Mom interrupted my thoughts with a tap on the shoulder. I turned around and stared first at Dad's fingers. They weren't black—no smell either. *Thank God.*

His face looked just as blank as it had the last time.

Not even electricity could energize him.

⚘

By late October 1972, Dad had started visiting us every other weekend at home in Centreville. I was nervous about having him home again, but I quickly realized he was so drugged up, sometimes it was like he wasn't even there.

We still attended St. Timothy's, but Mom also found a Protestant "home church" for us to attend as well. The congregation apparently rotated to various members' homes throughout the year. Would they ever come to ours? I hoped not. I wasn't sure what to expect. *I mean, what kind of church is held at a person's house?* I was hoping it wouldn't be too weird.

It was Indian summer when we drove up to a one-story, gray house situated on a wooded lot in the middle of nowhere. There was a line of cars parked in the street, and Dad had to circle a few times to find a spot for the Biscayne.

"Why are we here? I don't want to go to this!" Ann said on behalf of both of us.

We exited the car, and Mom reminded Dad to grab his Bible, pen, and notebook, which was sure a lot more than what we needed to bring to the Catholic church. I was happy that at least we didn't need to get dressed up. Mom said the people of this church were not concerned about what people looked like or what they wore, only about people having a heart for God.

Okay, cool. I hate wearing dresses.

Mom knocked boldly on the metal screen door. It opened with a "Praise the Lord, sister. C'mon in! I'm Brother Jim, and this is my wife, Helen."

Mom introduced us with a friendly, "This is my husband, Dick, and my daughters, Ann and Susan."

Dad mumbled a "hello" or two and I nodded and smiled as best I could. Ann just stood there and clicked her heals. There were about twenty adults and five or six kids sitting in chairs situated in a circle around the living room. Everyone seemed extremely happy to have us there, and they all shouted out either a *Hello* or an *Amen* or a *God Bless Ya*. Some even hugged me. I figured, if nothing else, at least they weren't as boring as our old parishioners.

I looked at Brother Jim's face and focused on his flabby jowl that jiggled back and forth while he talked. His smoker's cough interrupted prayers and reminded me of Poppy. His bushy eyebrows furrowed into a uni-brow as he concentrated on the morning's blessings and prayers.

I zoned out completely while gazing at a tall oak outside that bent under the weight of decades of storms. A woodpecker pounded a rhythm that was answered by the bark of a distant dog. The congregation startled me out of my daydream by singing what I later learned were called *Praise Songs*. After a few rounds of *Hallelujah*, people started raising their hands and ad-libbing the words.

"Hallelujah, hallelujah, hallelujah. [Some sang Alleluia]
Lord we love you, lord we love you, lord we love you, lord we
    love you.
Thank you Jesus, Thank you Jesus, Thank you Jesus,
Thank you Jesus... You are Holy, you are Holy, you are Holy,
    you are Holy... "

This went on for what seemed like three days, and then we moved into prayer time. Mom said her request was for peace for my father and our whole family.

"Can we get an *Amen?*"

Someone else prayed for their Aunt Ethel who had cancer. Another needed a job. Someone else said they were praying for the salvation of their whole family. Did I feel better? Maybe. Any time Dad wasn't just sitting and staring was good at this point. When we took him back to the hospital that night, he seemed slightly better.

Two weeks later, as the whole family watched an Ohio State football game, Dad seemed uninterested but mentioned that he was looking forward to church in the morning. Mom seemed pleased. At half-time, she asked him to get milk and bread at the grocery store. I volunteered to go along, thinking it didn't seem right for him to go unsupervised. We drove along silently to the store. When we arrived, I told him I'd go to the back of the store for the milk while he got the bread. We met at the checkout counter, and on our way out, I took hold of the brown paper bag as we headed for the door.

Back at the car, Dad unlocked the driver side door, got in, and reached over to unlock the passenger side. I fumbled with the bag

while pushing up my glasses, busted up and bent from collisions on
the soccer and football fields. As we settled into the car, he made no
attempt to start the engine but instead began to talk about his father.
He said it'd been a while since he'd seen him. Then he asked me about
a springtime picnic Mom, Ann, and I attended at Aunt Nora's before
we moved to Centreville. Grandpa Joe was living in a nursing home—
paid for with public assistance and supplemented by the children he
had abandoned—but Nora had brought him over to the picnic.

"So how did Grandpa seem?" Dad asked about his father.

"Grandpa? He seemed like he always does. You know, he sorta just
sits there and asks about the price of meat and tells you that pork
chops cost thirty-five cents a pound when he was a kid."

"Yeah." He actually chuckled.

I gave him a sideways glance and felt good about his response. His
cobalt eyes still shot an occasional spark. I wound up for another
pitch, this time with an accompanying impersonation of diminutive,
bald, and toothless Grandpa Joe.

"I mean, he even says stuff out loud like, 'Woe is me, woe is me!
My eyes, my eyes! I can't see, and I haven't had a bowel movement
in weeks.'"

"He said that at Nora's?"

"Yeah! But doesn't he say that everywhere?"

"What did Grandma say about it?"

"You know Grandma. She didn't say anything. She just sort of pats
him on the hand like he's a kid and finds another conversation. Did
you know Uncle Art was there?"

No answer. Just the usual *UncleArtLook* that crossed his face as he
stared off to the left corner of the sky. He coughed a short, nervous
throat-clearing and bent over slightly as if in pain.

I'd said the wrong thing. As if my air had been knocked out, I
tried to breathe in deep and then another slow breath.

"I feel bad about putting Grandpa in that home," he muttered. "And
Mary Ellen...poor Mary Ellen! I should've been there...done something differently. I mean, my mother was so..."

I hung on that pause, waiting for an explanation, some key to fall out of the sky—one that would unlock the box of trouble in my father's head.

Nothing.

He stopped himself and after a few seconds, lowered his hand from his head, looked up, and scratched his nose. Without saying another word, he exhaled loudly, started the ignition, and we headed for home.

Windows, doors shut. He was locked away inside again. And I went back to feeling powerless, watching, hoping, waiting, afraid.

Nine

El Greco and Me

THE NIGHT BEFORE MY ELEVENTH birthday, I lay in bed and listened to my parents' conversation, alert for clues as to how Dad was doing. The light of the moon shined on the poster of my favorite Redskin player, Larry Brown, as my mother pleaded with my father to stop feeling so guilty. I drew my pale green blanket up and rubbed the smooth satin border on my cheek, wishing we could just go "home"—to Cleveland.

I heard the mattress springs squeak and Dad's feet hit the floor. I took in a quick breath and sat up. He knocked something over on the night stand, probably reaching for the glasses that everyone said made him look like Steve Allen, and mumbled words I couldn't understand. A door opened. *He must be getting his robe out of the closet for his pacing ritual.* I imagined the way his legs looked too short for his long body, straining to hear the *why* of it all as he made what had to be no more than four or five steps and then a turn, four steps and turn. Pacing and muttering went on for hours while Mom sniffled and cried. Ann was sleeping in the bedroom across from mine and never stirred.

❧

"Dick, get in bed, please! I can't take this anymore. You need your rest, and so do I!"

"What could I have done? I should have known she was so upset. Why did she do it?" he asked himself out loud as if he'd heard nothing Mom said.

"That's enough. Stop feeling guilty for things you had no control over!"

I pictured the way his facial muscles had gone on vacation since he began to stare blankly into a soup of memories. His steps shuffled along until Mom started to cry even louder.

"Get back in bed!" she commanded.

I quietly slipped out of my bed and crawled to the door for a better chance to hear. I lay down on my stomach and listened.

Poor Mom. I had to think of some way to help her. Images of happier Ohio days and nights took me away from the tension and lured me to sleep where I still lay by the door. I awoke to daylight and the sound of Mom getting ready to go to the airport to pick up Grandma Marie. I pushed myself up off the floor and to my feet, rubbing my neck as I stumbled to my bed for a few more minutes of sleep.

When I awoke again later that morning, rain was pounding against my window. I said "good morning" to Dad as I passed the hall bathroom, and he grunted back as he stared in the bathroom mirror, like it held some answer he couldn't remember. I knew I wasn't imagining that things were seriously wrong.

I walked downstairs for breakfast to the rhythm of clinking dishes and silverware. Mom was a whirlwind of Pine Sol, Murphy's Oil Soap, and Windex. Grandma Marie was drinking her coffee and reading the Sunday paper. Neither seemed alarmed in the least by Dad's behavior.

I looked out the kitchen window at the falling rain and wished it could wash away all the weirdness.

※

Back in our family room that evening, I realized that we had made it through the day without incident. Church, Dad's driving, the pharmacy, birthday dinner, cake, TV, and now he was reading his Bible. It was dark outside, and I let out a sigh of relief. *All my worrying for nothing!*

Kung Fu, my favorite show, was about to begin, I wondered if Dad might enjoy watching *it* with me. I was about to ask him when he excused himself to the bathroom upstairs. Grandma said she wanted to finish her book. Ann joined her in the living room while Mom started doing the laundry. I was lost in the exploits of the protagonist, Caine, when I heard Mom screaming.

"He took his pills! Ohmigod! He took his pills!"

I raced to the living room to see her standing there crying and screaming hysterically. This was no ordinary crying. I had grown accustomed to that. No, this was completely different. Her face was contorted, and her already big brown eyes had widened. I was so caught up in the moment and in her face, I don't remember anything about Grandma or Ann. The next thing I knew, Mom and I were running to the bathroom at the top of the stairs.

Dad was lying on the floor in his Fruit-of-the-Loom underwear. She held up the orange-tinted medicine bottle and pointed at it.

"The pills, the pills! Did you swallow them all? Omigod! How can you do this to me?"

He was on his side and his legs were bent and scissored. His arms were splayed out while his head rested partially on the green bathroom rug and partially on the beige linoleum floor. His skin, undershirt, and briefs looked especially white against the green walls, like a white and elongated subject of an El Greco painting.

I knew he was going to hurt himself today, I wanted to shout.

Why hadn't they known?

"We have to keep him moving! He's taken all of his sleeping pills!" Mom cried.

I bent down and touched his arm and recoiled at first because his skin was clammy and pasty white.

Mom tugged on her hair and screamed hysterically. "Get up!"

I reached down and pulled on Dad's right arm. She lifted under his left side, and we somehow got him to sit up on the cold bathroom floor. Then I pulled, Mom pushed. Together we picked him up off the floor.

"How could you do this to me?" she screamed again.

The scent of her perfume clashed with the smell of bleach and Pine Sol in the always-clean bathroom of our always-clean house.

My head felt thick, and I couldn't find a single word.

"We need an ambulance! Just keep him moving!" Then she left the room.

I thought she went to call an ambulance, but I would later found that she ran down the stairs and *out the door of our house.*

Dad leaned against me, and I struggled to keep him upright. I pulled his arm over my left shoulder and put my right arm around his waist. We shuffled from the bathroom to his bedroom like two drunks on Bourbon Street. The light from the hall kept us from bumping into furniture.

"What, Dad? Did you say something?" I asked.

I sat him down on the bed so I could rest.

"Daddy, please, please don't die."

He mumbled again. I looked into his eyes and knew he saw no one.

"You know I wouldn't trade you for all the baseball cards in the world!"

He blinked and looked at me like I was some nice girl he couldn't quite place. His silvery hair was matted to the left side of his head, and he had a five o'clock shadow that looked past midnight.

"Please, Dad, let's get up."

I hoisted him up again and walked him in the darkness to the other side of the room. How can I turn on the light without him falling? *Jesus...please help me! I promise I'll do anything.*

I tried to tell myself it was going to work out, that he'd be okay, all the while wishing I'd been born *someone* else—someone who didn't have to do *this.*

We walked a few more steps and a wave of invincibility hit me. Mom had left me there. And Grandma—where was she? Like Mom, nowhere to be found. If I couldn't do this, it wouldn't get done. It was only me. I, a day away from actually being eleven years old, summoned my *Susan to the Rescue* persona to fight for Dad's life.

"Come on, Dad, keep going. That's it...put your right foot out. Take another step...I gotcha."

It was my will against his. The voice in my brain repeated to my super self: *He'll be all right, he'll be all right.* We walked him around the room. Round and round and round.

An ambulance arrived. The emergency technicians said something about pumping his stomach, and Mrs. Bowen steered me out of the room. I panted as if I'd run for miles. I was a little shaky, but I had done my job. I'd done it!

Now, I could go off Daddy duty. I walked down the driveway with Mrs. Bowen's arm around me, into the cold rain, and past the onlookers and flashing sirens. We headed to her house, and I remember wondering how I would explain the commotion to the neighborhood kids. I didn't really know what happened when it was happening. Later I learned that my mother ran out the door and went to Mrs. Bowen's house where they called the ambulance. So I was left alone with my dad. My grandmother and Ann were downstairs. I suspect my Grandma just couldn't deal with it so she stayed downstairs with my sister, but who knows?

That night, I wanted my dad to live more than anything, but once I got to the Bowen house, I just wanted to see my friends and be a kid again. Mary Beth said something about being sorry that my dad was sick, and we ran upstairs with her brother, Russ, to flip baseball cards. I couldn't wait to tell them that I had won a Willie Mays rookie card the previous day.

I awoke the next morning in Mary Beth's room and momentarily forgot where I was. A glossy, black and white photo on the wall reminded me. Mary Beth loved that autographed picture of her home state's governor, Ronald Reagan. I used to look at it, not because I was particularly interested, but because it was at eye level when we kneeled on her bed and sang pop tunes out the window.

I don't remember much about that next day except the most important thing—the inner voice didn't always lie—Dad had survived his suicide attempt and the night. I overheard Mom say the hand of God slowed the shipping department at People's Drugstore long enough to save him.

Maybe. Or maybe God had empowered young *Super Susan* to regain her lost confidence and help Dad live to see another day.

That evening, I returned home to a house that held a temporary sense of relief—but no father. The hospital people would watch him now.

This should have been my transition back to being an eleven-year-old. The problem was, I'd experienced a scary taste of adulthood, one not so easily swallowed. Something had been lost in that walk around Dad's room. Whatever it was had been replaced with profound fears that would not be addressed, and instead, would fester below the surface.

Divers get the bends from surfacing too quickly, molecules of nitrogen expanding and exploding delicate membranes. My dad had no defenses against the sad realities that led to Aunt Mary Ellen's brutal death. Steady doses of truth might have brought a healing decompression to my dad, but truth was something my family suppressed.

I had detected the danger of his condition, but not my own. I too would eventually get the bends, the long-range effects of this weekend holding me under long enough to allow my fears to take up primary residence inside. Years later, truth, long held back, would surface suddenly and shatter the delicate strands holding me together, strands connected through layer upon layer of family histories laid over raw places in my heart. I didn't know that I, too, was underwater, walking around in the deep end. At age eleven, there was only one place for me to turn.

At least I have Jesus, I thought.

Part Two

A Closer Walk

Ten

Guidebook to Sanity

MY PARENTS NEVER MENTIONED DAD's suicide attempt other than to say it was a *miracle* that he had survived. God had saved him through the intervention of a shipping delay.

Somehow I forced myself not to think about the whole episode, but Hal still tormented me at school and new worries landed on the pile. Mom said Dad was getting "sick pay," but I worried it would run out, and the loss of his regular paychecks scared me. Worries often upset me so much, I needed to sprint down to the basketball court at London Towne Elementary or cycle up and down Kamputa Drive, fantasizing about kicking a soccer ball through Hal's bedroom window. Devouring a Hostess lemon pie, Mom's peanut-butter cookies, or a Hershey bar helped even more.

One month after Dad's suicide attempt, Mom said he was feeling much better and doing well enough for a visit. But did she really know? And would she really say if he wasn't? *Would he be wearing some kind of crazy white jacket to keep him from committing any more self-destructive acts?*

We arrived at the specified visiting hour, and I was pleased to find him in a regular shirt and pants. No restraints. He smiled and hugged us hard, as though he'd been away at sea and we were visiting him at the port of call to his sanity.

"Hi, Dad! How are you feeling?" I asked while Ann crawled up onto his lap. I watched her hug his neck and scratch her face on the bristle of his stubbled cheek. He looked almost normal.

"Well, I'm pretty good, but these people here really need to know the Lord. There are a lot of evil things going on here. White and black witches who can make things float around the room."

Stuff was flying around the room? I scanned the area, but gravity seemed to be doing its usual job. "There are black and white *witches?*"

"Yes, practicing white and black magic—not talking about skin color. The white ones have good intentions, and the black ones don't. Either way, it's dangerous, and although they might not understand the danger, we need to pray against those forces of evil they're toying with."

The only witches I wanted to hear about were in *The Wizard of Oz* or the Halloween costume aisle at K-Mart. My stomach started to hurt. Other little girls in fifth grade didn't have to visit their father in a mental hospital. I walked over to the record player and picked up a Jim Croce album, turned it over, and read the song list over and over until the letters started to blur. Mom and Dad began chatting about the hospital food and the weather. I tuned out the rest, my mind adept at disconnecting from the rest of me since my constant vigil too often brought more than I could handle. Eventually, I tuned back in and realized that Dad was talking about Jesus as if He were a guy living right there at the mental hospital. My father apparently saw himself as some sort of missionary to the mentally ill.

I tried to change the subject. *Do they have art classes here like we have at school?* Yes, once a week, and he was helping teach the others.

"Wait here and I'll show you some of what I'm working on." He came back with three small sketches and a watercolor—all with religious themes. "See, here's how I'm signing my name now—with the fish symbol that symbolizes Christ Jesus."

His previously scribbled signature now incorporated a symbol I'd seen before, one that looked like a fish heading vertically out of water. I wanted to know why all this happened. Why Mom had run out the door. Most importantly—*Would it happen again? Was*

I safe? Instead, religious symbols and talk of missionary work in a mental ward replaced any explanation I might have expected for *ThatSuicideNight.*

Back in my own room that night, I tried to understand the "forces" that had "toyed with" people like my dad so I could make sure they wouldn't return. Meanwhile, somewhere deep inside an inner place I didn't want to go, I worried that those same forces might also get a hold of me.

⚜

In May, 1973, Dad had been home for a month, I started thinking we could finally have a regular life in D.C. I loved being with Mary Beth and Russ, loved playing soccer and baseball in the neighborhood. Even though it bothered me that I never stood up to Halitosis Hal, at least the bastard never caught me. I had never said a word like "bastard" out loud, but when I heard that one, it seemed to fit Hal perfectly. The school year was almost over, and I was looking forward to the summer with Russ, Mary Beth, and other neighborhood kids. Everything changed when Mom called Ann and me into the family room one Saturday morning. I sat on the far side of the green plaid couch, tracing the crisscross of the pattern with my finger, thinking over the previous day's game of baseball while Ann fidgeted next to me.

"Kids, your father and I have something to tell you." Mom looked nervous.

I looked up to see a muscle twitch, right above the corner of her mouth. Her dark brown eyes darted back and forth. Dad cleared his throat. This wasn't going to be good.

Mom drew a deep breath. "We've decided to move back home to Cleveland, and we'll be putting the house up for sale in a few weeks."

Even though this wasn't an emergency of the kind we'd already lived through, it was another blow that felt like I'd been tackled and held down. I couldn't breathe.

Ann said, "Oh, good. Are we going to move back to our old house?"

Dad looked down at his hands. "No, sweetie, there's another family living there now."

"What about the neighborhood and our old school? Can we go back there?" I asked.

"No, honey. We want a fresh start, and, well, you know how it is." Mom avoided eye contact. "We won't be going back to the east side."

Of course, Mom must have been ashamed, worried how she'd recount the tale of Dad's self-induced ambulance ride to our old neighbors.

"We might as well be moving to a whole new city!" I moaned. "And what about all of your friends *here*? Your Bible study ladies and all that?" Mom had acted like she couldn't do without her circles of support that had kept her sane during Dad's breakdown.

Mom sat down and put her arm around me, and I smelled her perfume. "God's people are everywhere, and He'll be wherever we go in Ohio too," she said.

Yeah, but Mrs. Bowen won't be there for you, and Russ and Mary Beth sure won't be there for me either. We weren't even going to have a place of our own, but Mom and Dad said we were blessed; when the time was right, we'd look for a new house on the west side of town where Aunt Nora and Dad's other relatives lived. In the meantime, we were going to move in with Mom's parents for the summer. The move was as welcome as the acid rain that had been so much in the news lately. I ran out the front door to the garage. No one followed. I thought about riding my bike to Mary Beth's house, but I'd just start blubbering. I fought back tears that eventually won, and I kicked the garage wall.

❧

More moving boxes, more good-byes. We sold the Biscayne and headed back to Cleveland in Mom's Chevy Vega, putting most of our possessions in storage so we could move into Gramma's house in an east-side suburb of Cleveland, ten minutes from our old neighborhood.

Dad seemed happy with our getaway from D.C. He even started drawing again. I joined him, and we set up our supplies on Gramma's kitchen table. As I worked on a watercolor landscape, he sketched scenes from Bible stories on scraps of beige vinyl wallpaper he planned to use as "canvas" for the final paintings when we moved into a place of our own. I picked up his latest—a drawing of Jesus hanging on the cross. It wasn't bad, but I wanted to see his old stuff. Gone were the majestic trees and serene lakes, the detailed technical drawings. Had Dad been artistically lobotomized? His creativity zapped by shock therapy?

He read the Bible as though it were the guidebook to sanity. Sitting across from me one morning at Gramma's, he studied the Gospel of John.

He looked up at me. "I'm thinking about going into the ministry," he said.

I couldn't think of a response I could say out loud.

Me? A "preacher's kid"? *Please don't let that happen.* I didn't understand how you could take a bottle full of pills one day, clap along to "praise songs" a few months later, and then decide to be a minister. Now his head was down and he was deep in scripture

"Dad..." Are the bad times gone for good? "I mean, are you...?"

He didn't hear me, so I continued to try imagining what life as the First Family of Faith might be like. I thought about how stupid I'd look in one of those starched prairie dresses churchy females seemed to wear. *Oh God, no!* I didn't want to bother him with questions or nudge him into a dive into the deep end of his mind, a place that couldn't possibly match his new, outward serenity, so I left it in the hands of God.

❀

Spending time with "Gramma" and Grandpa Frank, or "Poppy," as I had named him when I was too little to say "Grandpa," made me feel safe and gloriously normal. At first, I believed that staying at their house might fix things. Gramma loved to cater to me as if I were royalty.

"Here, my little dolly," said Gramma as she tied her apron. "Why don't you have a seat at the table. Let me cook you and your sister lunch before you unload any more luggage from that car."

"Ma," Mom protested, "they can help—"

"Oh, I know, but it was a long drive from Virginia, and they must be tired. If you and Dick won't take a break, at least let the girls have lunch."

Poppy coughed and mumbled something about going to the hardware store.

Gramma's sugarcoating dissolved. "Get going, Frank. You can't tell me you're going to some store right now! Go help with the car."

Poppy's shoulders drooped. "Okay, okay, I'm going."

Whether Poppy was aware of it or not, Gramma decided when he could come and go. She also told him where he could sleep.

"He snores so loud. I told him to go to the other bedroom. I mean, what can I do?"

That meant when we arrived, there was only one extra bedroom for our whole family. Dad and I slept on cots on the side of the basement that Gramma used for laundry, while Ann stayed with Mom in the third bedroom. Dad didn't seem to mind. I didn't either, even though the last time I was left alone with Dad, life hit the skids and we nearly crashed. I don't know why Mom and Dad didn't sleep together; maybe Ann was afraid of the basement. Or, maybe Mom was resentful of what Dad had put us through and reluctant to return to intimacy until Dad proved he wasn't going to try to kill himself again.

I'd slept in late the next morning and awakened to find myself alone in the basement. I dressed and hurried upstairs. "Where's Dad?"

Sitting at the kitchen table, Poppy grunted and barely looked up from his newspaper.

Gramma appeared with a what-did-Poppy-know-about-it stance. "Your father went to the library, and your mom and sister went to the store. I told them you'd rather stay here with us. Was that okay, honey? How about some bacon and eggs? Then afterwards you can have a Snickers bar." Health food, Slovenian style.

Never one to turn down chocolate, I quickly ate my eggs and toast, and then nibbled on the candy to make it last. Poppy went outside, and Gramma got right to the point as she dropped spoonfuls of cookie dough onto a baking sheet, blackened with decades of use.

"You know, dolly, I know what it's like to be torn up by the roots." Grandma's voice was soft, her tone sweet. "When I was your age, we still lived in Newark. We moved to Cleveland when my father found a new job in a factory where his brother worked. There was a pretty big Slovenian community in Cleveland, then and now, but I was so lonely at first. You'll have to give your new home a chance."

She described the Slovenian Home where young couples talked over plates of stuffed cabbage and blood sausage. She popped cookies in the oven and told of the older women who cut freshly baked *potica* and brewed coffee while the men played bocce ball or threw horseshoes in between puffs on cigarettes and swigs of beer.

The few times I'd been at the Slovenian Home the previous year, I loved the smells, the families, the old people, and the homey atmosphere. There was a connection; a part of something solid and enduring with the stability I craved. Old folks speaking in another language made me wish I could speak it too. I didn't mention that Poppy always gave me a taste of his Schlitz beer while we listened to Frankie Yankovic (Weird Al's father) play the accordion.

"The only socializing I ever did was at the Slovenian Home." Gramma handed me the spoon and bowl to lick. I loved the feeling that—for once—all was right with the world.

"I never went without Joe and my sisters—not before I was married, anyway. My mother wouldn't allow it." She looked out the window, as if she could catch glimpses of the past. "Poppy was so handsome back then—not so fat like he is now! The day he walked up to our table, well, I could barely talk."

My tiny grandmother giggled like one of those little people on *The Wizard of Oz*. Again, I bit into the cold and chewy Snickers bar and felt lucky to be sitting with her, seeing a different Poppy through her eyes. Gramma was still staring out the window.

I loved Gramma and considered her wise, but as religion became more of an obsession with my whole family, I questioned the evangelical world view and worried about Gramma's soul. I wanted the impossible: an inclusive faith we could all agree on. "Did your parents take you to church?" I asked her.

"Oh yes, every Sunday—to the Catholic church, of course."

"Do you believe in Jesus?"

Gramma looked at me like I'd just landed on Earth. "Of course, honey—why do you ask?"

"It's just that people, you know, the Born-Again people we've met, don't think you're a real Christian unless you accept Jesus as your Lord and Savior."

Gramma had been looking out the window and then abruptly turned her head and looked at me. She leaned in and said in a quiet voice, "Well, but honey, we all know Jesus is our Savior, so I don't know what all the fuss is about." She pulled the cookies out of the oven. "How about a cookie? You'll love the marshmallow and the chocolate together. You want milk too, right?"

A surefire dodge. After finishing the extended breakfast and our conversation, I ran outside to play with Duchess in the backyard. As good as all the hominess felt, I still wanted a friend or something to do. Poppy was in the backyard and saw me coming. He quickly threw down his cigarette, thinking I didn't notice. He didn't seem happy very often, and I wondered if he was a different person after his breakdown so many years ago. Duchess bolted over to greet me; I roughed-up and then smoothed her fur, thinking about Gramma's saying Poppy had been a handsome young man once. It was hard to imagine. I knew he'd grown up in Yugoslavia. It always seemed to me that he had one foot in each country. The seesaw of his life hadn't been between his family and career, but between the two countries.

I tried to see him as the young father of my mother and Aunt Joy. Mom said he used to pick her up and hug her after coming home from work. If she was lucky, he took her bowling or brought her with him to watch him play bocce ball at the Slovenian Home. During World War II, he worked long hours in Cleveland factories, churning out bolts, screws, and other fasteners for war planes, tanks, and God knew what else.

I wanted him to tell me what it was like to have a breakdown and then come back to a wife and two daughters, just as Dad had done. I knew not to ask this, but maybe he'd tell stories as Gramma had done, and I could sneak in some questions. "Do you miss Yugoslavia?"

"Every day." He looked me in the eye and reached down and picked up a handful of soil from his garden. "But an uneducated man like me could *never* own *this i*n Yugoslavia." He cradled the soil like it was a newborn infant. And that was all he would say.

⚘

After dinner, I headed downstairs to read. Nancy Drew didn't hold my attention that night, though I loved her adventures. I'd moved my cot to the "rec room" side of the basement where I could poke around in things. In the corner of the room sat the Victrola that Gramma cranked up every once in a while. She'd told me Nelson Eddy and Jeannette MacDonald danced across her youth, making her believe life and love were beautiful. Why couldn't things just stay that way? I walked over to Poppy's desk where I'd left one of our photo albums and found a picture of our former Ohio house, now occupied by another family.

I almost cried. I needed Duchess and called for her. She came running down into the basement from upstairs, always happy for some attention. I climbed into my cot and stroked her fur, closing my eyes, wishing I could transport myself back into the world we left behind. Gramma probably wanted to crawl into the world of that old 78 rpm record just like I wanted to crawl into that picture of our old house.

Eleven

The Sign of the Fleece

❦ WATCHED DAD FROM THE driveway as he swirled suds onto the hood of the Vega to the sound of Tony Orlando and Dawn singing about oak trees, yellow ribbons, and missing people you love. Dad wiped sweat from his forehead and smiled at me. Me. Not something strange that was going on in his head. I removed my sandals and splashed my feet in the cool water.

He even knew I was antsy. "Mind taking the dog for a walk? She could use the exercise."

As Duchess and I worked our way up and down the street, I longed for the tall Dutch elm trees of my old neighborhood, but there were no elms, no old oaks, or trees of any kind. Our former house stood only a few miles to the south of Gramma's, but I felt like it would take a time machine to travel there. Duchess pulled me away from the property my grandfather owned on Swetland Boulevard—which needed another *a* to be aptly named. Few children lived in the plain, one-story homes of this eerily quiet, shade-less street without lawns or sidewalks. Neighbors didn't say "Hello" as we passed. There were no neighborhood ball games; there was no one to play with.

Mom didn't seem to miss either of our old neighborhoods; she preferred order to nostalgia or introspection. When we weren't going to the grocery store or the library, we were running other errands or cleaning the house. *Keep moving and don't think about anything*—that was her solution. But I needed more. I wanted to find the path back to Normal, and no one knew how to help me, so it was a summer of pesky questions and snooping as I tried to sort things out for myself.

After our walk, I gave Duchess some water and went back inside. As I entered quietly through the front door, I heard Mom on the phone. I moved silently toward the green-carpeted steps leading to Gramma's attic of old treasures. Ever since I was five, I had liked to spend hours in the attic, looking at Mom's old paper dolls, sitting on Aunt Joy's English saddle, or reading through old Christmas cards. Today though, it was far too hot for that. Making my way to the third step where I wouldn't be seen, I sat and listened. Voice muffled, Mom said something about Dad's job. I leaned forward, but still couldn't make out what she was saying. Her voice changed back to a pleasant tone, and just like that, her conversation was over.

I jumped with the click of the receiver. Mom turned quickly around the corner and saw me perched on the steps.

"What are you doing here?"

My throat went dry. I tried to think of something that would make sense and make her go on with her afternoon and forget about me. "Nothin'."

"Well, it looks to me like you're eavesdropping, and I don't like it." Her eyes flashed an anger I hadn't seen in a while.

"I'm sorry. I was just...well, I just wanted to know if..."

"Come on, honey, spit it out. I'm really tired." She tapped her foot like she did when she needed things to be moving along.

I ground my toe into Gramma's green carpeting, trying to switch gears. I'd wanted to know if there was some other terrible event about to happen, but was afraid to ask. "I wondered, ya know...um...what you liked to do when you were my age."

Her mood softened. "Oh, honey, let's see....I liked to play with my paper dolls and talk to my friends about clothes and music. I wanted to get as far away as possible from the Slovenian Home, that's for sure! It was a time of Rock and Roll—Elvis!"

I didn't get Elvis. I liked James Taylor, Three Dog Night, and Elton John. I also didn't get why she didn't like the Slovenian Home.

Mom continued. "But of course, those were the years Poppy had his nervous breakdown."

Breakdown. That word again. I still didn't completely understand what happened when a person had a breakdown. "Did he...?" The anxious look on her face stopped me. I quickly changed the subject to another safe topic. "Did you like to play ball?" I knew that she did, but hearing about it always made me feel good. We had *something* in common.

"Oh, I loved softball. My friends and I would play every day during the summer, in the vacant lot next to the house." She gestured toward the houses now standing on her ball field. "At night, we'd all bring a potato and start a fire and use the burning coals to warm the ground so we could bake them in the hot earth. I loved that first taste of salted and buttered potato. We'd stay out late until my dad came for me 'cause Gramma worried about the dark and all."

Hearing that made me feel good. She'd had fun playing with kids in the neighborhood, just as I did. Like me, she also adored her father. When she was little, she used to wait on the front stoop for him to come home from work.

"I felt invisible sometimes." Mom's statement suddenly humanized her for me. She became, not my mother, but a little girl. "Every so often, my dad made time for picnics at Lake Erie or at Pymatuning Lake in Pennsylvania. I was six or seven, and my dad carried me into the lake—I think it was Pymatuning—and let go of me."

Dad would never have done that to me. She must have been panicked. "What happened?"

She was looking off into the distance and finally said softly, "He laughed and grabbed me just when I thought I would drown. He said I'd never learn unless someone threw me in."

Neither Poppy nor Gramma seemed particularly interested in understanding her feelings. Poppy had certainly had to bury his. Maybe somewhere along the way, she grew to realize they looked at emotion as one of those luxuries or conveniences they couldn't afford as they focused their attention on hard work, frugal living, and home ownership.

I felt bad for her, knowing that now she had to deal with my father, thrown into the pool of his depression. Maybe she felt like me.

❧

No home, no friends. Down in my grandparents' basement, I worried. I was afraid that everyone looked sideways at my father and whispered about the nearest mental hospital. I, too, was looking sideways at him as he steeped himself in scriptures in the basement with me, trying to become a preacher. I often sought comfort in the bounty of Gramma's kitchen.

Every now and then, Dad emerged from his Bible study to help Poppy with minor repairs around the house or to take us to K-Mart for packs of gum, Kit-Kat bars, or the balsa-wood airplanes that we assembled and flew in the front yard. Still, I kept thinking of the fun I'd be having at that moment with Mary Beth and Russ if we hadn't moved.

I turned to the most reliable fun source I knew. Baseball. Despite its long history of losing teams, Cleveland was a rabid sports town. America's pastime kept me occupied with trading cards, Indians games, and Hank Aaron's quest to beat Babe Ruth's long-standing home run record. I spent hours poring over articles in *The Plain Dealer* that detailed Hank's pursuit. I recorded his stats and drew pictures of Hank, "The Babe," and Roger Maris until I finally had my sketches looking as lifelike as I could muster. Dad even put down his Bible and religious tracts long enough to help me start a "1974 Cleveland Indians Journal" that I filled with my commentary and portraits of each player on our roster. I carefully arranged it all in a green scrapbook Mom purchased for me at K-Mart. No one pressured me out of my tomboyish ways—at least not to any extent that made me doubt myself. My dad seemed proud of my sports knowledge, so as a child of eleven, I could still bask in the glow of parental approval.

Old men often preempted baseball that summer, however. I'd try to watch a game on TV, only to find endless testimony about a thing called *Watergate*. "I have no recollection," they all seemed to say over and over again. Ann and I played board games and bickered.

Some of those summer nights held all the wonder any child in a *normal* family could hope for, though. We ran around outside, catching fireflies in our hands and keeping them in jars they lit green. Dad emerged from the basement and helped us put holes in the tops of the jar lids. He didn't want to see his girls get hurt with a sharp object. Some nights he built a charcoal fire in Poppy's barbecue grill so we could roast marshmallows. Dad seemed to enjoy those days without work and worry. He returned to being such a good dad that summer, and I wanted to believe he was truly his old self.

Didn't he need to find a job though? I hadn't noticed him going to any interviews yet. Mom circled classified advertisements of jobs he might try, but he didn't seem interested. Was it because he was still considering the ministry? I took up my post, listening to their conversations every chance I got.

"Listen, I told you, I've been praying about this," Dad said to Mom in the kitchen while Gramma and Poppy were in the backyard. "I'm waiting for a sign about what I should do. I've put out a fleece—"

"A fleece?" Mom sounded indignant. "How will that work? Just because God told Gideon to do it thousands of years ago, doesn't mean you should do it now! You need to find work!"

"Well, I'm waiting for a sign. I'm feeling even more called to the ministry."

"We have savings to put down on a house, not for you to go to divinity school!"

"Who said anything about school? There are plenty of pastors and assistant pastors in non-denominational churches who didn't attend the seminary."

If our future depended on a piece of wool, I'd better find out how reliable it was. That afternoon, when Gramma and I were perched in the cool of the basement, reading through stacks of old copies of *Reader's Digest* on Poppy's desk, I looked it up in the Bible. I found the reference to a fleece and Gideon in Judges 6:36–40.

Then Gideon said to God, "If You will deliver Israel through me, as You have spoken, behold, I will put a fleece of wool on the threshing floor. If there is dew on the fleece only, and it is dry on all the ground, then I will know that You will deliver Israel through me, as You have spoken."

And it was so. When he arose early the next morning and squeezed the fleece, he drained the dew from the fleece, a bowl full of water.

Then Gideon said to God, "Do not let Your anger burn against me that I may speak once more; please let me make a test once more with the fleece, let it now be dry only on the fleece, and let there be dew on all the ground."

God did so that night; for it was dry only on the fleece, and dew was on all the ground.

I sat there for a moment, trying to understand the confusing words. Wait. So the ground was wet, but the wool wasn't, so somehow Gideon had proof that God was in favor of his idea? (Whatever that was.) But how would Dad do it? Did he really need to get a piece of fleece? I wished I could ask, but I'd get in trouble for eavesdropping. I also wished I hadn't overheard the fleece thing because it seemed weird and unreliable to think about setting up tests to find out what God wanted. It seemed more than a little loony.

Mom and Ann returned home from the mall and interrupted my thoughts. I jumped in my seat and closed the Bible with a start as they came downstairs to enjoy the cool air.

"Did you find anything?" Gramma asked Mom and Ann.

"Well, I found this dress I thought would be good for my next job interview," Mom said, removing a royal blue dress out of the bag and holding it up for us to see.

"How much did you pay for it? It looks expensive! Maybe you should go to K-Mart and see the sales they have there next time. That blue light they have is really good."

Mom's face fell. Mine did too.

An hour later, I was bouncing my basketball in the driveway when Mom's sister, Aunt Joy, and her son, Sam, drove up in a green Volvo station wagon. I had never seen such a car; it was boxy and sturdy. Different. We lived in the land of the American car, the region of our country where Chevys, Chryslers, and Fords were manufactured with pride and well-paying factory jobs were expected. Other than Volkswagen Beetles, I'd seen only a few foreign cars in my life.

"Hi, sweet girl!" Aunt Joy greeted me. She looked so pretty. Her big blue eyes sparkled, signaling to me that she was glad to see me.

"I like your car! It's really different!"

"Thanks! I thought I needed to get something a bit more sensible than that '66 Mustang I had," she said.

Just thinking about that red Mustang with the white leather interior made me smile. "Yeah, but that was a cool car."

My grandparents hurried out the door of the house to meet Joy. Mom followed.

"*Yo*, what is dis?" bellowed Poppy.

"A Volvo, Dad—one of the safest cars on the road." Joy responded, as she opened the driver-side door.

"Safe? Were you unsafe before? So expensive!"

"Do you know how expensive it'll be to maintain it?" Gramma added as my mother nodded her agreement with that assessment.

Joy exhaled and suddenly seemed tired as she climbed out of the driver's seat and stood next to me.

"Oh, Joy, what were you thinking?" Mom asked.

Why did Mom just put Joy down in the same way Gramma just did to her? I wanted to slink back into the house to escape their misfiring communication, but stayed out of politeness.

Joy looked at Mom, then Poppy and Gramma. She opened the car door and climbed back into the driver's seat. "Why can't you all just be happy for me? Why do you care if it costs me a bit more to service? Just never mind." She closed the door and started the engine; our visit with Aunt Joy finished before it started.

I stood in the driveway, feeling stunned.

Why couldn't they see what they had just done to her? Wasn't there anywhere we could all just *be*? I wanted to land somewhere safe, where family could protect me from the outside world and its diseases and inner worlds didn't break down, but I was learning that if you held an individual liking for something unconventional, even something as trivial as a certain dress or type of car, you'd better not look to this family for support or congratulations. Imagine the disapproval over a social deviation, a political idea that ran counter to their world view—or a different religious idea.

⚜

The Catholics in our family probably thought our newfound Born-Again faith was a passing fad or even that we were part of a cult, but I doubt they knew how serious we were or how certain we were that we were right. *The Catholics don't count.* That's what we Evangelicals really believed. *They* were not *real* Christians, and so they were just as ripe for evangelizing as Atheists, "Secular" Christians, Hindus, Muslims, or Jews.

"Are you going to Mass?" Gramma asked Mom, trying to pretend she was focused on dusting the coffee table, rather than worrying that her daughter was abandoning her Catholic faith.

"We don't go to Mass anymore. I told you that," Mom snapped. "Look, I'm sorry, Mom, things are just different—and I wanna wait to find a church until after we get into our own place."

"Well, I just don't think you should so easily leave your faith behind."

"Mom, I'm doing what I believe is best; please try to respect that."

"But how can you leave The Church?"

Their bickering continued. I'd be scolded if I put my hands over my ears, so I listened nervously. I'd heard a TV preacher say, "Going to church doesn't make you a Christian any more than going to a garage makes you a car." I guessed that meant that just because Gramma had been going to church all of her life, she shouldn't think she was a Christian. The Good News of the Gospel was that Jesus died for you, so if you accepted Him as your personal Savior, well, then Hell and Damnation were not to be yours. The trouble was, it sounded more to me like bad news than good. How could I be happy about being saved if Gramma was damned to hell?

At least one controversy cleared up. Apparently, Dad's fleece revealed that he was going to have to get a real job to support the family. I watched him as he wrote his resume and numerous letters on legal-sized, yellow note pads that he handed over to Mom to type. Weeks went by and still no job for Dad.

He called his old boss. I heard Mom tell Aunt Nora that they could only offer him a position at a lower rank and pay than what he had before D.C. The department head worried he couldn't handle the pressure. But Mom said that wasn't right since he had held his Cleveland job for several years prior to his breakdown. Dad turned down the offer.

Discrimination. I was learning about it for the first time. Finding a job would not be easy. People still thought Dad was crazy. *Would anyone hire him?* I looked for signs of insanity or weirdness in his prayers, Bible reading, Christian radio and books. He trusted Jesus, and hopefully, some boss somewhere would see that he wasn't nuts— except about the Lord.

Two months at Gramma and Poppy's house seemed more like four with the cramped quarters and no playmates, and it was long past time to move into our own place. I lay my head on my pillow at night and prayed. *Please God, keep us all safe and happy. I don't know how to do a fleece. Is that really what You want? Please help Dad and Mom find jobs, and they'll be all right without Gramma and Poppy.*

Amen.

Twelve

Nerves

FINALLY MOM AND DAD FOUND a house. Neither of them had found work, but their nest egg allowed a small split-level in a west-side suburb in a good school district. Mom didn't seem to care that the house was much smaller than our home in Centreville. She was grateful for our own place. So was I.

Shortly after Ann and I arrived at Pine Elementary, I discovered that things at this new school were going to be far worse than they had been at my school in Centreville. Obviously, I had landed on the low end of the food chain, probably walking with a lack of confidence that bullies sensed and seized on—as Grandma Marie would say. My Super Self hadn't returned, and an outbreak of acne didn't help.

The leader of the pack at my new school was like a nastier, big-nosed cousin of my nemesis in Centreville. His name was Stan Stakich, and unfortunately—at the time—it didn't dawn on me that his surname rhymed with *jock itch.* Little Stanley took great pleasure in calling me pizza face, crater face, or whatever else his genius brain could come up with.

"Hey, crater face, where's your short, fat friend?" Meaning my new friend, Lisa. "You two look like a pizza-faced version of Laurel and Hardy waddling down the hall!"

I wanted to knock his block off the way I did to opponents in the *Rock 'Em Sock 'Em* boxing game I'd gotten for Christmas a few years back. *Pow!* I imagined his head knocked clean off his neck. *Imagined.* In reality, I lost my nerve. I took his abuse. I still hadn't been able to rehabilitate my spine. Things got worse as the year progressed and adolescence hit me like a bat on a ball. It didn't help matters that my acne grew angrier and my body ganglier.

I didn't mention my troubles to my parents because Dad seemed so happy, even though he was still unemployed. I figured if you strung enough happy days in a row, you'd get a roll going and have a better chance of staying that way. I had to make sure that the delicate balance held.

Within the first month after our move, Mom burst through the front door with a smile. "I GOT THE JOB at the nursing home!"

"That's great news, hon!" Dad hugged her, and Ann and I cheered.

"Well, it isn't going to be for a lot of money, but you never know what it could turn into. I just know that the Lord has a plan for me there because I haven't been able to find any secretarial work, so at least it's something."

Dad said it would be fun for him to make our lunches, keep the house tidy, and help us get ready for school while Mom went to work. He seemed relaxed about it, and Mom didn't seem too worried about the fact that he wasn't working. I wondered when his sick pay would run out.

The next morning, we got up early to wish her well and eat breakfast together.

A sparkle from the old days lit Mom's brown eyes. "Before I go, I want you to each pick out a scripture. I want us to each read one every morning," she said as she held out a little, brown box shaped like a "Bread of Life" loaf. It held yellow, green, blue, and orange "slices" of scripture. I reached for my "slice," feeling a little silly but happy to know that new family traditions were replacing mental hospitals and electric shock therapy.

"Go ahead, honey, read it for us," Dad encouraged me.

"For God has not given us a spirit of Fear, but of Power and Love and a *sound mind.*" I looked at Dad with a *Got-that?* look and put it back into the plastic loaf.

After Mom returned from work later that day, she told stories about the elderly and lonely residents of the nursing home. It was obvious that she was well suited for the work: generous and personable, with the kind of people skills that always tempted others to tell her their life stories. She recognized her job as an important opportunity to minister to the old and lonely residents, and she seemed to feel good about giving. She was what The Church would call a *joyful giver* and remained that way her whole life. Mom cleaned bedpans, lifted patients out of their wheelchairs, and listened to the elderly talk about their families that never visited. I admired her for taking on work with such a good attitude. I also saw that a person could make a difference in the world, no matter their job. Mom seemed to have found a new dignity and sense of meaning and purpose in addition to the steady income.

I was proud of her and even began to think our family tableaus could turn into Norman Rockwell portraits after all. That was until I went to school.

My sixth-grade math teacher, Miss Harper, didn't make things easy. She was an overweight and angry former nun who belittled nearly everyone, making it clear we were a bunch of little brat losers. Miss Harper didn't call your name, she snarled it. She terrified me. I hid from her as best I could from my desk near the back of the room. Her contempt for her students and her job was obvious—this clearly wasn't what she'd envisioned for her life.

I tried to pay attention in her class, but sometimes I just stared at her, wondering what went wrong. One Friday, I watched from my seat as she dug her wide hand into the candy jar on her desk. She was tan, like someone who played tennis regularly—only I couldn't picture her running, so it must have been golf. She never offered any candy to her students or apologized for eating it in front of us. I was thinking I wouldn't mind a piece when Miss Harper interrupted my thoughts and jolted me back to reality.

"Susan, come to the board and finish the problem, please."

Nervously, I approached the blackboard, and on the way, whatever knowledge I had of square roots flew out of my head. I stood at the board trembling. After what seemed like an hour squared, I mumbled, erased, and scribbled.

"What's wrong with you? Oh my God! You're terrible! Don't you know this yet? Are you *stupid* or what? Go sit down. I can't handle you right now!"

My stomach cramped up, and my heart raced so fast, I felt winded. At least I succeeded in one thing—I held it together and didn't cry like a baby in front of the whole class. She was mean. *Was that what they taught her at the convent?*

When the final bell rang, I quickly gathered my things and nearly bumped right into Jock-Itch in the hall. Before he had a chance to react, I met up with Lisa and hurried outside. I was about to remind her I wasn't able to walk home with her as planned since my father was picking me up for a dental appointment, but before I could tell her good-bye, Stan Stackich reappeared.

"Laurel and Hardy! What's goin' on, girls?" His smirk took up his whole face.

"Get out of our way." I wished I could squash the big-nosed bastard. Yeah, the B-word had become a vocab essential.

"Sure, no problem, but let me make sure I leave enough room for your friend, *Fatty Fatkins* to pass." His friends laughed, and Lisa pretended not to hear, her eyes on the asphalt.

I pushed by Stan and headed toward the front of the building to wait for Dad. Miss Harper appeared at the corner of the building. I ducked just inside the doorway and watched her waddle toward a blue Mustang ragtop. Her huge, polyester-clad thighs made a chafing sound as she plodded along in black, rubber-soled shoes. Her legs looked like tree trunks. It wasn't nice to think, but had she not been so mean, I might have felt sorry for her. The convertible passed with Miss Harper on the passenger side. I couldn't help but stare; it was so hard to imagine her as a real person outside the four walls of our math class. She touched the cheek of the slight, shorthaired blond woman who was driving as they passed. *Was that a loving touch?* I wanted to tell someone that I saw Miss Harper with her girlfriend, but I felt too embarrassed. Besides, maybe I was seeing things. After all, who could imagine Miss Harper doing anything at all like a regular person— much less something so taboo. She was a former nun, for God's sake.

Dad's car pulled up and interrupted my thoughts. I climbed in the car and noticed the classified section and a book on resume writing. He was still job hunting. Clean-shaven, well groomed, he'd finally lost the "nobody's home" look. That was the main thing. I didn't have time to think too much about the personal lives of mean teachers or plan the demise of an enemy. Even thoughts about what I might get for Christmas or my birthday didn't matter. Vacations and new clothes? Not so important. The fact that King-of-the-Mountain-Super-Susan had become a wimp? Who cared? None of it mattered if Dad didn't stay sane.

※

"...Nerves," Mom said. "So go tidy up your room."

It was mid-October and I was concentrating on my homework for Miss Harper. "What?"

"Aunt Joy is having some troubles with her *nerves*."

As in nervous breakdown?

Yes. Mom's sister, Joy, was "sick," but Mom was certain the Lord would help. Dad was going to pray with her. Since he'd been sick in the way Joy now was, maybe they thought his prayers would weigh in more powerfully than Mom's. As I shoved shoes and my boxing game under my bed, I hoped that mental illness was something like the chicken pox—once you got it, you didn't worry about catching it again. Yet now it had popped up on Mom's side of the family. So was it contagious after all?

Aunt Joy was coming to dinner, ostensibly to celebrate Ann's seventh birthday. As soon as she walked in, I knew that Mom was right about Joy's condition because of the look of disorientation and the same vacant stare I'd seen in my father. Her auburn hair looked messy. She'd once been a model, and I'd always thought Aunt Joy was pretty and full of life. Gramma said that when Joy was little, she'd lie on the floor of a store and kick and scream if she didn't get the doll or dress she wanted. Mom said Gramma was a hostage to Joy's wishes. As she grew, so did her demands. She talked my grandparents into buying her a horse and paying for boarding and riding lessons. I remembered seeing pictures of her on "Billy Boy," sitting straight and tall with a look of sheer joy on her face.

In her twenties, Joy married a pilot and moved into a house not far from Gramma's house in rolling Willoughby Hills. My cousin Sam was born six months after Ann; everyone said they looked alike, some even confused them as twins. I liked to pretend Sam was my little brother. Before our move to D.C., Sam, Ann, and I had climbed up a huge oak tree in their backyard and pretended that we lived like the Swiss Family Robinson. Aunt Joy made lemonade and ham sandwiches with the crust cut off and sliced apples for lunch, saying, "Tell your mom and me what terrific adventures you've had." Aunt Joy was one of the few adults I knew who seemed interested in what a kid had to say, and I loved her for it.

Mom handed her a Pepsi. "Joy, have a seat."

She stared at Mom and squinted like she couldn't quite catch the dialect. She didn't take the drink, so Mom set it down on a lamp table. Ann gave Aunt Joy a limp hug, trying to hide her disappointment that she hadn't brought a present. Joy didn't seem to notice.

"Hi, Auntie. Isn't Sam coming?" I asked.

She fumbled around in her purse, pulled out a pair of glasses, and sighed as if she'd just heard bad news. "No, he's with his father," she said, looking at me like she barely knew me.

I hated reruns.

Thankfully, Dad came up the stairs to greet her. "How's the painting coming along, Joy?"

Joy didn't respond at first, her delay like those at the United Nations when the audience awaits the interpreter's translation. "Oh, I'm just dabbling. Nothing really coming to me at the moment."

Dad looked over at Mom. He knew Joy was out of it too. Did he realize he used to be the zombie she was now? I pictured her artwork: watercolor landscapes and Japanese florals, all peaceful in a way she couldn't seem to grasp for herself.

Our dinner conversation started and stopped in all the wrong places, like a bad phone connection. Usually, I enjoyed the grown-up banter about art or politics, but now we all struggled to bring up an acceptable topic. My once beautiful aunt was overweight and laughing too hard at the wrong times or gazing into the distance. I knew about the divorce that she hadn't seen coming. Mom kept giving Dad sidelong glances, clearly worried about her sister.

"The Lord's really taken care of us and brought us through a lot. Dick is a changed man," Mom proclaimed, hoping Joy would want to drink at the same heavenly fountain too.

No response.

"Ya know, Joy, you may not know it, but God's in control. He'll take care of you and loves you. You need to trust in Him," Dad added.

"I don't trust anyone right now." She put down her Pepsi and resumed her stare out the window.

"You don't mean that!" Mom nearly shouted. "God is—"

"Excuse me," Joy interrupted, "I have to go to the bathroom."

I poked at my mashed potatoes, and Ann asked for another piece of bread and butter. Joy returned, coat on, purse in hand. "Listen, I really appreciate dinner, but I need to be going."

"But we need to talk." Mom pleaded. Dad was silent.

"Sorry, gotta go." She turned and hugged me so hard it made me sad. I wanted to say something that would help, but what? Something was horribly wrong, and Joy wasn't interested in hearing about any possible solutions, not from my parents and especially not from hers. She'd made it clear that she saw Gramma and Poppy's point of view as a useless one inherited from the Old Country, the Depression, and Convention, none of which interested her. So, if she wouldn't listen to anyone, could she just snap out of it on her own?

No.

⚜

Six weeks later, I caught a cold and had to miss school. Staying home alone while Dad went job hunting wasn't an option, so Mom asked Gramma to keep me at her house. I was only too glad for the break and stayed in Gramma's spare bedroom, the one Mom and Ann had shared the previous summer. I awoke on Monday morning to the smell of fresh coffee and fried bacon.

"Good morning, my little dolly," Gramma chirped. "How's your cold? Did you sleep okay? That bed isn't very comfortable, I'm sorry. Oh, my little sweetie, I wish you didn't have that cold!" This she said, all before I could get a word in.

"No, don't worry. I feel much better. I slept well too."

"Are you sure? I'm so worried you didn't get your rest."

"No, Gramma, really, I'm fine. Don't worry."

She set up a tray for me in front of the television so I could eat my bacon, eggs, and toast while I watched *The Price is Right*. Gramma scurried around the house, getting me whatever she thought I might need: blanket, pillow, magazines, Kleenex. *This was the life!*

Later that morning, the phone rang. After a greeting and a long pause, I heard her say, "Oh no! Yes, yes, of course, I'll be right there." She hung up quickly and grabbed her purse. "Do *not* answer the door while I'm gone. I have to pick up your aunt; she's not feeling well. You'll be all right here, won't you, honey?" She looked tense.

"I'll be fine, Gramma. Don't worry." I knew she would have never left me alone unless it was something serious.

When Mom came to pick me up, I heard Gramma recount the details of the day's events, how Aunt Joy had shown up at her son Sam's school, hair in curlers, wearing only her bathrobe. She wandered up and down the hallway, calling his name, demanding to see him. The staff assured her he was fine, he was busy in class, she needn't worry. Joy, though, continued to call his name. Moments later, when the bell rang, seven-year-old Sam emerged from the art room. At first, he didn't notice his mother, distracted by a friend who jokingly punched his arm as they walked back to their homeroom. His mother called for him again; he stopped for a moment, and his friend's jaw dropped. She screamed his name again, and he turned and walked away. By then, Gramma had arrived, trying her best to coax Joy home.

"Joy, honey, why don't we go to my house and make some coffee and have a good breakfast?" Gramma had pleaded.

"I don't eat breakfast. What are you doing here? I want my son."

Gramma had insisted, "I came to pick you up, honey. Now c'mon, let's go."

"No, I don't feel like it," Joy had insisted just as doggedly. "I came here to see Sam. I need to talk to him about some plans I'm making for our vacation. I don't care that his stupid father has run off with some other woman. Sam and I can have loads of fun without him! Now leave me alone so I can plan this thing out!"

I heard Gramma tell Mom that the principal eventually called an ambulance, and they took Joy to the psych ward of the Richmond Heights Hospital. Days later, I heard Mom say something about "manic depression." I made a note to look it up in the dictionary, hoping it wasn't any worse than *breakdown*.

Joy stayed at the hospital for a while. Sam came to live with us for the rest of his second-grade school year. Although I loved his company, I worried that Aunt Joy would self-destruct. My cousin didn't say a word about it; instead he jumped on furniture, hit Ann and me with a pillow while we watched mindless cartoons, and rode his bike into the flower beds, crushing Mom's pink and white peonies.

Five months later, Mom let me know that Joy's medication was working and she was getting better. Sam would be going home soon. Did that mean Joy was okay? And Sam? I didn't know what to think, knowing as I did at age eleven that *anything* could happen. For some reason, bad things happened too often to my family. The people I loved best, the ones I most wanted to emulate, were fragile. And I knew I shared something with them. Was it that fragile part?

Thirteen

Jesus '76

I'D BEEN ON A SUICIDE watch nearly the whole year that I was ten, and now nearly twelve, I wanted to believe what our family believed, that God would take care of things because He'd taken care of Dad. Yet I still worried. He hadn't protected Aunt Mary Ellen from herself, and now Aunt Joy was in trouble.

I lay on the couch in the living room of our small house and listened to Mom's phone conversations, hoping to learn the latest without arousing her suspicions. One Sunday afternoon, while Dad was running errands, I overheard her talking to Aunt Nora, Dad's sister.

"Well, Nor, God is Good. So far, Joy seems okay—she's working and taking her medicine and looks much better too." A pause, and then more from Mom. "Yes, Dick's been reading the scriptures and praying for her. We're claiming a victory." There it was again, another one of those little pre-programmed phrases my parents had picked up like: *God-willing, Praise the Lord, Let Go and Let God.* It was as if a jingle writer had inhabited our faith.

At least my parents felt inspired to once again create a welcoming normalcy in our home, so I was okay with the Evangelical twist. Our new yard was the best kept on the street, a statement that our household was under a caring control. Yet I remained constantly alert. Something inside of me was keeping tabs, looking for proof of a secure future I could never quite have faith in, no matter how pleasant our life seemed on the outside.

That winter, Dad was always one of the first in the neighborhood to shovel the drive and walkway. One cold morning, I awoke to find him outside already, not shoveling, but working in the backyard. Uh...was that normal work he was doing out there in the cold? Or was he doing something with fleeces?

"Look," he said when he saw me watching him. "I'll just lay out the plastic and then set the borders with these two-by-fours. Once I get that set, it'll be time for the water, which should freeze tonight with what-all the weatherman is predicting. It's prob'ly better to wait a few days before skating on it."

Our own private ice rink! "Thanks, Dad." I hugged him. My real dad was truly back. Wasn't he? "I can't wait to try it out."

The ice set solid and smooth two days later. I put on my white figure skates and glided around a rink half the size of a basketball court. Ann came outside to shuffle her feet on the ice. I wiped my nose with my sleeve, skated across the ice, and hit a water-bubble bump and caught myself before I nearly plowed my little sister over. She slipped and fell, and we both laughed. Duchess barked her bewilderment, wondering what it was we were doing, going in circles and laughing steamy cackles that circled up into the cold, normal air.

❧

Sometime in the summer of 1975, Dad gave up on finding a job outside of the government and reapplied to HUD. They rehired him at a lower rank and for less pay, even though he'd been perfectly responsible and normal for over a year. Mom and I went to the grocery store to purchase steaks to grill in celebration. On the way home, the radio played an old Buddy Holly song that reminded her of her high school days of poodle skirts and bobby socks. She turned up the volume and sang along, letting the music spirit away any worries that her faithful soul might have kept hidden until the moment he got that job offer. When we got home, I helped Mom with the grocery bags and then slipped back outside to empty our mailbox, hoping, as usual, for letters from Marybeth or Russ. *None today.* Mom quickly found something of interest.

"Well look at that! The Lord continues to look out for us. Here's an unmarked envelope with fifty dollars!"

I never knew what to say when she said those kinds of things. I felt grateful, yet worried. *Did we really need that money? Who gave it to us?* Surely it wasn't some big, giant Divine Hand from heaven. It must have come from a neighbor or church friend, someone who knew Dad was unemployed. The thought made me feel uneasy and vulnerable, even though Dad was still doing well. My dad, who'd always had short hair and looked like Steve Allen or maybe even Buddy Holly, was now sporting dark gray sideburns and wire-rimmed glasses. He was allowing for the kind of self-expression that the seventies seemed to encourage. To me, these were signs that he was overcoming his demons, proof that God was strengthening Dad. I watched as he repeated scriptures, verses that I too claimed when I faced my own troubles. "I can do all things through Christ who strengthens me," I whispered under my breath when Miss Harper harassed me. If I saw Jock-Itch in the hall or in the cafeteria, I felt better after reminding myself that "God has not given us a spirit of fear, but power and love and a sound mind."

That part of my faith was a help and comfort to me. There were other things I wasn't buying, but this, *this* was shoring me up in ways that I needed. I was deeply grateful for that.

After a year of steady paychecks, Dad talked about travel again, expressing renewed interest in seeing the paintings of Europe. I knew our budget didn't allow for European travel at the time, so I thought maybe we could go to New York, to MOMA or The Met. But no, my parents arranged for a trip to Pennsylvania for something called *JESUS '76*, a sort of a Woodstock for Jesus Freaks. Not exactly a top cultural event.

I wanted to point out that New York really wasn't much farther away than eastern Pennsylvania. "Dad, ever thought of going to see the museums in New York?" I asked him, holding my breath, hoping for the answer that would tell me we'd soon be on our way to the Empire State.

"Well, yeah, remember, I told you I saw them when I studied at the New York Art Students League."

"I know, but *I've* never gone; neither has Ann, and I think she might like that. Might be a good learning experience, ya know?"

"Oh, yes, well you're right, but well, ya know, it's pretty pricey to go there. Maybe some other time."

Mom walked in, evidently having overheard. "Sweetie, we've decided we're going to *Jesus '76,* and you know, the Lord has been so good to us. It will be really good for us all. You'll see."

Other kids with less-religious parents certainly weren't vacationing at places that shared the name of the Son of God, but what could I do? My desires grew numb the way my foot sometimes did when I sat cross-legged when I watched TV. Sometimes, by the end of the show, I could hardly feel my foot at all. Mostly, I didn't care; I had no idea just how good I had become at ignoring what was important to me.

So off we went in a summer heat wave to the Jesus show. Dad carefully mapped the route along the Ohio Turnpike. I slept through part of the trip and awoke to the sound of our tires on gravel. I rubbed my eyes and looked out the bug-smudged window to the sight of thousands of long-haired hippy types with signs and banners saying things like "Jesus Loves You" and "Praise the Lord." We parked, unloaded the car, and headed for the lawn near the stage so we could carve out a slice of heaven in a place as hot as hell.

Dad set up our folding chairs and a blanket while Mom, Ann, and I went through the cooler to calculate the sog-factor of the ham sandwiches, apples, grapes, and chocolate chip cookies. Phil Keaggy and Larry Norman jammed in the background.

Next to us stood a young, long-haired couple maybe in their twenties, wearing *Jesus Loves You* T-shirts. They raised their hands and sang along while I stared at them, wondering if what they'd been through to bring them here was as bad as what we'd been through. I didn't recognize the song, but Dad did. He sang notes that just missed the tune and clapped to a rhythm that was only in his head. He even made a little jump on a particularly upbeat part of the song.

Then he smiled and raised his hands in prayer and song like the throngs surrounding us. I was about to take a bite into a ham sandwich, but stopped—I was amazed that my father felt so free. I put down my food and focused on the stage.

The song leader led us in prayer, and then, "C'mon and sing with me!"

God is so good. God is so good. God is so good, He's so good to me.

"Now with more emotion.... C'mon, sing it like you mean it!"

I looked around me at the thousands of people who had come to sing this song. They looked to be from every walk of life. They were sincere. I, too, believed that God was good, but singing about it here in a rock-concert-like setting felt weird to me. I didn't want to raise my hands just because they were. *Jesus, do you forgive me? I AM very grateful and I DO love you, but this feels too weird.*

I can't say that I heard a reply, but a peace welled up inside me. No, we weren't in New York thrilling at the great art in The Met or feasting on lasagna in Little Italy, but we were together, happy to be a part of God's universe, surrounded by a bunch of long-haired Jesus lovers. I chuckled to myself, grateful for this God who could stand the sound of so many people singing off-key.

My family would take the momentum and fervor of this gathering away with them and try valiantly to build it into their lives—and into my life. Somewhere, though, among the slogans and phrases sprinkled into our already stunted dialogue, a false note would begin to ring, faintly, clearly, incessantly.

Fourteen

Hallelujah

Ⓘ WAS FOURTEEN AND IN the spring semester of ninth grade. It was Sunday. My family and I walked across a gravel parking area beside two schizophrenic buildings of a church edged in weeds and tall grass. The first building was an old, white clapboard church, and the second was a steel, prefab job. Along with my family, I entered into the newer building.

"Hallelujah, thank you, Jesus. Let's give him a hand clap this day. Hallelujah, Hallelujah...Amen, Hallelujah," the man at the front said, drawing applause.

Mom said he wasn't a priest or a pastor, but a Worship Leader. Dad had announced that from then on, we'd be attending an Assemblies of God church. Having never heard of the denomination, I wasn't sure what to expect, but I was glad to see that the pews had cushions. The congregants of North Olmsted Assembly of God were definitely better groomed than the parishioners at St. Timothy's and St. Richard's.

The congregation sang, "This is the day, this is the day the Lord hath made, the Lord hath made. We will rejoice, we will rejoice and be glad in it and be glad in it...."

When the song was over, a long-haired woman to my left called out, "Amen, Hallelujah, Lord. Thank you, Jesus. Let's just praise the Lord" over and over. I couldn't stop staring at the dishwater blonde hair that fell past her hips and had more split ends than I'd ever seen in my life.

Other members of the congregation threw out comments as people hummed and shouted out thanks in a cacophony of praise.

"Hallelujah! Hallelujah! Hallelujah!" a man near the altar cried out, hopping in punctuation.

After I picked my jaw up off the floor, I checked Mom and Dad. They and the rest of the church had joined a woman with outstretched arms, singing sweetly, hands raised to heaven. I didn't see any hymn books, but the repetitious verses miraculously faded in unison into hundreds of ThankYouJesuses and YesLords. A new song began in the back of the church and spread through the congregation. It went on for what seemed like days.

I leaned over to Mom. "Is this almost over?"

"Shhhh."

The Worship Leader introduced the pastor and led us in another prayer. "We ask you to bring those whose hearts are hurting to a place of peace, Father. And we ask your Holy Spirit to convict those who are not saved."

Convict? Like in a courtroom? What exactly did that mean? It was another example of the new vocabulary in this new world. *Oh my God, what are we doing here?*

A voice cried out from the other side of the room, "Ash na dalala nuke do ra. Mandanda alahem."

Silence fell over the sanctuary while a phrase rang through my head: *Holy Shit!* I soon realized this was when we were supposed to await the translation.

A man in the back with a deep voice that seemed appropriate for channeling God, boomed, "My people, I hear your cries and I will answer them. I Am that I Am. You have come to me, and I will honor you, for my mercies are great."

A groundswell of appreciation for God's personal message caused another round of *Amens* and *ThankYouJesuses*. Okay, maybe I had higher standards, but I was looking for something a bit more specific.

"Thank you, Jesus," Mom repeated, once, then twice, and yet again.

I looked over at Dad. His hands were raised high and his eyes closed. The whole thing was giving me a headache. I wanted to run for the next train to the conventional life we'd left far behind.

A fresh round of noise grew like a wave into a babbling crescendo. Most of it was in English, some in Tongues. Interestingly, the translations never consisted of God telling us to sell our homes and feed the poor. They always came and sounded about the same. It was uncomfortable and made me feel as different from the kids in my neighborhood and school as if I were eight feet tall. *What if they found out?* Mom had asked if I wanted to invite a friend to church; I politely declined. Did I look like I planned to commit social suicide?

I sat on the blue upholstered church pew and dreamt of being somewhere—anywhere else. Arms close to my sides, shoulders hunched forward, I tried to bring my tall self to the smallest possible and, hopefully, invisible space. And yet, the morning held still another surprise.

People babbling in tongues soon began falling over all around me. *Shit! Was I the only kid here who was freaking out?* I looked to my parents for an explanation, but they were in their own little trances. The minister said something about being "slain in the Spirit."

What? As in killed? Murdered? It was weird and frightening. I wished my parents could be normal enough to skip this televangelist training ground. I glanced around the simple church, evaluating the congregants' faces as I'd learned to do with my family. Some looked bored, but mostly, they looked happy with devotion and sincerity plastered on their mugs. I couldn't relate to the theatrics. My own thoughts of Jesus comforted me in a way that made the lunatic fringe seem unnecessary.

Unfortunately, Dad became adept at the whole Speaking in Tongues thing and even practiced his new skills at home.

"Alla maka savey na-ha" rolled off his tongue as he shaved his beard and trimmed his sideburns. "Hamma la, hama la, Asha baga ma, OO shee manna gaza," he'd say while ambling down the drive

for the newspaper. *What in the hell am I going to do if the neighbor-hood kids hear this?* It was embarrassing, scary, and nutty, but no one else in my family or at church seemed to think so. I wanted to say something, but I felt guilty for thinking that maybe all of them were whacked.

After several months of this, I learned I'd be attending a summer camp in southern Ohio for kids in junior high—an Assembly of God church camp. I welcomed the time away to see and experience something new, but I did not want to be stuck for a week with whackos.

When we pulled into the gravel parking lot that sat in the middle of a large field, I was pleased to see that we wouldn't be staying in tents. Our accommodations looked like a whitewashed cinder block Motel 6—with air-conditioning even. Camp counselors had come from various Assemblies of God colleges around the country. They were fresh-faced, good-looking, and straight as the lines of a crucifix.

My new friends—Laurinda and Roberta—and I carried our luggage from the church van to our room, lamenting that the pastor's wife would be rooming with us.

An hour after we arrived we were given our first instruction. "Girls, get ready for church," Pastor Wife said. "A lady always looks her best."

Not this one. I was there to have fun. Acting like a "lady" was not what I had in mind.

Nevertheless, we primped and preened and sprayed hairspray and cologne on ourselves until the room was filled with an aerosol cloud. All that ladylikeness made me cough and try to blink gunk off of the contact lenses I was now wearing.

Two hundred campers shuffled into a cavernous building, the *Tabernacle*—yet another new religious word. Loud Christian rock music played in the background. On stage stood a thin, pinched-faced, bald man who introduced himself as the camp director.

"Good morning, campers! PRAISE the Lord!"

Those of us who weren't talking looked around, wondering if he really wanted us to shout "Praise the Lord" back at him. I just couldn't.

"I said, Good Mooorning, Campers! PRAISE THE LORD!" He repeated the routine until we complied just to shut him up.

"Well, that's *much* better, people. I'm Bob Miller and I'm here to welcome you to Camp Maranatha. You're in for a *great* time in the Lord! Put your hands together as the band leads us in worship."

"In the Lord" was another new Born-Again phrase that allowed us to recognize other fellow ("True") Christians. Eventually, the man assigned team colors and counselors.

A tall and handsome college guy named Charlie introduced himself to our team with an enthusiastic Southern twang, nurtured in Waxahachie, Texas. "I'm here to have a good time in the Lord."

Okay, here's hoping that means we'll actually have fun and not just more churchy stuff.

Edie, a brunette from Mount Vernon, Ohio, was the co-leader of our Orange Team. She began sharing her *testimony*—a well-worn, evangelical word that meant she was about to recount the story of how Jesus had saved her. It wasn't as dramatic as my family's, but it was reassuring to know that it wasn't just post-suicidal fathers who gave such accounts.

At the mandatory, twice-daily services at the Tabernacle, we were encouraged to pray to receive the Holy Spirit and the gift of Tongues. These Pentecostals were telling me to pray and plead for the Holy Spirit to come down and enter my body. *Plead?* As in beg? How would I know if it happened? I asked. Easy—the gift of Tongues was evidence of the indwelling of the Holy Spirit.

The next day, during morning devotionals, Charlie asked "You wanna be baptized by the Holy Spirit and speak in Tongues, don't you?"

I wanted to tell him that I'd rather speak Spanish, but didn't have the guts to say it. So instead, I found my way to the altar and found my place next to several other Spirit-seekers. I was nervous, having reserved this kind of God-begging for those moments when people were dying. Nevertheless, I began to pray, although I was unable to raise my hands and cry out loudly like those around me. Still, I did beg. Please, please, please, I said, stretching the vowels like a TV evangelist, begging for the ability to babble with the best of them.

Twenty minutes later—nothing. Kids to my left and right were successfully speaking in Tongues, tears of gratitude streaming down their faces. Some even fell over, "slain in the Spirit." For some reason, I never *got it* and figured that maybe I just wasn't meant to sound like a stuttering native of Latvia.

℘

By the end of the third day of camp, we had been to church six times. I still didn't speak in Tongues, but I was having fun at the many competitive activities and more social events than I'd had in my life. To top it off, our Orange Team held second place in the over-all camp color wars competition. We found that we were pretty good at sports, Bible verse memorization, and wacky games like Ketchup-WhippedCream-PeanutButter fights. I was chosen as the team's co-captain, along with a strong and handsome kid name Sam.

Being voted co-captain didn't surprise me too much; I was used to being a leader on the sports field. What stunned me was that later in the week I was voted onto the Court of the "Big Church Banquet." Each team voted for one boy and one girl to participate in a con-test, sort of like the Homecoming King and Queen festivities in high school. What we would rule over, I never knew. I mentioned to Sam that I couldn't believe I was chosen, and he said, "Why not? You're the prettiest girl on our team." I didn't feel pretty, but I was happy that Sam thought I was. All the girls were hoping to be asked by someone to go to the banquet. I wished that Sam would ask me. I think maybe he was looking for someone who appreciated his strength—not some-one who matched it. As it turned out, the boy who asked me was shy and hardly capable of uttering a word in the presence of a girl. Still, I liked his big smile when I said I'd go with him, and it felt good when he took my hand as we walked in.

The banquet turned out to be fun, but I couldn't help noticing that despite the supposedly *unworldly* view of us Christians, there didn't seem to be much difference between church camp banquets and high school dances. The pretty and thin girls got invited to the banquet, the less-than-thin and ordinary ones did not. It seemed to me that people who claimed to love Jesus really didn't want people to be *just as they were,* but just as the world wanted them—at least in terms of social status and looks. Why were we trying so hard to kid ourselves?

Despite my questions and my lack of holy-language skills, I was still sorry when the week ended. It had been fun to meet kids from other schools, to play sports, and to compete as a team. I loved the sense of shared community, the "oneness" we had sung about and even occasionally accomplished. The school year was about to begin where nobody wanted anybody (except the in-crowd) to be just as they were. At least they didn't pretend. It also meant hiding my family's spirituality and religion—not because I didn't truly believe Jesus was who He said He was, but because all of the people and the associated weirdness that sometimes created more problems for me than they solved.

Trying to want to be a young lady when I had no such image of myself, trying to feel a fervor I couldn't feel, trying to conceal my father's problems from the world, trying to glean the truth from my mother, trying to silence my own innate curiosity—all made me fear that I was hopelessly out of sync.

Fifteen

Focus On the Family

Dear God,

Can you please find us some other church that doesn't feel so weird to me? This new church, well... it's just not for me. I'm not trying to be disrespectful or anything, but please, if you think it's a good idea, I'd appreciate it if we could go somewhere else.
Thanks,

Susan.

ASKED THIS ONLY ONCE, not knowing for sure if it was okay to ask for something like this. Living under the influence of Tongue-speaking, Holy Ghost-inhabited, charismatic church members made me feel like every Sunday was a staggered walk through a carnival fun house. I muddled through the dogma, the bizarre behaviors, and simplistic views, trying to remember to give thanks for the miracle of sanity and good health. This was well before the days when being Born-Again was a political statement or advantage.

I worried that people outside the church, especially kids at school, would start thinking our whole family was nuts. It didn't help that Dad advertised our affiliation with a yellow "Praise the Lord" bumper sticker—something that was uncommon in the Rust belt of the 1970s. My first day of tenth grade, on the high school campus for the first time, was a very big deal for me.

High school promised to be a welcome change from the dingy, drugged-out junior high school of ninth grade, where blue clouds of marijuana smoke often permeated the bathrooms. I'd heard that the high school principal "solved" that problem by offering a "smoking courtyard" where nicotine was enjoyed legally and cannabis illegally. Mom said Uncle Art graduated from the same high school in 1965, almost twelve years earlier (when there'd been no smoker's courtyard). At the breakfast table the morning of the first day, I sat there wondering about my classes while Mom busily cleaned the kitchen and Ann jabbered on about what she was going to wear. I was wearing a pair of Levi jeans and a lightweight, brown-and-white striped sweater. My biggest challenge was deciding which pair of my new Earth shoes to wear. Of course, I also had to think about my face, knowing that covering my acne could sometimes be a chore. Since I turned thirteen, I'd been careful to conceal my blemishes with foundation and cover-up, adding blush, eyeliner, and lipstick as I got older. I was pleased with the results that morning.

Dad switched on the small GE radio that was mounted under one of the kitchen cabinets, its dial continually poised on WCRF, the local Christian radio station. He and Mom drank their coffee and readied themselves for our daily dose of Dr. James Dobson's program, *Focus on the Family*. My parents weren't alone in believing that Dr. Dobson taught Christians how to raise children using *Biblical direction*. I believed it too; at that time, "Biblical direction" meant something to me. Dr. Dobson wasn't shy about using the Bible in his diagnoses. That morning, he talked about the growing decadence in our society, and although I couldn't concentrate on the whole program, I caught some of what Dr. Dobson said about Family Values and child rearing.

"From Genesis to Revelation, there is a consistent foundation on which to build...parent-child relationships."

The Bible. I hadn't before considered it to be the foundation for parent-child relationships, but I was willing to. I didn't have the insight to see that you couldn't take the Bible and stamp it on every circumstance and come out with an answer that was a perfect fit. I thought

Dr. Dobson was knowledgeable and trustworthy. He called himself a Born-Again, Evangelical Christian, and at the time, I didn't think any Born-Again would lead us astray. I wanted to believe he provided direction and answers for the *social turmoil* in the world. Besides, I knew that I was about to be thrust into some social turmoil of my own as I readied myself to walk the halls of North Olmsted High School.

That first day of school, I exited the bus and nervously scanned the area for someone I knew. I recognized no one. I headed inside toward the hall where I would find my assigned locker. The hall teemed with girls in flared pants, flowered tops, and platform shoes and boys wearing Levi's and football jerseys. In a million years I wouldn't have put on platform shoes. At five feet ten inches, I was already a head taller than most students, save the boys' basketball team. I didn't want to stick out any more than I already did.

As I fumbled in my pocket for the small piece of paper on which I'd written my locker combination, I noticed a group of older boys gathered in an alcove across from the school's sports trophy case, laughing and shouting. As I walked by, trying to appear confident, they held up a placard. I avoided their eyes and didn't read it. Having made it a safe enough distance past them, I turned and watched them hoot and holler as they raised their numbered placard, rating another girl from one to ten. She was a seven. *What had I been? Who the hell did they think they were judging us like that? Did someone say "Holy Roller" and mark me down even lower?* What if the hallway boys ever found out about Dad's mumblings? I could only imagine the results. I wished I could hold up placards of my own with their low IQs for all the school to see.

On the bus ride home, I sat with my neighbor, Sandy, a thin, blonde girl who was desperately shy. I asked her if she'd seen those boys. She hadn't; I knew she would have been mortified if she had. She was more interested in telling me about the *youwouldntbelievethis* book her parents had confiscated from her brother: *The Joy of Sex*.

"Come over after breakfast tomorrow, and I'll show it to you," she said.

I was surprised both by her bold offer and by my interest. The next day, as I looked at the pages of the book, an undeniable stirring of hormones surprised and excited me.

"Where did you say you got this book?"

"My brother. I saw my parents hide it on top of the kitchen cabinets, and as soon as my mother left for work yesterday, I pulled it down. I guess having a brother finally came in handy."

"Yeah, definitely."

In school later that day, I thought about the scenes in the book. The hallway boys continued with their ranking system. They scared me and made me feel angry and hopelessly inadequate. It bothered me that the game of love and attraction seemed to be so complicated. This was the first time it really hit me that I was only worth my sexual potential in these boys' eyes. They were simply more blatant about that particular agenda than the boys from church camp had been.

⸙

Only two months had passed since my prayer about attending a new church when Dad announced that he'd found one. I held my breath, hoping it wouldn't be even worse, with snake charmers or some other weirdness my parents' search for spirituality and Biblical Truth might bring us. I was relieved to hear that *Christ the King Lutheran* was our next stop. At least it was part of a denomination I had heard of. Grandma Marie would be glad to hear it. Dad said that the new pastor was known for his public-speaking skills, passion, and commitment to Christ.

That first Sunday, the pastor marched into church like a warrior headed for battle. His white robe flowed in his wake as he strode behind the procession of pimply-faced, teen-aged acolytes in the "high church" procedures originating in the Catholic Mass. I almost felt at home. Ward Mott was in his early forties, handsome with wavy, white hair and a red face that grew increasingly crimson as he preached. I tried to listen to his sermon, but the sunlight shining through the stained-glass window projected a colorful design on my hand that distracted me. He was saying something about Jesus loving us and then he shifted gears. Pastor Mott's loud admonition made me jump.

> "Wives, obey your husbands, submit to them as you do the Lord. For a husband is the head of his wife as Christ is the head of his body, the Church; he gave his life to be her Savior."

OBEY? Are you kidding me? Imagine if my mom obeyed my dad! And who said men were automatically better equipped to be leaders than women? Had someone mistranslated that passage? My bogus-meter started clicking around Pastor Mott.

In the Sundays to come, he harped on personal responsibility, morality, and fidelity, warning us against the sins of premarital and extramarital sex. It made me feel uncomfortable to hear those topics discussed at church. I admired his ability to connect with the audience and turn a phrase, but a warning bell rang in my head when I shook his hand—his eyes were eerily unseeing orbs, blind to individuality, unless it came with a substantial tithe. I "saw" this because I'd studied both mental patients and "normal" people. Gestures and expressions often revealed the truth when words didn't. Pastor Mott possessed an empty charm and didn't remember names of congregants, including those in my family. But how could I complain? No one was being slain in the Spirit or shouting in Tongues or providing interpretations that were as predictable as "Jesus Loves Me."

Besides, who was I to question the new church God had provided in answer to my prayer? I felt God's presence and an umbrella of his care, so I could sit through simplistic sermons that were as wishful as a Lucky Charms "magically delicious jingle." I felt fortunate to have met new friends in the youth group who "loved me in Christ." Definitely better than the days when Halitosis Hal or Big Schnoz Stackich tormented me just because they felt like it.

I found comfort in knowing that the creator of the universe equated Himself with love. As I shuffled along in the leaves that had fallen in the park, I felt it in the beauty of His creation: in lakes, trees, and animals; in the goodness of people who'd helped us; in great art and music; and in the love of home, despite my parents' flaws. Even as a fifteen-year-old, I recognized that my father's yellow bumper sticker proclamation was a response to the flood of love and acceptance he felt from the creator of the universe. A man whose parents had left him, Dad had found a home "in Christ."

Just as it would be hard to say why I loved a particular painting by Van Gogh or Murillo or why my heart jumped a little when I walked under a canopy of trees in autumn, I couldn't account for the way God's love, bliss, and glory swelled inside me and filled my heart and soul in quiet moments.

Our family had been through hellish experiences, but I felt grateful about what *didn't* happen. Cars that never careened over the dividing line, illnesses that didn't ravage our bodies, and psychopaths who never made it to our neighborhood. I didn't expect God to show up as some sort of apparition, but I did believe that He sent people to us, people with a purpose in His Kingdom, like Mrs. Bowen. And I believed He trusted me enough to give me a purpose and a mission to be there to help others—a concept outlined in what the Bible called *The Body of Christ*. We were to be His hands and feet, doing His work here on planet Earth. For me, that meant showing love and kindness to those in our path. Unfortunately, I'd learn that it meant we Christians also sometimes did the wrong things with good intentions.

Although Hollywood, church camp, and my high school each defined my worth in a narrow way, I believed then and continue to believe that God gives us gentle approval and acknowledges our character, individuality, and purpose. He accepts and even cherishes our uniqueness while leading us to grow in a positive direction like tall sunflowers seeking light.

If Pastor Mott were to ask me about any of this, I'd have to explain to him that neither his sermons nor the traditions of our church did this for me. They were more distractions than celebrations of what the connection to God was really all about.

Sixteen

Scandal and Night Fever

I WAS RESTLESS BY THE end of tenth grade, bored with the *Christ the King Youth Group*. We focused on the same tired Bible verses, the same selections from Paul's letters to people in civilizations that had long-since morphed into orthodoxy. I wasn't against The Bible, but I thought it equally important to pay attention to the stories and viewpoints all around us. By then I had become an avid reader of all kinds of historical novels and fiction. I sped through *Anna Karenina*, *Wuthering Heights*, and *Gone with the Wind* with a hunger for more. The power of people's stories captured my imagination. My parents also unknowingly inspired me by opening our home to people with all kinds of stories and backgrounds. "When you do good for someone that can't pay you back, it's like you're doing it for Jesus Himself," Mom had said.

I remember one lady in particular, Alice Graney, a lady Mom met after she started a new and better job as a secretary at a nearby hospital. Alice was in her fifties and worked in housekeeping. She was developmentally slow, although sweet and loud with a crooked wig and lipstick that ran all over the borders of her mouth like she had applied it while riding the bus. She lived alone in a trailer and would have spent every holiday that way if not for Mom, who invited her over for dinner, and Dad, who picked her up and took her home.

One morning, I tuned out Dr. Dobson and read an article in *The Plain Dealer* about a woman in East Cleveland who had adopted five kids whose parents had been killed in a house fire. Did we need to read any more Bible stories and verses to know she could use our

135

support and action? I knew we couldn't help everyone, but couldn't we do more?

I had the growing sense that we Born-Agains were like dazed people sitting in our driveways, puzzling over the Bible like it was a road map but never really going anywhere, let alone doing anything to make this world a better place. We were supposed to "testify" and "witness," but they felt formulaic and inauthentic. I thought that if we really wanted to demonstrate our "changed lives," we should be doing more to make a difference in the world for those in our immediate path and to right the wrongs and social injustices in the world at large. Integration was beginning to affect our formerly white neighborhoods. Shouldn't we be out there, working to help people get along? Inviting black people to our church? Going to theirs?

The world was changing, and it appeared that the Church feared the changes were for the worse. When women like my mother increasingly committed to working outside the home, the Church resisted, saying it would contribute to the breakup of the *family.* My experience told me that women should be prepared to take care of things, as my mother had. That side of the argument wasn't touched, though. Pastor Mott and Dr. Dobson never thought about women like Mrs. Adams, two blocks away, a woman who'd lost her front teeth and often sported a black eye following one of her husband's drinking binges, or women like my mother, who needed to work because their husbands had gone off the deep end. They preferred to confine women to the nursery, needlepoint socials, and potluck dinners. Sometimes we did good things, ministering to lonely people, repairing the home of a widow, baby-sitting for a sick mother, or bringing food and condolences when a congregant passed away—which was more than we'd ever done at the Catholic church.

Even though my mother was too busy with her job and our home to go along with all of the events at church, our family continued to attend church functions that seemed outdated and corny. Pastor Mott designed a program to welcome visitors, called "PIE" for *People In Evangelism.* (*You can't* be serious.) "We'll deliver a home-made pie

to every visitor, so they'll feel welcomed and want to come back."
We all knew *he* wasn't going to bake a pie. That was women's work.
"We" meant "you women" will bake and deliver and welcome people
to *his* church.

Since I'd dropped out of the youth group and refused to bake pies,
my parents thought I needed to find a new church-related interest so
I could meet Christian kids my own age. I argued but finally gave in
just so I wouldn't have to discuss it anymore. I tried the church's teen
gospel choir. I wasn't a great singer, but the group surprised me. it
was led by a loving couple who avoided the usual pretense and "religi-
osity" that made so many other Christians seem so phony to me. Rhe
mixed group of about a dozen teenagers called the leaders "Mom"
and "Pop." They opened their home to us whenever we wanted to
stop by. "Mom" didn't hide the fact that she smoked cigarettes and
said that if anyone had a problem with it, they'd have to take it up
with the Author of her faith, because so far, He hadn't said anything
to her about it. Spiritual wiggle room at last.

During the summer, we toured other Lutheran churches, riding a
yellow school bus and singing gospel songs in Wisconsin, Minnesota,
and South Dakota. Who knew why any other church would want to
hear a bunch of kids from Ohio sing the same songs their own youth
sang? I never really stopped to think about it, but I was happy for the
chance to do some traveling. There was another benefit too—the food.
We ate like half-starved bovines as the miles passed by. *Granola bars for
the road? Cheese in Wisconsin? A&W burgers in South Dakota? All part
of the Fellowship, so pile it on!* (I have since eaten steamed octopus and
roasted bull's balls in Spain—it's all good to me.) When we got back
from our three-week trip, I waddled off of the school bus, ten pounds
heavier. I tried to ignore the disappointment on Mom's face when she
picked me up, but it was impossible. She took a deep breath.

"Ooh, well, you had fun—I guess, huh? Did you snack a lot?
Looks like you did."

"Yeah, we pretty much ate everything in sight the whole way there
and back."

"Wow! Do you think everyone did that?"

"No, I *know* they did! Do you want to hear about the trip?"

"Well...yes. Of course...I was just wondering...."

"Mom, forget it...just get us home. Please!" Of course, *I* didn't forget it. Her attitude hurt. It was the beginning of a chasm that opened up between us and intensified my self-doubt. All aspects of *Super Susan* had turned tail and run. My sense of justice and sincerity counted for very little. What mattered were my thighs.

The Sunday after we arrived home, we sang a concert for our congregation. Seeing American teenagers looking so sweet and innocent and singing about God seemed to encourage the congregation. Pastor Mott even recognized me when he greeted me. At the end of the service, we received slaps on the back, and the praise-the-Lord-sisters carried a bit more emotion than usual. But uttering them in our nasal Midwestern accents, we sounded like Southern Baptist wannabes with cotton up our nasal passages.

Our family attended *Christ the King* for several years, proudly boasting about the talents and faith of our handsome and brilliant pastor. Aunt Nora and her family also attended the church. Everyone said that Pastor Mott was *anointed*. It was the highest of compliments, meaning he was ordained by God with special gifts and abilities to preach the Truth.

One Sunday, Pastor Mott didn't appear, and the church Elders called a meeting. An uncomfortable silence fell over the congregation. Brother Tom went to the pulpit and cleared his throat.

"I have some very regrettable news about our church leadership," he said solemnly.

Had the pastor been killed in an accident?

"It has come to our attention that the pastor has been unfaithful to his family, and after learning that this situation has been ongoing, involving an administrative member of the church staff, the Elders had no choice but to ask for his resignation."

A collective gasp. Then silence.

"Please be respectful of both of the families involved and refrain from the gossip that would surely make this situation worse."

We found out later that his affair with the church secretary had been going on for several years—all during the time he had been so vehemently preaching fidelity, honesty, and sexual purity. The great fall of our beloved pastor didn't seem to affect our family much. Why would it? We were no longer fazed by the suicide of Mary Ellen or what we'd experienced in Washington. I looked to my parents for their reaction, but there wasn't much to see. They weren't the gossiping kind, and the hypocrisy was probably too overwhelming to reckon with. We didn't say much because our newfound faith took care of everything. Worried about your family acting crazy again? Feeling sad? Hormones going crazy? No problem: *read the Bible.* We took our spiritual answers and applied them to biological and emotional questions and just kept going. For me, that wasn't nearly enough.

※

I made the girls' junior varsity basketball team in my sophomore year, and my success on the court gave me some much-needed social confidence. I couldn't believe it when some of my teammates and their friends asked me if I wanted to hang out.

Me? The Born-Again geek with acne? Yeah, I think I can fit you in.

Jodi was the central force of our group and one of the most popular people in our high school. She wasn't popular in the way that cheerleaders and homecoming queens were, but she was popular. Freaks, Jocks, Nerds all flocked to her. One day I noticed two beefy football players making fun of little Lenny Carzen. They towered over him, sneering and jeering, making fun of his too-short pants and K-Mart striped shirt. As I stood there feeling helpless, Jodi swooped in with her usual good humor.

"Guys, guys, what's goin' on? Have a good summer? Did I tell you about the party I'm having soon?" She gave the biggest guy a giant hug as Lenny silently slinked away. It was like distracting a gorilla with meat on a stick. With Jodi around, all of us—the foot-ball knuckleheads, Lenny, and I—could see that the world wasn't such a bad and boring place after all.

Apparently, my mom was also impressed by Jodi's social skills. Her reaction to one of Jodi's calls to our house sounded something like, "Oh yes, okay, yes, thank you for calling, I'll go get her. Thank you, thank you so much." The first time Jodi and the others came to pick me up for a night on the town, Mom continued to want to please.

"Are you thirsty? Can I get you girls something to drink? Eat? How 'bout an apple?"

An apple? Oh God, we need to get out of here. "Thanks, Mom, but we've gotta run" I said as I pushed them toward the door. We climbed into Jodi's mint green Nova. She backed down my driveway and started driving to the movie theater where we would anxiously await the start of the new John Travolta disco movie. Laura offered me a beer, but I declined.

"Suit yourself," said Laura with the same kind of wickedly amused tone I would get from Jodi. She cracked open a *Bud* and passed one first to Molly and then to Julie and MJ.

"Here ya go, Jod, let me get that for you," Julie said as she opened a beer for the driver of our vehicle.

No one seemed fazed by the little thing called drinking-and-driving. Jodi sipped her beer and rounded the corner. I wasn't sure how long it took someone to get drunk, but I hoped we'd be okay since I lived blessedly close to the movie theater. Jodi parked the car, and everyone else chugged their cans dry while Jodi hid hers in her purse. While MJ reapplied her lipstick, Molly started telling a long, drawn out story about the last time they went out drinking. No one seemed to listen. As we exited the car, they all lit cigarettes for the walk to the building. After a few long drags, they flipped their cigarettes into the parking lot, then we walked inside to buy our tickets, popcorn, and soda.

After we sat down, Laura dropped her popcorn all over a cute guy in front of us. She turned bright red. Molly poked me in the ribs, and

I laughed my cola through my nose the way Ann used to when I did something funny at the dinner table. Julie did an impersonation of one of the residents of the old-age home where she and her sisters, Jackie and Jeanne, worked—a place that had turned out to be a candy box of good stories.

"Hey, Susan," Jodi said, giving me a sideways glance, "tell your mother she doesn't need to thank me anymore for coming by."

"What's that?"

Molly guffawed.

"You heard me." Jodi chuckled.

I felt my face go red as I stuttered for something to say. Then, for the first time in a long time, maybe ever, I laughed at myself and my family.

It felt good.

On the way home, we sang *Saturday Night Fever* and discussed how sexy John Travolta looked. Everyone worked on the twelve-pack and smoked a few more cigarettes while Jodi drank and drove for another half hour. We picked up Laura's sister, Carol, from work and they drank some more, laughing about everything and nothing. It felt real and unforced. I thought, *This is good—illegal, but good.* It was the year of *Saturday Night Fever.* I had caught it, and there was no going back, kicking off my teenage dilemmas around the "right" that felt disastrously inadequate and insincere and the "wrong" that often felt sincere and satisfying to the spirit.

With my new group of friends—Julie, Jodi, Molly, MJ, Laura, and Carol—I felt accepted for all of the right reasons. They seemed to really want to know me, and once they did, they liked me, laughed with me, and made me see the humor in nearly everything. At first, I didn't drink their Millers or Budweisers—after all, this was an opportunity to "witness" to nonbelievers—but the more time I spent with them, the more I realized that they weren't nearly as "lost" and I wasn't nearly as "found" as I had thought.

Church activities that amounted to beauty contests at camp, biases favoring wealthier church congregants, and fake smiles with canned phrases made Evangelicals seem off the mark and inauthentic to me. Could it be it was because they were hiding the same sort of buried feelings that I had? Didn't Jesus want us to be real? Honest? Accepting? I thought that He did. From what I could tell, my friends on the team, for the most part, were more authentic and loving than people at church.

We laughed about our fears, our families, and our feelings about boys and the pressures of it all. Sometimes we talked about God. I told them that Jesus was my Savior, although I didn't explain all that He'd saved me from. I knew that Carol understood the basics of what I was talking about, because I had first met her at the youth group at *Christ the King*. My salvation message was well received at times, though at other times they just shrugged like they were glad it worked for me but didn't want to hear much more about it.

Despite my new social life, *home* was still a sanctuary where I basked in the knowledge that our family was back to normal—not normal to the point where we didn't have a "Jesus Loves You" bumper sticker plastered on the family car, but normal in a post-Jesus kind of way, courtesy of the fallible Pastor Mott—maybe. Dad hardly ever practiced the gift of tongues while he was shaving or mowing the lawn any more.

One evening, Dad mumbled something, interrupting our usual dinner chatter. Something about Uncle Art. It was odd since my parents hardly ever mentioned him.

"You say he's bringing his *girlfriend*?" Mom asked.

"Yes, that's what I said," Dad replied.

"Why don't we go see him," I said. "Philadelphia seems like a good place to visit."

They didn't hear me.

"Hmm, I'm just...you know, surprised that he...you know, has a *girlfriend*. What was her name, again?"

Dad paused, then looked at her as he lifted his fork. "Jill."

I wondered why Mom and Dad acted so differently—less engaging around Uncle Art. Aunt Nora did the same thing around him.

All three seemed *pinched* with pursed lips and loud exhales that demonstrated a willingness to tolerate him, but not much more. I thought it was unusual since they were hospitable people, prone to helping others until it hurt.

I was the first to greet him on the day of his visit. He waved at me as he exited his white Buick and ran around to the passenger side. He bent down to offer his arm to Jill and helped her out of the car. While brushing a strand of his sandy brown hair from his face, he introduced me to his slim and brown-haired girlfriend.

"Hey there, darlin'," he said to me. "So good to see you! This is my fiancée Jill, and her son Trevor." I was surprised to hear him use the word. None of us had realized that they were engaged.

"Oh wow, well congratulations, I didn't know you were engaged," Mom said.

A slim boy of about thirteen stepped out from behind them. Art and Jill walked up the driveway toward our house, holding hands, while Trevor dawdled, probably hoping the visit wouldn't be too boring. My parents met us at the door, and we went inside.

The adults commenced on the usual introductions and niceties. Trevor and I escaped to the basement rec room, where I showed him my baseball card collection. He reminded me of Russ Bowen when his eyes grew wide as quarters at the sight of them.

"Here, have these," I said as I gave him a stack of doubles.

"Are you kidding me?"

"No, they're doubles and you're welcome to them. I used to use them for flipping—you know where you bet your cards—but I'm too old for that now."

He hugged me like I was his new best friend. Ann joined us and spent ten seconds looking at what she considered a whole lot of nothing.

"Do you wanna see our bunny rabbits?" she asked him.

Poppy had given us two rabbits for Easter, guaranteeing Mom they were both males. How wrong he was became apparent when a litter of babies was born six weeks later. Mom agreed to let us keep them in the garage. We hurried out to see them, removed the rabbits from their cages, and spent a half hour playing with them before starting a game of "Horse" in the driveway.

Just as Trevor missed his layup, Mom called us to the backyard patio for dinner. We sat down to steaks, potato salad, and corn on the cob. I felt happy for Uncle Art and his new "family-to-be" and looked forward to their wedding and having a new cousin in the family.

Two months later, Mom told me that Uncle Art's wedding had been called off. I wondered how he was taking all this. It had been obvious that this relationship had been important to him. No one said too much more about it, but I worried about him. *Would he be okay?* Or would he crumble the way his sister and brother had when they faced tough times?

Years later, I learned that Uncle Art was gay, Jill and Trevor his one foray into the straight world. When that didn't work out, he decided to be more open about his unchangeable orientation—that which the Church tries its best to annihilate, but which is ultimately as natural and insistent as the night fever. Timidly or boldly, gays were sneaking, stepping, squeezing, dashing, and escaping from the family closets of America, challenging basic identity, exposing the hypocrisies in Christian brotherly love. Our family didn't discuss it, and I didn't know what to think, unable to articulate how I felt about the gay issue in general and certainly myopically incapable of envisioning how it might affect me in particular.

PartThree

The Fall

Seventeen

The Good News and the Not So Good

$\mathfrak{S}$ITTING IN CHURCH ONE DREARY Sunday in 1978, I put on my brakes, skidding into rebellion, arguing with almost every message I was being asked to take into my heart and soul. It started with a simple hymn I used to love back in my Sundays in St. Clarence.

We are one in the Spirit, we are one in the Lord...

Wait a minute. I was singing it, but what did it mean exactly? Were we really *one*? I'd been to more than a few denominations and hadn't noticed a lot of togetherness. Why did we need so many denominations anyway? Though the people singing next to me seemed sincere, singing along and doing as they were told, I realized I felt so much more connected to my friends. I sighed. Maybe I just needed to try harder to be like these good folks. I cleared my throat and sang:

And they'll know we are Christians by our love...

Will they? Lately, my fellow churchgoers and family members were excitedly quoting Pat Robertson, Anita Bryant, James Dobson, and others who seemed more judgmental and discriminatory than loving—despite the fact that the Bible clearly dramatized a story where Jesus commanded us: *Judge not, yet ye be judged.*

I'd stopped singing, trying to sort through my turmoil. At seventeen years old, I had no idea of the damage I'd been through when I was younger, at a time when children in "normal" homes feel more or less secure in their age of innocence, but I did understand on some level that something had been lost, and it made me feel that something dark would catch up with me if I didn't figure things out. The desperate curiosity of ten-year-old *Super Susan* ferreting out truth for myself in an adult world run amok had transformed into a compulsive need to find spiritual answers for myself as a young adult. I hungered for stability, a place to land that felt like a spiritual home. And I wanted things to make sense. Was that too much to ask? If I were to anchor my soul to a Christian Church, its message had better feel true, loving, just, and right.

The minister that morning stressed the gospel passage that for me had always reflected God's love: John 3:16—"For God so LOVED the world that He gave his only begotten Son, that whoever would believe in him would not die, but have eternal life." I loved that passage, but this "Born Again" type pastor had a different interpretation: people who didn't believe in Him—in the precise way that he prescribed—simply went to hell. I knew he would not consider my friends, whom I loved, to be real *Christians*.

How could I reconcile unending punishment for nonbelievers—especially those like Native Americans who'd suffered genocide at the hands of so-called Christians? I figured if God so loved the world, He'd find a way to include all good people in heaven. Mom wouldn't tell me I couldn't live at home if I didn't follow all her rules and then cast me into a bonfire, insuring my existence through all eternity as a crispy critter. What would she get out of that? It didn't make sense, and I couldn't picture her saying it. I couldn't picture God saying it either.

Friendship evangelism was born in the seventies, and our minister said, "To spread salvation, you must make friends with nonbelievers, earn their confidence, and then share the gospel message in hope that they would see the Light." Onward Christian con artists.

We Christians had always tried to reach people in faraway lands who had never heard of Jesus—except maybe at the end of a sword or rifle—so evangelism wasn't so tough at a distance. But when it was up close and personal, I saw it from a different perspective. I would not allow my friends to think I was simply after their souls.

I tuned out the rest of the service and flipped through the little Bible I always brought, looking for some confusing passages I'd recently heard about on a radio debate. I'd jotted down the references in the back of my Bible. This was as good a time as any to look them up. These were mostly Old Testament ideas that we apparently ignored, passages that were so "out there" we didn't dare ask for explanations. That morning, I dared. In Leviticus 11:10, I found a section discussing what was edible:

> And all that have not fins and scales in the seas, and in the rivers, of all that move in the waters . . . they shall be an abomination unto you.

Abomination? I'd only heard that word in reference to homosexuals. So, was I going to hell for eating shrimp? Was eating shellfish as high on the damnation scale as being gay? How could I believe any of this myself, let alone witness to friends?

And in Leviticus 25:44, there was something about slavery:

> As for your male and female slaves whom you may have: you may buy male and female slaves from among the nations that are around you.

Surely it couldn't be saying that God thought it was important for us to buy local, that we could have slaves from Mexico and Canada, but not from France, Spain, or Africa. But, wow! Good thing Dad hadn't read this little Levitical gem:

> When a man sells his daughter as a slave, she shall not go out as the male slaves do. (Leviticus 21:7)

That Sunday, I couldn't have explained the extent to which the Bible and its interpreters fermented the mix of old ideas, names, cultures, and traditions, all of which we drank in with our non-alcoholic communion grape juice. Nor could I have articulated the way our faith had morphed into a political and social gospel that sometimes pitted "Real Christians" against downtrodden minorities, as well as tolerant, forgiving, kindhearted souls. But I was beginning to sense that my faith held some major flaws along these lines. Something profoundly disturbed me, and that Sunday was the first time I consciously acknowledged it. I began to question everything.

The minister was a nice enough man, but old Pastor Mott and high profile Evangelicals seemed to obey a different gospel than the one they quoted, something more like:

> Thou shalt judge others for sins I preach against but secretly commit. Lo, I shall maketh sure to inspire fear and hatred, so the coffers stay full. (12:1 Jumpin' Jehosaphat)

Wouldn't that explain a lot—the rock star preachers with TV and radio shows, books, and seminars creating a feeding frenzy of Christian spin, packaged in slick American marketing?

Still, questioning the Bible made me feel guilty. I'd been carefully taught that *The Bible said it. I believe it. That settles it.* There were times when that seemed acceptable to my young mind, but maybe we were really worshipping the Bible more than Jesus.

Many Evangelicals had helped our family though, taking time to care about us. I didn't remember any such care from Catholic parishioners. So I tried to overlook the pre-programmed behavior that seemed so incongruent to the very nature of Jesus Christ, the individualistic, Middle Eastern founder of our faith.

A line from that first hymn ran through my head as we left church that Sunday.

And together we'll spread the news that God is in our land...

Two thousand years of spreading the news and still, in many ways, we Evangelicals didn't seem capable of being honest about our contribution to hate in the world. A child of the 1960s, I was just beginning to understand what had gone on in our country and in the world, yet I sensed that our evangelistic efforts offered inadequate solutions—especially if we weren't going to face reality.

゚゚

"Have you met them?" asked my neighbor, Larry Voorhees, as his buddy David Daughtry looked around and scratched his balls discretely, thinking I didn't notice.

"Who?" I replied.

Larry looked at me like I was the village idiot.

"The black family," David said, apparently finished correcting his dangling itchiness.

"Yeah, why?"

"What are they like?" Larry asked. I could tell he was after dirt. A few months earlier, while I waited my turn during a game of Horse in my driveway, Larry mentioned something about a World War II documentary he'd seen. He called Hitler a great leader who did what he had to do for the sake of his country.

A buzz had started when the Elkins family moved into our neighborhood. It grew louder with the news that there were two teenage boys in the family. It didn't seem like a big deal to my parents, and so it wasn't to me either. As they passed by our house, Mom and Dad waved to them, but it wasn't until we got to know them at *Christ the King* that our families starting spending time together. I noticed at church there was a lot of See,-I-Like-Black-People behavior that was probably annoying but preferable to other attitudes they faced.

Their oldest son, Duane, was a year younger than I was, handsome and athletic, slightly shorter, although his afro gave him some added height. Terry was a year younger than Duane, more talkative, less athletic, but just as handsome. A few weeks before school started, the youth group planned a beach party at Lake Erie. Duane called and said his mother was making them go.

"Are you going?" he asked.

I laughed to myself, thinking of the way their mom ran the show. She did it in a way that demanded their respect though. "Wasn't planning to, but if you guys are going, I'll go."

The trip went well. Duane and I made faces at each other on the bus ride, and Terry interrupted us with a story about a girl he liked. After we got back from the party, we waited for Mr. Elkins to take them shopping. When they left, I was sorry to see them go as I stood in our driveway and waved good-bye. I turned to walk back into the house, but Larry Voorhees startled me. He was perched on his bike, staring at me with his head cocked to the right.

"Hey, what's up?" I asked him, trying to hide how frightened he'd made me.

"Not much. Just hanging out." He chewed his gum and eyed me.

"Uh-huh. Well, I gotta get inside. See you later." I turned.

"So, are you a Nigger-lover now or what?"

"What?" I turned back to look at him and make sure I'd heard correctly. My knees felt weak. Larry and his family were staunch Catholics who were forever commenting on the downward spiral of moral decay in our society—much of which they blamed on black Americans, Jews, or "women's libbers."

"You heard me," Larry replied. "Well, *are* you?"

I finally snapped out of my stupor. "Shut up and go home, you fat idiot."

It was the best I could muster. Clearly not the TurnYourCheek kind of response Jesus would have given. I was furious—not just at Larry, but at all of the stupid, ignorant questions of my neighbors and just the whole stupid, hypocritical planet. I walked into the house, wishing I could hit Larry. Pious little shit. (My vocabulary had expanded in a certain direction.)

At breakfast the next morning, I struggled with how to bring it up as I buttered my toast and glanced at the sports section of *The Plain*

Dealer. Dad finished up the front page, which featured the story on John Demyanyuk, a local autoworker, originally from the Ukraine, whom the government alleged was Treblinka's "Ivan the Terrible." If it was true, he was a death camp guard responsible for hundreds of thousands of Holocaust deaths. *Larry probably thinks he's a great guy too.* I sat back in my chair and tried to shake the skeletal images of the concentration camps out of my mind.

Mom interrupted my thoughts. "Honey, Aunt Nora and everyone are coming over today—can you help me clean off the patio furniture?"

"Yeah, sure. Hey, Mom...?" I told her about Larry Vorhees. "He's always saying bad things about black people and Jewish people."

"Well, you know, God is in control, and He'll show Larry how wrong he is someday."

I wanted to explain how it made me feel both sad and angry, but I didn't want to swim through the God-Loves-Everyone platitudes. So, instead I settled on questions about someone I didn't know— someone whose black and white picture was plastered all over *The Plain Dealer.*

"Dad, do you think Demyanyuk is Ivan the Terrible?"

"I don't know, sweets. Could be. Many Holocaust survivors seem to think so. I guess we'll just have to see how it all turns out. If it is him, he needs to be brought to justice."

"If he's not Ivan, he's guilty of something," Mom said as she set her coffee down. "There are years of his life that he can't account for. Those Nazis were just so *Satanic.* Anytime you go against God's Chosen People, you are *not* going to win."

I wanted a harsh justice, but Dad tried to explain that as a great orator, Hitler stirred up the emotions of the German people because they felt so defeated and were looking to blame the Jews for their problems.

Mom added her final word. "How people like Demyanyuk and others followed him is beyond me. Hitler was a devil-worshipper and a *homosexual.*"

This confused me, because when we studied World War II and the Holocaust in Mr. Barrett's history class, a different picture was presented. Mr. Barrett told us that homosexuals and abortionists were among the first people Hitler sent to concentration camps. Surprising since people who were against homosexuals or abortion were usually "on our side," sitting in our pews. Did that mean they were like the Germans who followed Hitler?

❧

"Now take a look at the leaders in the next photo," Mr. Barrett instructed in world history class. "Mr. Miller, name them please."

Jay Miller, the class burnout, was half asleep at his desk. "No idea, man—none whatsoever."

"Mr. Miller, graduation may never be in your future."

"I know, man, that's what my old man tells me."

The class laughed.

"Hitler, Mussolini, and Franco. Anyone want to tell me what they had in common?"

Jodi spoke up from the back of the room, "Fascist, twentieth-century European dictators." Despite being such a party-er, Jodi almost always had the right answer.

"Right. Hitler and Mussolini supported Franco during the Spanish Civil War, which left a million dead, and Franco, in turn, supported their aggression." He went on to tell us about the Mauthausen labor camp, one of Hitler's first. Spanish political prisoners who were enemies of Franco suffered among its early populations.

I sat at my desk and wondered how a country's leader could ship his own countrymen to another country for punishment. Mr. Barrett described a town in Spain called Guernica, where the Germans bombed some of Franco's enemies, the Basques. I perked up. Dad and I discussed Guernica.

"Who knows what artist depicted that heinous act in a famous painting of the same name?"

I raised my hand, proud to be in the know in such an adult discussion. "Picasso."

"That's right. Picasso was living in France at the time, but it was his way of showing solidarity with his countrymen and drawing attention to the carnage."

Mr. Barrett pointed to a certain photograph in our textbook. I squinted at a close-up of the Nazi uniform belt buckle inscribed with *Gott Mit Uns.*

"It means, as I'm sure you can guess, *God With Us,*" Mr. Barrett continued.

"But why would it say that? I thought they were the bad guys," a boy in front said.

"Good question. What do you think?" Mr. Barrett often answered questions with questions.

"I have no idea...just didn't think Hitler was a religious guy."

"I'm not saying he was. There are some things we don't know for sure. We do know that millions of people went along with what he did. Let's find clues, then, of *how* he was able to commit so many atrocities while a whole nation looked on, or at least, looked the other way."

That blew me away. I thought about people in Germany, going to church on Sundays, turning the pages of the same Lutheran hymn book we used, genuflecting and singing while their neighbors shuffled into gas chambers.

"We know," Mr. Barrett said, "that he was baptized a Catholic and attended a monastery school whose coat of arms bore a medieval symbol you'll recognize as one he'd later hijack."

"The swastika."

"Right. In fact, each of the fascist dictators we've mentioned was Catholic. Interestingly, despite their actions, they were never ex-communicated by Pope Pius the XII. In fact, the pope gave all three veto power over the appointments of bishops in their respective countries."

How pathetic was that! Was the Pope Christian? Why didn't he do something more? And what were my fellow Lutherans doing—

besides singing "A Mighty Fortress Is Our God?" My parents once told me about Dietrich Bonhoeffer, a Lutheran minister who opposed Hitler's anti-Semitic policies. Few people had listened, though, and it eventually cost him his life. He wrote:

> First they came for the Communists, but I was not a Communist so I did not speak out. Then they came for the Socialists and the Trade Unionists, but I was neither, so I did not speak out. Then they came for the Jews, but I was not a Jew so I did not speak out. And when they came for me, there was no one left to speak out for me.

"Now take a look at this," continued Mr. Barrett. "It's what Hitler's party adopted as its constitution. There were twenty-five points. What you have is point twenty-four."

> We demand liberty for all religious denominations in the State, so far as they are not a danger to it and do not militate against the morality and moral sense of the German race. The Party, as such, stands for positive Christianity, but does not bind itself in the matter of creed to any particular confession. It combats the Jewish-materialist spirit within and without us, and is convinced that our nation can achieve permanent health from within only on the principle: the common interest before self-interest.

"Surprised?" asked Mr. Barrett.

Surprised? How about horrified? I raised my hand. "I'm shocked to see the 'positive Christianity' comment. I'd always thought Hitler was some kind of Satanist or something."

Mr. Barrett reminded us that part of the reason it was important to study history was to ensure it wasn't repeated. We discussed the influence of religion on politics, and someone mentioned that

President Jimmy Carter called himself a Born-Again Christian. I looked around, wondering how many others in the room could speak on the topic as well as I could. I wanted to say that of course the United States would never pervert the Christian message as badly as the Germans did, but considering the hatred spewing from Christian Talk Radio and Christian leaders like Falwell and Robertson, I didn't feel so sure anymore. I said nothing.

❧

That class haunted me so much that I began my own research into Hitler's writings and speeches. I copied pages I'd found at the library and took them home for further study. One night, I sat in my room and read a quote attributed to Hitler in the 1920s.

> My feelings as a Christian point me to my Lord and Savior as a fighter. It points me to the man who once in his loneliness, surrounded by a few followers, recognized these Jews for what they were and summoned men to fight against them and who, God's Truth!, was greatest, not as a sufferer, but as a fighter!

His Lord and Savior? That was a *Born-Again* tag line. What was Hitler doing saying that? *Adolf Hitler considered Jesus his Lord and Savior?* I needed to read on. What's this? Something about Hitler being influenced by Martin Luther?

> Moreover, they are nothing more than thieves and robbers who daily eat no morsel and wear no thread of clothing which they have not stolen and pilfered from us by means of their accursed usury. Thus they live from day to day, together with wife and child, by theft and robbery, as archthieves and robbers, in the most impenitent security.
> —Martin Luther

What? The founder of our denomination *and* the Protestant Reformation called Jewish people thieves and liars? I fumbled through my papers and found that the quote was a passage from a book Luther authored in the 1500s entitled, *The Jews and Their Lies!* I laid my head on my pillow and braced myself to read Luther's sickening rant suggesting that Jews' homes should be destroyed, their synagogues burned, their money confiscated, and their liberty curtailed.

Had Pastor Mott known about Luther's anti-Semitic writings and the inspiration it had provided Hitler? Did our new Pastor What'sHisName know? If people at church had any clue, I never heard it. No one demonstrated any moral outrage at the thought of any level of Christian responsibility for The Holocaust. Was anyone ashamed? Shouldn't we be apologizing to someone? A lot of Someones? I was in shock. I got up from my bed, did a circle around my room, and then sat down to read it again and again.

It wasn't a huge leap to see how both Catholicism and Protestantism influenced Hitler and the events of Kristallnacht in the 1930s. Why didn't we talk about it?

Did the whole human race have the ability to develop blind spots so as not to see the beast in the room with them? As with my family, who discussed banalities in the presence of a loved one bent on self-destruction, was it simply easier to pretend everything was fine, or to confront, say, the loosening sexual mores of the 1970s than to face any responsibility for the Holocaust? And where did that leave a seventeen-year-old girl who was hungry, desperately trying to find something worthy of allegiance and devotion?

Maybe the Evangelical call for a return to our country's "Judeo-Christian" roots was supposed to suffice. Hal Lindsey and others wrote books that foretold that the End Times were near. The Heritage Foundation, The Christian Voice, and later The Moral Majority urged us to send donations so they could stem the tide of our culture's godlessness.

Even though the constant fear-mongering seemed overblown to me, it was unnerving to hear their predictions. I knew our culture was becoming increasingly sexualized and violent. I hated that. I also wasn't comfortable with the thought of millions of aborted babies. *And why couldn't we pray at school?* What if they were right? Maybe a combination of prayer and political action *was* the answer.

A pendulum swung inside my head from horror about the hatred perpetrated in the name of God and back to submission to the Evangelical battle cry to fight against de-humanizing promiscuity and selfish behavior that felt wrong to me. I wanted to be faithful to Jesus, the One I believed to be the incarnation of God. But I also worried about blindly following leaders who could be taking us down the wrong path for their own benefit. Most of all, I feared that the consequences of making the wrong choices would cause my world to fall apart the way it had when I was ten.

Eighteen

Jodi

WE STOPPED TALKING TO LISTEN to a news report on Jodi's car radio about a Ku Klux Klan rally in a nearby town. "I can't believe there are Klan members in Lodi!" Jodi said.

"Yeah, and they probably think they're doing some sort of walk for Jesus." I looked out the window of Jodi's car at the passing Ohio scenery.

The greens of tall maple and oak trees blurred as she drove a little too fast past wood frame houses with swings on the porch, grammar-school kids playing catch in the yard. If the world was in a mess, there was no evidence in these neighborhoods where naïve church people were safe enough to believe whatever they wanted.

Social injustice didn't seem to trouble Jodi and Laura for long, and they'd already moved on to a discussion of Todd Rundgren's latest album, *Real Man*. I tuned out.

Dear God, I'm kind of a mess. Really confused. Why does it seem that so many religious people act like they KNOW everything, when they just don't get it? Help me figure things out and know what to do...

The conversation of two deejays interrupted my silent prayer.

"Okay guys, if you had to choose between a girl who was fat, but with whom you had a lot in common, or a thin, beautiful girl with whom you had zero in common—which would you choose?"

The calls came in one after the other. It was unanimous. Fat meant failure. Fat meant disdain and disgust. Fat couldn't beat thin regardless of the rest of the picture. I looked down at my thighs and Jodi switched the station. "Assholes."

It was Thursday night, and that meant drinking and dancing barefoot at The Corral. This was the first time I'd been invited, so I wore my white jeans, cutest red top, and hooped earrings. My excitement about dancing that evening fell flat after hearing the survey. Although the time had long since passed when I could be characterized as a "tomboy," my interest in sports often attracted boys, despite the fact that I could still beat many of them in a game of one-on-one basketball. I wanted to be asked to dance. I wanted a boyfriend, someone I could hold hands with and be proud of. Unfortunately for me, my affinity for carbohydrates outweighed that desire. I was gaining weight, and *that* scared them off more than anything.

No one was looking to redefine beauty back to the days of Rubenesque proportions—the male population and the media made that very clear. Through my jeans, I grabbed the fat on my inner thigh. I loved food and hated my body. From what I could tell, American body-hate was as common as double cheeseburgers and fries. We were fat and getting fatter. Food, which had been a loyal friend during times of family crises, was starting to look like my enemy. The deejays set me up to expect rejection at The Corral that evening, and I was afraid my friends would think I was a detriment. Fat by association. Would they fear not being asked to dance because of their fat friend and want to leave me behind?

The Corral didn't always check IDs, and when they did, those of us who needed them were sure to have fake ones. In those days, once you turned eighteen, you could drink the low-alcohol, "3.2" beer. Either way, they were thrilled to serve both eighteen-year-olds and other minors alike; the cops rarely bothered them. We all drank at the bar acting nonchalant. Even when Jodi and some others went to dance, Carol and I ordered beer and talked at the bar. The girl laughed at everything I said, which made me especially love hanging out with her.

We scoped out the most handsome guys, figuring we might as well start there. I was surprised to find that there were plenty of interested parties. We chatted with a few guys before Flatbush began their first set. On the first note of "Driver's Dream," we were on the dance floor with two tall guys from nearby North Ridgeville. I let the music flow through me and stayed on the dance floor for a slow dance with a guy named Bill. The beer was going down easy. Before the night was over, three more guys had asked me to dance. *Guess I'm not as fat as I thought I was.* Carol and I both left the bar with the phone numbers of five guys. I only kept one, and she pitched all but two of hers in the trash as we left the bar in time for our 1:00 A.M. curfew.

⚘

All that beer added to my already large caloric intake of regular meals, snacks, and pizza with friends. My weight was on the rise. I noticed many overweight people at church and wondered if the pastor thought the sin of gluttony wasn't as bad as the others.

When I reached a size fourteen, Mom suggested that I consider Weight Watchers. I felt embarrassed but agreed, especially after she offered to send me to San Diego to see the Bowens—who had recently moved there—if I lost forty pounds. Within four months, I'd weighed, cut, and measured enough low-calorie food to reach my goal. The Bowens were just a flight away, and I packed eagerly.

Shortly after my arrival in San Diego, Mrs. Bowen announced we'd need to get ready for Wednesday night church. "You're gonna be so blessed to hear our pastor." I found their church to be similar to ours and not as mesmerizing as Mrs. Bowen suggested. On Sunday, Mary Beth told me we would be volunteering in the Sunday school class for young adults with Down's syndrome. I was impressed by her obvious love of the class and her ability to comfortably interact with the students.

In the Bowen household, Wednesdays and Sundays were for the holy trinity, and Mary Beth made sure that Friday and Saturday were for a less holy trio: Marijuana, Kahlua, and Cream. That weekend, when we returned home from a pool party in time for Mary Beth's ten-thirty curfew, we were tipsy, laughing, and totally reconnected.

Thirty minutes later, she announced it was time to exit her bedroom window.

"What? Are you sure we should be doing this?" I asked.

"Don't worry; I do it all the time . . . they never know."

Her boyfriend, Mo, was finishing his beer at her street corner when we approached.

"Take us to the taco stand," Mary Beth ordered.

"How do you do it?" I asked after watching her put away three tacos and a large frozen yogurt. "You must have great metabolism."

"No, I just throw up." She said it as if she were telling me about the way she applied her make-up. "Yeah, it's really not that hard. You eat foods like ice cream or applesauce to make it easier. I don't even have to put my finger down my throat."

I had never heard of such a thing. Throwing up had always been something to avoid, but it struck me that it would be great to eat all the foods I loved without consequence.

The following weekend, we camped at the beach with her family. After a dinner of hot dogs, chips, candy, and ice cream, I told her I was ready to try barfing away my calories. The whole idea registered somewhere in my head as the ultimate in "hurling your cake and eating it too."

We walked over to the beach-side bathrooms and I nervously entered the stall, hoping I could make it work.

"Nothing's happening," I told her.

"Just keep trying to burp."

After fifteen minutes, I gave up, resigning myself to weighing and measuring every calorie-filled bite for the rest of my life.

❧

I don't remember how I eventually "succeeded" in throwing up on cue. My brain was too disgusted to register the memory. It probably happened when I started working at an ice cream parlor after returning home from my trip. Mary Beth had said that ice cream made things come up easier. Standing in front of all that free ice cream was probably the trigger. Afterwards, it didn't seem weird to me to want to throw up all that I'd eaten. Food wasn't about nutrients for my body; it was salve for my wounds, a drug to calm my nerves. I couldn't feed my soul what it craved, so I fed my body.

I learned to eat strategically—applesauce and ice cream facilitating the purging process that pigging out on thousands of calories necessitated. The idea was to eat and not gain weight, but I found that although I could purge myself of most everything, I couldn't get it all out of me. Eventually, more and more fat clung to my thighs and legs. This sent me into a panic that sent me running for more food and more purging. I chose not to think about what the calories would do to me until after I'd found in of two Snicker bars, a piece of lemon cake, eight chocolate-chip cookies, two cheese burgers, an order of French fries, and two vanilla shakes.

The food fix helped me avoid dealing with my thoughts and feelings. Don't want to feel confusion and anxiety? Then don't. Don't want to think about any of it? Then don't! The world is full of all sorts of things to feel and think about, so just think of the good stuff! Go for it! Binge! Eat whatever you want. You only live once! A wicked, internal name-caller that verbalized its disgust invariably overcame my bravado about eating, however, shaming me into a purge session.

"Look at you, you fat cow! Omigod, what have you been thinking? How could you have done this to yourself? You cannot eat anymore today!" Before Homecoming, I spun left and then right, focusing on my fat ass in the mirror. "It's bigger than yesterday—and my face, it looks plumper too!" I ran my fingers through my hair.

Tension built up inside of me as I tried to navigate the high-wire walk between what "The World" wanted (lithe beauty) and what "The Church" wanted (blind devotion). On both sides lay a kind of convention and a message that females were subordinate, as if it was a man's job to make things happen, and a woman's job to find a man. *Conventional* ideas such as these didn't work for me, and it wasn't just because of my weight, my feelings of geekiness, or even the tomboyishness I couldn't outgrow. My misgivings about trying to fit in to shallow, limiting, or dogmatic situations ran deep, but I buried them along with my childhood fears about people running out the door or going crazy, spinning them into a growing addiction to binging and purging that provided both comfort and suffering.

At Thanksgiving, Gramma's chatter about the price of groceries hung in the air over the gravy. My family would have preferred to read the phone book rather than talk about anything unpleasant that was going on. We could argue over the minutia or the conceptual, so long as we never talked about *us*. Aunt Joy, why don't you smile anymore? I wanted to ask her. Isn't your life still worth living without a husband? And Dad, when you ask the blessing, do you believe that God will really bless us and protect us from disasters now even though He didn't stop Aunt Mary Ellen from going off the bridge? Mom, when you eye every spoonful of mashed potatoes I pile on my plate, does it mean you think I'm unlovable if I get overweight?

"Mary, the turkey is really delicious!" Dad said.

"Oh, Richard, it's just not fresh like meat used to be. Oh, it's so expensive now too!"

"Mom, can't you just say, 'Thank you'?" Aunt Joy rolled her eyes at Gramma.

Since the bathroom was close to the living and dining room, I had to plan my strategy carefully. First, I needed to be sure that the menu included foods that would be superior accomplices. I slurped some applesauce down. Then, like a mugger spotting a mark, I waited for the right moment. Gramma kept passing everything as Joy protested.

"Mary, bring me some more ice cubes," Poppy interjected. "And make sure I get one of the turkey legs. I like the dark meat."

Good. They were preoccupied. "Mom, can I be excused?"

"Sure. Are you finished eating already?"

"No." *I'm actually just getting started.* "Just have to use the restroom."

No one seemed to notice how often I was excusing myself to the bathroom. I didn't want to face the reality of my eating disorder, and therefore couldn't bring myself to pray for help or ask anyone. My faith in Jesus was dangerously low. I lied and hid in shame, throwing up ten or twelve times a day, wishing for an earthly/heavenly savior without turning to God.

※

I lived in the black haze of my bulimia, working around it somehow, laughter my lighthouse, thanks to my friends—principally Jodi.

"My mom said I could have a New Year's party for a 'few' friends." Jodi said.

"How many are a few?" asked Laura. I looked at Laura, and we both smiled. We all knew Jodi wasn't capable of inviting only a few people.

"Ten or twelve...tops." Jodi laughed.

"Jodi! Your poor parents!" added Molly.

I noticed Jodi had turned the corner onto my street and drove past my house.

"What are you doing?" I asked, knowing she was up to no good, knowing I'd soon be nervous, but laughing.

"We're not done with our conversation." She looked up into the rearview mirror at Julie. "Okay, so maybe it'll be more like a few dozen."

Jodi rounded the next corner, and I held on tightly. Laura and Julie laughed loud and hard as Jodi drove over the curb and onto the snow-covered yard. Up and over the sidewalk and across three frozen lawns, she aimed for a few bushes, turning at the last second, heading back to the street.

"Oh my God, my parents are going to kill me," I groaned.

Jodi let out an evil chuckle I'd hear for years to come. Although sober, she kept driving, swerving on both sides of the road and turning around in one driveway and heading toward the other side of my neighborhood, crossing over three and four lawns at a time. Laura and Julie cheered her on. I sweated. Everybody was nuts.

By the time she turned into my driveway, I was ready to hit her, but I was laughing.

"Can you NOT do that next time?!"

"Hey, who said there's gonna be a next time?"

They all laughed harder still. I looked at them all and broke into uncontrollable, tear-stained laughter, shook my head, and opened the door, thankful to put my feet on the ground—but even more grateful for having found such free-spirited friendship.

❧

On new year's eve, the first dozen guests arrived at Jodi's house and the next several dozen soon joined them. And then more people showed up for the party.

"Guys, we have a problem."

"Oh, let's see—could it be that there are now two hundred people mulling around your parents' house?"

"No—I mean, yes, but that's only part of it."

"What now?"

"Well, my dad went out, but it's my mom...she wasn't feeling well, and stayed home. She's upstairs, sick, in bed."

Julie and I covered our faces. MJ, the cheerleader I'd mistakenly typecast as silly and shallow, burst into laughter. As time went on I found her to be well read and capable of debating me into circles.

"How sick is she?" Laura asked.

"She'll be a lot sicker if she comes downstairs," Julie chimed in.

Jodi looked worried. "Well, she's pretty sick, but so far as I can tell, the flu doesn't affect a person's hearing. She knows there are more than twelve people here."

Julie laughed. "Oh my God—do we even *know* all these people?"

No. I chuckled to myself, remembering that Jodi invited two couples we met at Denny's, two Strongsville football players at the Sunoco station, and many more.

Minutes later, Jodi's diminutive mother marched down the steps like a bathrobed Napoleon. "Get these people out of my house."

Julie, Laura, MJ, Molly, Jodi, and I went from room to room, tapping the shoulders of kissing couples, cajoling them with road beers, and coaxing people to leave before the cops came. Dozens of teenagers grumbled and sulked off; some arranged other gatherings, while a few called us names or pelted the house with snowballs after exiting, but soon things quieted down. We laughed it off and rang in the New Year with our usual circle of friends.

At breakfast the next morning, I was surprised to find that Jodi's parents were surprisingly good-natured about the whole thing. I stirred a cup of tea and noticed that her little sister had written a breakfast "order" on a small chalkboard that hung on the kitchen wall.

"Does she really think someone is going to make her a special breakfast every day?" Laura asked.

Jodi laughed. "Someone usually does—but that someone is never me. I just hand her a Popsicle."

I stared at her and then laughed. The girl made everything funny—and maybe everything was. *Maybe all families were weird and funny too.* Maybe I'd get by with a little help from my friends.

Nineteen

Precious in His Sight

🖗 COULDN'T HAVE GOTTEN THROUGH what happened next without friends and family.

In May of 1980, my twenty-one-year-old cousin Mike crashed his motorcycle into an on-coming van and died on impact. Three days later, I sat in the padded funeral home chair, staring straight ahead, hoping no one would talk to me while I talked to Jesus in my head. *Please be with Aunt Nora, Uncle Roy, and my cousins. I feel so bad for them. I'm not blaming you, but why do these kinds of things have to happen? Where were you when Mike's motorcycle crossed the yellow line?* I imagined crying with my head on Jesus' shoulder. He would carry me to a light-filled place where I could see Mike one last time to say good-bye.

A crying baby startled me out of my vision. I shifted in my seat, wanting to get out of there even more. I noticed an old woman trying to offer comfort to Aunt Nora, as if there was any way to console her. The open casket lay directly in my line of sight. *Could I make myself look at him?* I lifted my gaze from the floor and saw that no amount of make-up could make Mike look like anything but a dead guy I didn't recognize.

The buzz in the room was getting louder, nervous energy growing. A toddler twirled in a circle at the far end of the room, her dress a navy blue parasol over little girl legs. Across the room, Uncle Art stared at the ground, but he looked up every once in a while, his glance darting around the room as he politely chatted with the crowd of mourners. I could see the red rimming his eyes. He wanted to escape as much as I did.

The next day, we sat through Mike's memorial service. The pastor's hopelessly inadequate words slipped into the air, not reaching any place of comfort inside my mind. As I listened, all I heard was people using the occasion of Mike's death to remind themselves that there really was a heaven. Grief was what sank in. Uncle Roy's eyes were red, and for the first time, he seemed like a real person to me. All his meanness melted under the terrible reality of his son's death.

Family and friends trudged across the cemetery to the freshly dug hole that would house Mike's coffin. I was numb. That evening, my friends decided it would be a good diversion to drink and dance at The Corral. Uncle Art and Mike's girlfriend, Becky, joined my friends and me. We met up in the parking lot and hugged each other, glad to be away from the funeral home. The heavy air in that place had permeated my clothing, my hair—all of me—with its grim truth that Mike was gone forever. The night air softened the harshness a bit.

It was a weird sort of dance we all did, socializing to the tunes of our grief and feeling vulnerable as we opened up to each other. We told stories about Mike, and then we told stories about ourselves. I felt an odd need to confess my bulimia, but then held back. Uncle Art talked about his job and how his firm retrained disadvantaged clients in new job skills. He loved the sense of purpose and accomplishment it provided. The evening had a kind of glow of shared experience.

For the first time, my uncle opened up about his love life. He had a longtime boyfriend named Wayne. Now I knew why my parents and aunt had acted so strange around Uncle Art. I told him that I wished I had known earlier. Maybe I could have made him feel more included. *Maybe.* He nodded, like he knew that kind of openness was only for some families and definitely not ours.

The truth was we weren't open to people who were different in the way my Uncle Art was. Anyone who deviated from the *conventional* was lost and hurting, negatively influenced by "Culture" and deceived by the Devil.

Later that year, when I attended a youth group event aimed at younger kids, I watched a slim puppeteer as he flitted all over the stage, singing and chatting with his cast of puppet characters, representing all the kinds of people that God loved. *Black, Yellow, Red, and White, All were precious in His sight.* Diverse puppet characters told us in happy little stories and songs that Jesus loved us regardless of whether we were tall or short, young or old, slim or wide, boy or girl. One group the puppets didn't mention consisted of skinny, gay puppeteer boys. And girls who preferred to be Zorro for Halloween. Gay boys and girls went unacknowledged, the church too embarrassed to hear about people who were different in *that* way. The puppeteer didn't push the issue, even though he was clearly part of that demographic. He reminded me of Liberace or Charles Nelson Reilly. He didn't have to say it. It was hard to see his shame dancing on a stage. But where did that shame come from? Wasn't much of it from the very faith he proclaimed? The one that compared homosexuals to condemned criminals?

It seemed to me that although the founder of Christianity was accepting and loving, His followers weren't necessarily so. No matter what the Bible said, hating the sinner often went along with hating the sin—or the perceived sin. At that point in my life, I understood I was different, but not so different that it was a problem. I liked boys. I surely didn't think about girls in any "sinful" way. Wasn't capable of thinking along those lines then. So I was safe. I'd be okay. Yet Uncle Art and his life haunted me.

⁂

That fall, I started college. The day my parents and sister pulled away from the rolling Oxford, Ohio campus of Miami University, I stared at the shrinking image of our family's black Buick until it disappeared around the corner. A mix of feelings, from the thrill of freedom to the sadness of missing my family, tightened into a confused lump in my throat. I thrust my hands into the pockets of my overalls, kicked a pebble on the ground, and started off across the soft green grass of the East Quad. I felt as alien as if I'd been dropped off on a moon colony. Julie, my high school friend and soon-to-be roommate, was on her way. Hopefully soon.

Giggling girls wearing upturned Izod collars paired with plaid shorts and penny loafers stared at my overalls with as much incredulity as my face must have shown as I considered their attire. I felt both inferior and superior at the same time. I wandered near my dorm and found a nearby, on-campus snack bar and ordered the specialty of the house—a warm sweet roll that soothed my nerves enough to feel okay with my discomfort in a new and not-so-welcoming place. I'd soon vomit it away. This place was not going to help my bulimia.

I shot a quick prayer up to heaven even though I was embarrassed about asking for help with overeating and bulimia. I wanted God to magically fix it. The thought of going to a rehab program was out of the question. I had college classes to attend, things to learn, people and places to see.

Sweet roll devoured, I returned to Dorsey Hall in search of Julie or Molly. I wondered if Jodi was doing any better at Ohio University. Fortunately, Julie and her father were just arriving. I helped them unload their car, and after her father drove off, Julie and I got down to the business of meeting our dorm mates. I struck up a conversation with Heather, a girl from Connecticut, and her loud roommate, Lisa from Columbus. Despite the friendly attitudes of many of our dorm mates, it didn't take us long to feel the snobbery of Miami of Ohio.

Rich and privileged young people from the East Coast, who drove late-model BMW's and Mercedes, crowded into the cafeteria, clustered in the corridors, and paraded their assets everywhere. I hadn't considered that a college campus could be such a bastion of conservative values. Somehow I thought college was going to be about independent thought and speech, ideas and freedom to figure out who you were in a world that wasn't defined by your parents and their values. *Got money? Great! Old money? Even better! None? Then I don't need to know you.*

By then, I was used to my mom looking at me like I was a disappointment, but I wasn't accustomed to looks from strangers who saw me as someone beneath their class and level, someone who should be excluded from campus clubs and activities. It didn't take long to see that their trickle-down economics were not watering my world.

The blatant sexuality of college life also left me as shocked as if my shoes had suddenly short-circuited. In my naiveté, I wasn't prepared for the expectation of promiscuity. I hadn't realized that we were on campus not for our minds, but for our asses, breasts, and the in-between. Despite the interest I generated in social circles back home, there on campus things were different. Whether it was a lack of a pedigree or lack of blonde hair (or both), the dating scene wasn't what I expected. I developed a crush on a few guys, but things didn't go as planned.

"Hey, you wanna hang out this Friday?" asked Brad from New Hampshire, a classmate in my English class. We met at CJ's, a run-down bar filled with drunken students, spilled beer, and picnic tables emblazoned with initials and other testaments of true love. Brad bought two silver buckets of beer to the table and plopped down next to me. "Go ahead and dip your glass in the pail—it's too hard to pour it when it's full."

Classy. The night was a boring foray into stories about his exploits on the high school football field. I was ready to leave after the first round of beer. Brad was too.

"Let's go back to your room and have some fun." Apparently he thought that for the price of two buckets of beer, he'd bought the right to waste my virginity.

"No, I really need to be going. See you in English class." I walked home and wondered why he thought I'd be interested in sex when we didn't even know each other. No one bothers to prepare girls for how to deal with immersion into the sexual meat market mentality.

Thankfully, I hadn't gone through the sorority rush process, not even knowing what it was all about—another form of meat marketing—until it was half over. My high school friend Molly also lived in our dorm and was devastated to find that she didn't have the right pedigree for access into any of the sororities she rushed; the acceptance criteria had everything to do with the amount and quality of her gold jewelry, her car, and most of all, her daddy's job. Since Molly had been a cheerleader in high school, I thought she'd be a shoe-in at any sorority, but that was before I realized how much it mattered that she was an Irish-American Catholic from a blue-collar town. If Molly couldn't make it, I knew there was no hope for me.

The rejection blew her away. She turned her shock and disappointment about the whole thing into an opportunity to reinvent herself by cutting her hair and donning the same Izod, plaid shorts, and penny loafer uniform of the East Coast preppies. Within the first three months of school, she lost a startling amount of weight. Looking at Molly's anorexia was like looking at the other side of my bulimia. It made my knees weak to look at her hands, the bones protruding like crow's feet wrapped in thin skin. While my backside grew, hers was shrinking so much that my roommates and I thought her head looked too big for her ever-narrowing body.

I was on my way to meet Julie between classes one afternoon to talk about what we might do to help Molly. I stopped at a small grove of maple and oak trees, their leaves glorious with color. Their beauty and that of the campus enveloped me with a sense of connectedness to life. I breathed in brisk fall air and cherished this feeling, sensing its power. The heavenward reach of the trees brought a Biblical passage to mind: "Whatever is true, whatever is good, and whatever is beautiful, think on *these* things..."

I arrived at the designated spot near McCracken Hall where Julie and I greeted one another under the full canopy of red- and yellow-leafed maples. She seemed nervous, kicked a pebble, rubbed her neck. I studied her face.

"You okay?"

"Yeah, fine, just concerned."

"Do you think we should call her parents?" I asked, trying to get the ball rolling. "I'm so worried about her—the girl looks so thin, you can see every bone in her hands. She's a bird. And I think she's slowly killing herself."

Silence.

Julie stared at me. I shifted my weight. She exhaled loudly, stared at the ground, and finally said, "Molly's killing herself? Yes, I think so too. I think so too." She looked up, and I watched a tear travel down her cheek. She left it there for me to study. "But what about you? What about what *you* do? Do you really think I don't know that you throw up after every meal? Do you really think I didn't notice that you always go to the restroom after you eat *anything*?"

I tried to breathe, but it felt like someone was sitting on my chest. I couldn't speak. I had no idea that she knew.

Her shoulders shook, and she cried like I'd never seen her cry. "I can't take this, you know? Molly's dying, Jodi's drinking herself to death, and you, you...oh, I'm sorry, it's just all too much."

"I know, I know. I'll get better—I'll go do something. I'm so sorry."

"Don't tell me you're sorry. Go get help. Please!"

Stunned, it took me a moment to process what she was saying. I watched her sob silently, feeling like she'd grabbed me by the collar and hung me up on a coat rack. I was caught, and what was more, she was suffering on my account. That felt wrong, and the possibility of a heart attack or a bleeding esophagus didn't scare me nearly as much as the thought of upsetting her this way.

"Listen, I promise, I'll get help."

Julie shook her head and hugged me. We could talk about Molly another time; she needed to go. I stood there for a few minutes, shocked that she knew my secret. Three days later, I was sitting in the Student Counseling Center with a cognitive behavior therapist who gave me exercises that required me to write down what I was thinking when the urge to binge and purge came over me. I sat at my desk that night and wrote: *Desperate. Out of control. Nervous. Needing food more than air.* Then afterwards? *Panic-stricken about the weight all that food could cause. Desperate. Disgusted. Hating myself.*

At the time, I didn't know what the therapist would do to help, but this was indeed the first time I'd looked at my bulimia so closely. It wasn't until much later, though, that I realized I needed to take some responsibility for my eating disorder in the same way alcoholics did for their disease. Back then, I blamed society, the Church, and my parents. The truth was, my addiction was like an abusive spouse I couldn't bring myself to leave. I needed food to calm me. Being grossly overweight was not an option. So I hid my secret shame from everyone but the therapist with whom I visited only a few times. I just wanted to go home but then felt conflicted about that, knowing my mother would criticize my weight and make me feel worse.

❧

At Thanksgiving, Julie, Molly and I caught a ride home. I worried about my mother's reaction to the "freshman ten" I'd put on, but thought that she would be happy to see me after such a long absence. Dad and I talked about the history class I was taking, but within thirty minutes of my arrival home, Mom asked the Question.

"Have you thought about going on another diet?" This she said in a *bytheway* sort of manner that was a cover for the fact that my weight bugged the shit out of her.

"Yeah, but I've thought even more about becoming a fat cow."

"Why do you have to be that way? I'm just concerned about you."

I could feel tears starting to form, but I blinked them away. "Is there a reason you care about my weight so much?" *Did she understand how much I wanted to please her but couldn't?*

I wished she could be more like Jesus on this issue. Wasn't she supposed to see *me*—the real me? Not the one that was discarded by the rich kids at school? Jesus didn't care about my weight as much as the weight of my character; His love was unconditional. I had thought my mother's love was unconditional, but her disapproval increased with the girth of my thighs, making me feel like an unwanted foreign exchange student longing for my real home.

I felt close to Dad, but he didn't seem to notice that anything was bothering me. He asked me how school was going and seemed interested in my friends. Still, he trod carefully, playing it safe on the surface of our existence. Maybe he was afraid to know what was going on with me, or maybe he was too busy trying to keep himself from unraveling. I couldn't be sure.

The tension hung around me like a curtain. The notion that Mom might be trying to protect me from the suffering that went along with the extra pounds didn't matter to me then. I had internalized her concern as rejection and turned it into a stew of self-hatred I cooked up in my over-active and overly analytical brain. Looking back, I realize I may have wanted to feel like her victim so I wouldn't have to blame myself.

Perhaps there was an unreachable place where Mom and I could say what we wanted to say. If we had reached it, I think she might have told me that she had felt unattractive in her youth and was trying to spare me from a similar pain. But what came across to me, while I was in the midst of my illness, was a critical and unloving eye coupled with useless suggestions.

If I could have penetrated the invisible wall between us, I would have told her that even though I hated myself for my lack of discipline, I was trapped in a sick cycle of needing food to calm me down. I felt like it gave me control over any rising fears about whatever was happening in my life—except the fear of weight. I needed to purge then, terrified that I wouldn't be appealing to the man-boys who seemed to like me when I was slim and ignore me when I wasn't. My parents would have helped if they knew how, and if I weren't standing in my own way. In my bedroom, most of my things had been taken down; posters of Todd Rundgren and Bruce Springsteen now hung in my dorm room. There would be no spring semester at home for healing, no treatment program. I was unable to ask for help. I was too ashamed. I thought I had to tough it out myself.

Twenty

Miss Petrie's Wedding

LOST IN DORM LIFE, I partied, studied, binged, and purged, somehow managing to hold down decent grades. As spring semester drew to a close, and Julie, Jodi, and I planned for the next year by signing a lease on an uptown apartment, along with our friend Heather, from Dorsey Hall. Molly, now less anorexic, signed up for another year in the dorms.

I returned home in search of a summer job and some down time. After a luckless week on the job front, I was at home reading *Mila 18*, when the phone rang. Deliberately mysterious, Jodi's raspy confidence carried over the phone line.

"Get ready for the wedding. I'll pick you up at six."

I pushed the phone closer to my ear. "What? What wedding?"

"Any one we want."

Silence.

She laughed. I looked around the room, making sure my parents weren't eavesdropping. "What are you talking about?"

"Ah, it's so fun talking to you. Relax, have you forgotten that my dad owns a party center? We can get dressed up and walk into any or all of the party rooms."

"Oh, wait—why would we want to do that?"

"You're killin' me. To sample some of their alcohol, of course. Look, everyone is onboard—Carol, Molly, MJ, Laura, Julie—the usual. Be ready."

Two hours later, Jodi lurched her Nova into our driveway and tapped the horn. Wearing jeans, I was out the door, panty hose, shoes, and dress stuffed in a brown paper grocery bag. The other girls were already wearing dresses and heels. *Why was I was the only one who seemed nervous?*

"Jod, what are we gonna say if your dad sees us? Won't he kick us out?" I glanced nervously at the others.

Laura elbowed Carol and snickered.

Jodi laughed harder. "So, you wanna know what to say to him if he sees you? Just tell him *Hi*. Listen, it's no big deal. I told him we'd be here for Miss Petrie's wedding."

For one who'd held her own in tackle football, I had the savvy of a volleyball among these girls, who constantly set me up. "Who's Miss Petrie?" I asked, knowing I was heading for a net but not knowing any other way to play.

"What? You don't remember her?" Julie asked with a smile. "Laura, remind Parker about Miss Petrie, will you please?"

"Certainly. Don't you remember her? She was your eighth-grade teacher—the one who loved you so much she told you to invite your friends."

"Yeah," chimed in MJ, "and since she's marrying your neighbor's cousin's best friend, well, she felt it was only right that you get to bring extra people."

OhMYGod. I was going to have to lie. I spent the rest of the car ride trying to remember if the groom was my cousin's best friend's neighbor or my best friend's cousin's neighbor. We walked into the party complex, a modest group of ballrooms around a central court-yard. I slipped away to the restroom to change into my red sheath with white trim. Some instinct had told me to look my best.

Minutes later, Jodi led us into the "the big room" on the far side of the facility. The bride looked much too young to be my teacher. Jodi thought we should grab a quick drink from the bar, avoid eye contact with people we didn't know, and congregate near the back of the room. I asked the bartender for a rum and Coke and drank it quickly, letting it slide down my throat while a mullet-wearing wedding singer sporting a powder blue suit sang "Betty Davis Eyes." Two drinks and three songs later, we followed Jodi to the next party where we encountered a polka band reminiscent of Frankie Yankovic and The Slovenian Home. After ten minutes, Jodi winced, slugged her drink, and slammed her glass to the bar.

"Let's go. I can't take any more of this music."

I hurriedly finished my drink and followed. We headed to yet another party where I belted another rum and Coke before switching to a vodka tonic. The room was starting to spin. If I fell over or slurred my speech, my friends would make even more fun of me. I needed to sit down. I remembered the comfortable-looking couches in the ladies' lounge, so I slipped away to the restroom. I sat down, trying to be cool. My numbed mind studied the gold-flecked wallpaper that blurred and melted into dreamlike random thoughts. I was sitting upright, half asleep when Carol and Molly burst in.

"Dave Spence is here at another wedding," Carol announced. "He's with his cousin—really cute."

Carol and I regularly competed for who could "get" the cutest guy, and we had a running score. I finally grasped the opportunity. The gauntlet had been thrown—although at first, her words seemed to be spoken underwater. Dave Spencer had been on the football team in high school and was cute and friendly. His really cute cousin could only be good news.

"Great. I'm there." I got up from the red velvet chair and assessed my make-up. Not bad. If I could hold myself steady, Dave's cousin would see a way more relaxed version of my normally tense self. It looked good on me. Maybe even sexy. Some fresh lipstick. At the time, I knew I looked good despite the inner sabotage that accused me of being fat and worthless. After all, I was ahead in the score against Carol. I wasn't a glamour queen, but a guy could do worse. Part of me needed to do this. See, I could say to my demons, I've got proof you're not always right.

I staggered over to the party room, trying to pretend I wasn't drunk. I came around the corner, and Dave's cousin immediately caught my eye. He was slightly taller than I was, with feathered-back brown hair, a blue suit, white shirt, and red tie adding to his appeal. Definitely the best thing I'd seen in a long time. Both Carol and Julie were vying for his attention.

"Jack, tell us where you go to school." Carol moved closer to him.

"Miami University. Just finished my sophomore year." He answered Carol, but looked at me.

"That's where she goes!" Laura said, pointing at me with her thumb.

He smiled and then singled me out. "So I understand from your friends, you aren't really here for any one wedding party."

"Yeah, the whole thing makes me nervous! So much so that I drank a bit more than I should have. They just laugh at me though."

"Well, you're having fun, right?"

"I am now." Probably the boldest thing I'd ever said to a guy.

He smiled at me. Oh, he was so cute that night. Good-looking, well-mannered, fun, AND he was a Redskin—a moniker thankfully changed to the Red Hawks in the nineties. I couldn't believe my good luck.

Thirty minutes later, Jodi, Laura, and Julie found us after escaping from the reception they'd crashed. They were laughing, but scared, walking as fast as they could without running toward us. Julie laughingly described the way Jodi positioned herself in the center of the crowd of young women, and, jock that she was, caught the bouquet.

The story filtered from the blurry scene to my ears and into my head. It was background noise to the sight of the beautiful young man in the blue suit I had just met. Could it be that he wasn't like the vulgar and self-absorbed college-aged men that I'd so often met at school? I studied him as he went back and forth to the bar for our free drinks. Jodi went on and on as the others laughed about her Willie Mays-like grab.

Jack's blue eyes lingered on mine. I thought, *Jodi caught the bouquet, but I caught Jack.*

Back at Miami that fall, Jodi joined us, having transferred from Ohio University. Jack was a frequent visitor to the apartment I shared with my roommates. From the beginning, it was a haven from the on-campus beauty contests and panty raids of the previous year. I didn't care that it was furnished with 1960s-style furniture that had seen its share of bodily fluids and beer spills. With our limited funds and decorating skills, we tried to spruce up the place. Julie hung pictures and arranged green plastic foliage in baskets, and Jodi picked up a few decorative pillows at K-Mart. I painted a rainbow on my bedroom wall. What kind of taste did we have? None.

Our neighbors, Kevin and Jay, had other ideas about how to make the place more livable. They regularly stopped over with beers or marijuana that we smoked in small joints they rolled. In between puffs of marijuana, we talked about the Bengals and the Browns. I told them about my baseball card collection. They were impressed. Everything was right with the world.

Jack laughed along with us, joining in on bong hits and afternoon beer-drinking sessions around our kitchen table. Sometimes he brought a friend or two, and we improvised on the seating by using empty cases of Robin Hood beer, the cheapest, most rancid beer I'd ever tasted, laughing non-stop. If you had asked me then, I would have said it was one of the happiest times of my life. Things were simple, really. Just live for the moment, that's all I had to do. Still, I couldn't name the fear that gripped me. Something was in charge that didn't feel like the real me.

One Friday night, early in the year, Jack called to say he was going to hang out with his frat brothers before stopping by around 8:00 P.M. Julie, Jodi and I ate pizza and played "quarters." I got up for another beer, and as I closed the refrigerator door, I heard a loud noise coming from the bathroom. Heather was in there with the door closed, but that didn't obscure the loud retching noise.

"What the hell?" Jodi asked. "Sounds like something between a bark and a loud burp. Should I go see if she's okay? She didn't seem sick."

Julie stared at me, looking for any clue that I had returned to my barfing ways.

"She's throwing up," I said. "And no, she's not sick—at least not in the way you're thinking. She does it so she won't gain weight."

"Oh my God. What should we do?" Jodi asked, looking in my direction, oblivious to the fact that I was the last person who would have a solution.

Feeling guilty and panicked, I just shrugged and plinked the quarter into the glass. "I have no idea—wish I did."

Heather flushed her latest meal down the facilities and strutted out of the bathroom as if nothing unusual had happened. None of us could think of a thing to say. Julie stuttered something to break the silence, and then our doorbell rang. *Jack.* I jumped up to answer the door and gave him a hug and a kiss, happy for the diversion. I hadn't yet told him about my bulimia, worrying it would scare him off. I didn't want him to know about Heather's problem either; it could start a conversation about the eating disorder we shared. Since Julie already knew, I privately assured her that my problems were under control, not explaining it meant my episodes were limited to twice a week. To me, that was victory, like the former alcoholic turned social drinker. I was glad I had gone to see the therapist. He'd helped me enough to allow partial control over my bulimia; I thought I could remain relatively healthy without gaining too much weight. Julie's outburst had also helped me, and I didn't want to worry her any more. She'd faced enough difficult situations in her life. Her mother had died when she was only eleven, leaving her father to raise six kids on his own. Julie's maternal soul was the stabilizing force of our college home.

Both Julie and I began working at one of the campus dining halls. Free food came with the minimum wages. It was great for my finances, but not for my bulimia. Despite what I had told Julie, the temptation was too great. Soon I was back to throwing up ten to twelve times per day.

I awoke every morning vaguely anxious. I didn't want to think about it. Bagels. That's what I wanted to think about. Buttered rolls, mashed potatoes, or the chocolate chip cookies freshly baked at the cafeteria. By late September, my clothes were feeling tight, and although my weight had been on the downswing all summer, it was now clearly moving up again. I prayed Jack wouldn't notice, afraid that he'd soon find me undesirable. That prayer was apparently answered. Although my weight still fluctuated, I never overate in front of him. Being with him made it easier not to overeat. He never overate and was disciplined about food and pretty much everything else. He had a plan, studied every day from 2:00 to 6:00 P.M. without fail. Only when his studies were complete did he think about dinner or having fun. I so admired that and hoped some of his willpower would rub off on me.

One Monday afternoon, I planned to meet him at King Library. I had to get some me-time beforehand so I could get something to eat. I walked uptown for my quick fix, heading to the general store. I took the red-painted concrete steps two at a time and entered through the columns leading to the front door of the store. The sweet scent of freshly made bagels wafted from the shop next door. A bagel sounded good, but I thought better of it, reminding myself I only had a few crumpled dollars in my pocket. A muscle in my face twitched as my anxiety started to mount. My hands sweated and I glanced at the clerk. The man behind the counter was old with a butch haircut and jowls that flapped over the collar of his plaid shirt, a *Townie*. Another shopper pushed by me. I looked left and right and then made another circle around the store. I couldn't breathe, and so leaned my hand on a shelf and tried to suck in some air. When the sales clerk rang up a customer, I quickly slipped two Snickers bars into my right jacket pocket. Seconds later, I grabbed three packs of M&Ms and shoved them into my other pocket. Now the hard part. I stepped forward, wishing I could run for the door. *Be discreet. Don't draw attention.* I took a deep breath, and five long strides got me out of there. Down the steps and into a back alley, I ripped open the Snickers bar. A flood of feel-good chemicals hit my bloodstream like an injection. Relief. I repeated the process, scarfing down what I later estimated were 1700 calories in three minutes. When the last bite was gone, I wiped the corners of my mouth. I had never stolen anything in my life. I knew it was a sign that my bulimia was getting worse, but I shook that thought out of my head and went in search of a milkshake to make sure it all came up.

Jack told me to meet him on the second floor of the library near the reference section, but my first stop would be the rest room. Relief flushed my mind as I flushed unwanted calories. As I made my way to the sink to wash my hands, I avoided my reflection in the mirror, telling myself what I always did. It was the last time. *Tomorrow I won't binge and purge anymore.* A lie I'd keep telling despite the fact that I knew I had fallen deeper into the trap of my addiction.

My parents may have worried that my roommates and I were drinking too much. Mom often commented about the high caloric content in beer, but she didn't ask too many direct questions. If she had, I might have told her she was right. The truth was, I was grateful she didn't ask about the drinking, but I was also angry at her and my father for not knowing about my bulimia. How could they, since I didn't tell them? I had a nice little victim racket going.

I was good at hiding the truth. Jodi wasn't. She got drunk and passed out at other people's places on a regular basis, always swearing that she'd only had a few, but we knew otherwise. After the first few months, I no longer expected her home on weekends, and we were never quite sure when she'd show up.

I certainly didn't want to give up my own chemical aids. Drinking and smoking pot made me laugh and eased my mind of the stress of schoolwork and life. They gave me a feeling of connectedness and shared experience that I hadn't found at church or anywhere else. A beer buzz helped relieve my anxiety and the chaos that went on in my head when eating and purging didn't work. I'd swig a beer and listen to the blues, lost in guitar licks that reached into my soul. It was all the therapy I could manage. By then, I was too ashamed to talk to Jesus.

❧

I spent more and more time with Jack as the semester wore on. One cold winter Saturday, we planned a double date with his friend Roland, who'd recently started dating Jodi. After piling into Jack's silver Chevy Citation, a sawed-off octagon with wheels, we set off for Cincinnati. Jodi poked me in the ribs and chuckled when Jack paid for his and my cover charge at the club with rolled pennies. I chuckled harder when she had to pay for both herself and Roland; he had no money at all.

After a night of dancing, Jack pulled into the parking lot of our apartment at 3:00 A.M. As I exited the car, Jodi pulled me aside and made a smart remark about the "rich" boys we'd found. I tripped on the eroding asphalt, laughing but feeling grateful for a fun night outside our boring college town.

On the steps leading to our apartment, we ran into Kevin and Jay, who invited us in for a beer. Jack and I declined, deciding to call it a night. I fumbled for my keys in the unorganized accessory I called my purse. It was filled with an assortment of candy wrappers, receipts, hairbrushes, and pens popping out as I rooted around for my keys. Finally, I had them in my grasp. Jack kissed me, and the beer from our breath joined in a miasma of alcohol and pheromones. We entered the dark apartment, trying to keep noise to a minimum, knowing both Heather and Julie were asleep inside. We both knew what was about to happen.

"Wait here in the hallway," I whispered, "while I turn on the light in the living room and grab some pillows and blankets so we can sleep on the couch."

I was nervous. Out-of-wedlock horror stories and fear of sexually transmitted diseases tempered my desire for Jack. Admonitions by Dr. Dobson rang in my head, but I looked at Jack waiting for me in the doorway and thought about the nice way he treated me. My feeling that he was the best looking guy I'd ever seen hadn't faded with familiarity.

I walked toward him and fell into his arms. I was as hungry for him as he was for me. He took my hand, and we walked over to the couch. I tried not to think of how many others had repeated a similar scene on that old green couch. His kiss sent waves through my body. Maybe I wasn't morally ready for it, but my body craved him. I reminded myself he wasn't like the others who felt entitled to my body after a short conversation and a few beers. Was something missing? Maybe, but what did I expect anyway?

What was I looking for?

The next weekend, we slept together again, stealing a private moment at his fraternity house while his roommate stayed with his girlfriend. Afterwards, a combination of guilt and fear made me anxious.

"I need to get back to my place to study."

"I'll walk you home," he offered.

"No, I have to meet people at the library for my Eastern Civ project. I'll call you later."

On the way home, I felt panicked, like I was sliding down a hill into hell. How pissed off was God at me for having sex? What would my parents say if I got pregnant? My mind was flooded with a slide show of scenarios that made me want to go to bed and pull the covers over my head. What kind of Christian was I anyway? Between the gluttony, the bong hits, drinking, and the sex, wasn't I checking off an awful lot of sins in a short amount of time?

I felt guiltiest about the premarital sex. Was that because it seemed to be the sin the Church most strongly condemned? I wasn't sure. I told myself that at least I wasn't promiscuous—that was good—but then again, I felt conflicted about being in a relationship. I sometimes felt trapped. Was I promising Jack more than I could offer? Was I giving up too much freedom? The root word in relationship is *relate*. Did Jack and I *relate*?

"So, wanna grab a pizza and then play a few video games?" he asked one Thursday, stopping by my apartment after he'd spent the afternoon at King Library.

"Yeah, sure—let me get some money."

Purse in hand, and after a quick kiss in the foyer, we headed down the stairs and toward the pizza parlor.

"Do you have a lot of homework tonight?" he asked.

I wanted to explain that I was having trouble concentrating on schoolwork because of my eating disorder, but I couldn't muster the courage.

"Well, I have a paper to finish for my Spanish class. Other than that I'm okay. You?"

"Got everything done at the library."

"Excellent," I nodded.

He took my hand and smiled at me, and we walked on in silence.

Our conversations were mostly informational exchanges—we weren't connected in a meaningful way. He didn't seem interested in my deepest feelings or what I had to say. Was I interested in what he had to say? How he felt? Yes, although to be honest, I was more interested in him physically than emotionally but worried about hurting him if we were to break up. I spent hours thinking about it and concluded that neither of us was that connected to the other. If I was going to stay with him, I needed to find a way to deepen our connection. Maybe he was the best guy he could be, wanting to be enough, all without ever connecting on a soul level. That thought lingered for a while and sent my stomach into peptic panic. I pushed those thoughts out of my head, and replaced them with visions of his blue eyes and great body. *Maybe this is just as good as it gets.*

Sleep offered no escape. Night after night, in my dreams, a group of people whom I couldn't see waited for me. I knew they were there, needing me to hurry up and bring books or something with me. *I have to hurry. I think I have it all now. But wait—what's this? There's another stack of books. They're expecting me to bring these too.* I reached down to pick them up, and everything fell out of my hands. *I'm exhausted—how will I ever get there in time?* I can't do this, I said to no one. I had a sudden urge to cough. Then, a white Styrofoam-like substance started streaming out of my mouth. There was no end to it. I pulled it out one hand after the other like a magician pulling a scarf nonstop out of his hat.

As gross as that was, I awoke with a sense that purging helped me get rid of unworthy crap, leaving me a purified Self.

Twenty-one

Spilt Beans

BULIMIA TAKES ON A LIFE of its own. Guilt and shame are by-products that carry their own emotional pressure, which leads to more binge/purge cycles. After a few weeks of working at the dining hall, it was clear that my addiction had escalated, and the emotional pressure of my secret was increasing. Jack's attention seemed like it might have the power to feed whatever it was inside me that was starving. So I came up with a bright idea. Maybe Jack could help me. It might even spark a deeper connection between us.

One Sunday evening, I asked him to come over to talk. I waited nervously for him in the living room of the apartment, glancing out the window every five minutes, careful not to move my head too quickly and add to my hangover headache, courtesy of the raucous party broken up by Miami security guards we called Seekies.

Jack arrived, and I greeted him with a hug and a kiss. "Have a seat," I said.

He was quiet. *Did he suspect anything?* He seemed angry, but if I didn't get started on what I needed to say, I was afraid I'd chicken out.

"Listen, this is really hard for me to talk about, but I'm feeling totally out of control and don't know what to do. Years ago, I started overeating and then throwing up to keep from gaining weight . . . and well, I stopped doing it for a while, but it's starting up again and I feel like I need to tell someone. I need help."

There it was. I exhaled and picked at a stray thread on the green couch while the refrigerator hummed in the background. I waited and looked at him. He was still. My chest tightened, and I took in a deep breath. *Was he angry?* In slow motion—the way things go when you feel like life is about to end—he looked up from the floor and then at me.

"Got any more beans you wanna spill?" His acerbic tone signaled he was angry about something else, wanting me to know that I had hurt *him* somehow. The last thing he wanted to do was listen to my stuff.

To me, his comment was a fist to the gut. I leaned back and took in a breath. *Beans? Did he say beans?* I had admitted what I couldn't say to my own parents, bared my soul to him. He'd answered my deepest confidence with a flippant cliché?

Shocked and confused, I got up from the chair and circled the room. Then I had the sensation that I was falling. His voice was fading into the background, and the hum of the refrigerator seemed to get louder, competing with the voice in my head. *Fat ass. What'd you think he'd say? He'd make it all better? You're gross, deal with it.*

Jack said something about me talking to another guy at that party, his words drowned out by the ones in my head. I could no longer hear him. When I could talk, I choked out a short cry and the only words that came to me—words directed at both him and my demon voices.

"Get out!"

That night, I lay in bed, alone on the planet of the freaks. Maybe like me, Jack was in some sort of fight for his life. If I had known him better, maybe I would have understood. Maybe I would have found that he didn't have the strength to address my problems because he had enough of his own. The summer with Mary Beth had taught me that no one was as normal as they looked on the outside, yet no amount of logic could touch a fear eating at me and demanding some kind of nourishment to make it go away. I had hoped maybe love could.

The next morning, Jack called to try to salvage things, but I broke up with him, needing to believe that it was somehow possible to find someone who could listen and care, someone who wanted a relationship built on more than sexual attraction. Someone who could handle my secrets.

※

Jodi tried to get me out of my funk. "We're going to a party."

I could tell I didn't have a choice. After a month of my moping, my friends were sick of it.

We walked in that night, wondering where the beer was hidden. The first person I saw was a guy named Brian whom I had met briefly the previous year. Brian was smart and good-looking. I soon found out he was also a great conversationalist. We talked the rest of the night, and I left the party flying high. He called me the next day and we went to dinner. I wondered if this was a guy I could trust to love *me*, and not just want my body. We were together nearly every day after that first date, and we talked about everything—or almost everything. I wasn't yet ready for him to know about my bulimia. Maybe one day I could tell him, but in the meantime, we sat for hours, discussing spirituality, religion, food, wine, travel, and books. There was never enough time to get it all in.

The best, though, was the dancing.

One evening, he stopped by my apartment and caught me just as I returned home from the library.

"Hop in the car."

I looked at him like he was crazy. "Brian, I told you I have a ton of studying to do tonight."

"Come on. Life's short."

I gave in, and he drove toward Cincinnati. When we arrived at a lookout point near the city, he pulled the car to the side of the road where there was a view of the Ohio River, took his boom box out of the car, and turned on Celia Cruz.

He walked around to the passenger door, opened it, grabbed my hand, and said, "Come on, let's go."

We salsa'd with the city lights in the distance.

The following weekend, we stayed at his place. Brian was a great cook and, despite our meager funds, made sure we ate well.

"Whatcha got?"

"Well, let's see—eight quarters, three dimes, a nickel, and two pennies...that's $2.37."

"Cool, I've got $4.94 and chicken breasts in the fridge. We can buy some black beans and rice and we're good to go. Let's go to Kroger."

Upon our return, he turned on his stereo and placed a salsa record on the turntable.

"You're going to chop the onions and the garlic." He handed them to me on a cutting board. "And I'm going to season the chicken and start the water for the beans."

When the meal was complete, he set the table, lit a few candles, and poured two glasses of Chilean wine. I sat there thinking this was *it*. I didn't have to leave the real me or any of my real thoughts outside the door when I was with Brian. It was like finding my way home.

"What do you have going on this week?" I asked.

"Well, there are some Franciscan priests that I met the last time I was home, and they'll be at a conference in Cincinnati this week. I'm hoping to have dinner with them on Wednesday."

"Really? Why?"

"Well, because I'm considering the priesthood."

I put down my fork. "The priesthood? You can't be serious."

He took a sip of wine. "Well, yeah, maybe, I dunno, we'll see."

I wondered how serious he was about it, but could tell he didn't want to discuss it anymore. He took a bite of chicken and then asked, "Do you wanna go to a party Friday night?"

"Sure. Will there be any dancing?"

"With you and me there? There's always dancing!"

I loved it when he said things like that. It was almost perfect. The trouble was, he still hadn't even kissed me. I kept thinking that it would eventually happen—some magical moment would occur when he'd find me irresistible. The kiss would be perfect, and we would finish college, move in together, and then travel or join the Peace Corp. Live happily ever after.

Months later, the perfect kiss still hadn't happened, and I was growing increasingly frustrated, worried it might never happen. Near the end of the school year, one night in April, Jodi, Julie, and I visited his apartment. Two hours and six beers into the evening, Brian made everyone but me leave.

"Come here," he said as he took my hand and led me into his bedroom.

Moving close to me, he said, "I told my brother to take everyone uptown. You and I need time alone." He gently pushed me against the wall.

"I thought you were going to be a priest," I whispered back.

"I know, but you make it so fucking hard." My sense of humor about the potential play on words took a back seat to the moment. He finally kissed me. *Perfect.* Tears fell down my cheeks. He brushed them away, and then took my hand and led me to the small record player where he played soft romantic Latin music, stood behind me, put his arms around my waist, and kissed my neck. A tingling sensation rippled through my body. He led me to his bed where we kissed and held each other for a long time. He was loving and attentive, but that was it. We fell asleep in each other's arms. I thought we'd make love in the morning, but the next morning when I awoke, he wasn't there. I got up slowly, hoping he would hear me rustling and come back to bed. I heard him turn on the water in the kitchen, then smelled coffee. I put on his robe and headed for the kitchen where I found him emptying the dishwasher.

"Brian, what are you doing? Why don't you come back to bed?"

"Oh, hey, well, I'm busy. Gotta lot to do today."

Did I dream last night? No, it had happened…and then again, it hadn't. I went back to the bedroom, grabbed my clothes, threw them on, and washed my face in the bathroom. Now, fully dressed I returned to the kitchen.

"What's so important about what you're doing in the kitchen?" I asked him.

"Look, I just have a lot to do."

I fought back my tears and the impulse to beg him to tell me last night meant something. To kiss me. He just kept chopping vegetables. I grabbed the doorknob of his apartment door slowly, hoping it would give him enough time to call for me. Nothing. I headed out the door and back to my apartment in the rain, feeling like I'd been run over, squashed by some sort of existential trickery.

Brian couldn't love me for some reason.

Now I understood my parents' need to pretend, stuff emotions, and keep moving. I went to my room and alternated between pacing the floor and crying into my pillow. I emerged and determined that I would one day find true love and also find a way to beat my bulimia on my own, one day at a time.

A letter from Brian arrived days later. I laid it on the coffee table and stared at it. Finally, I shoved it in my pocket and went to my room. Sitting on my bed, I tore open the corner of the envelope, careful not to tear through the address.

I read the words, none of it good news. He was sorry. He cared for me. BUT there existed a wall between us that could never be scaled. He hadn't known how to tell me, even though he had known for a long time.

He was GAY.

I wasn't stunned by the news. It was something I wondered about after so many months without so much as a kiss. His consideration of the seminary added to my suspicions. Still, I knew he loved me, and somehow believed that was bigger than what physical problems we might have. My friends thought that was a crazy notion.

"Are you kidding me?" Julie said. "I don't get what you're saying."

"Well, what does he love? Me? Or my body? I mean, is it IMPOSSIBLE to think people might be turned on for reasons that are beyond the physical?"

"Yes, pretty much."

The rest of my friends agreed with Julie's assessment, but I still spent nights in the bathroom, talking to myself in the mirror, begging to know why he couldn't just love ME, the person inside the body. Why my gender mattered so much to him.

I should have been careful what I wished for. I had wanted someone who loved me for me and didn't focus so much on my sex appeal. Then came Brian. Trouble was, he didn't want me because of it.

Jodi tried to get me out of my funk again, and the next weekend, invited me to yet another party. I went, but I wasn't interested in dead conversations and drinking games. On the way home, I glanced out the window at the passing scenery of the campus. When we got home, I called Brian to deliver a tear-filled speech about God and His ability to deliver him from his *sin*. I cringe now to think of the speech I gave him. The awesome irony.

Brian listened to my rant without a word.

"I gotta go."

"Wait."

An exhale. "For what? See ya."

I hung up the phone and sobbed until no noise, tear, or pain could be squeezed from my body.

I needed a different self. A different life.

CHAPTER 22

Born Again in Sevilla

SOMETHING STIRS INSIDE, LETTING YOU know if you don't make a radical change, your life will veer off in the wrong direction forever. I was stuck, lonely and restless despite the great friends I'd met at Miami. Months after Brian dropped me, I had some success in willing my bulimia episodes down to a more "manageable" two or three times a day. The self-absorbed, sex-crazed creeps I'd met still seemed interested in me, but even the good looking ones held no appeal.

I wanted to see the world. All I'd seen had been Ohio. I loved the Spanish language, but learning the language was challenging, especially since all I did was sit in a Spanish class with thirty other students who mostly couldn't care less about it. I knew immersion in a Spanish-speaking culture would make a difference and allow me to see more of the world. To my everlasting appreciation, my parents gave me the okay to speak with my Spanish professor about options for overseas study. The deal was I'd pay for my wedding (if I ever had one), and they'd pay the extra tuition for a semester overseas. I chose Spain over Latin America because it would allow me to see Europe.

I met my professor after class and asked where the best place to study in Spain might be.

Professor Rogers removed her glasses and smiled as she looked out the tall window of our classroom. "Well, if you're looking for a top-notch university in a beautiful setting, there is Salamanca—it's a beautiful place—sort of like this campus in a way. If you want an urban university with the excitement of New York, or their version of it—go to Madrid."

I shifted my weight and smiled inwardly, thinking back to the days when Dad and I talked endlessly about Goya and all the other great Spanish painters. She swiveled her chair back toward me and said, "And then there is Sevilla. It's beautiful, not too big or too small, a center of art, history, and architecture."

A certain magic came into her eyes and voice when she described Sevilla, and that sealed it for me. She recommended a program, and I thanked her and headed over to King Library to start the application process. Could this really happen? I knew that my parents would be making a sacrifice by sending me, and I felt guilty about it, but Dad was especially excited for me. Mom and Gramma worried about me being so far away. Even my sister, Ann, said she would miss me. I knew I'd miss them all, but my desire for adventure, change, and maybe even a new me overshadowed those feelings.

I went home to Cleveland to talk about the opportunity, and Aunt Joy came over for dinner. She was excited about it too. "Go for it," she said, and then looked out the window as though she wished she had followed her own advice. She was thirty-eight and seemed a little less enthusiastic about art and horses and just about anything else in life that had once excited her. Still, as we talked, she grew increasingly more animated. She was happy for me and listened attentively.

"The whole group tours Madrid the first few days, including a trip to the Prado museum."

She looked over at me and something flashed over her face. Was it jealousy? No. Maybe more like a wish that she'd had the chance.

"Make sure you find the Miró collection. I'm not sure if the modern art is housed in the Prado or somewhere else. You'll have to let me know." She picked up her plate and went over to the stove for more spaghetti. "I know I'm putting on weight, but I can't seem to stop eating."

I could certainly relate, but didn't know what to say to her. When it was time for her to leave, she hugged me hard, like she always did—like she needed to.

I filed the conversation away and vowed that I would go to Spain with my head held high. I would stop my bulimia. I couldn't throw up in someone else's home.

៚

Back at Miami the next weekend, I struck up a conversation with a guy who seemed promising. I met him at an uptown bar, but I also recognized him from class. We spent the evening talking over Miller Lite and popcorn at CJ's. Afterwards, he drove me home.

"Can I come inside?"

"No, look, my roommates are home and I'm really tired."

He looked slightly disappointed, but confident enough to give it another try. "At least give me a goodnight kiss." He reached over and slobbered on my face and stuck his tongue in my mouth. He was good looking, but the kiss felt like I'd swished a goldfish in my mouth.

"Let's go in the backseat."

I honestly didn't want to, but I also didn't want to be a total prude. We got in the backseat of his Toyota, and the next thing I knew, his pants were unzipped.

"Grab it."

What? I felt like a whore. Maybe though, this was what I was supposed to want to do. I took his penis in my hand, and he groaned. Like a prostitute in it for the money only, I felt nothing. His jollies did nothing for me. Did this make me undersexed or otherwise abnormal?

"Faster."

Oh my God, when is this going to be over?

"Don't stop."

I didn't, not until he spasmed untidily, there in the back of his Corolla. The *afterglow* awkward, I told him I needed to be on my way.

The next morning, I woke up and the previous night's tawdry scene crowded my mind. *Think about something else. Go eat breakfast.* Later that day, my sister, Ann, called and told me about her new boyfriend. I told her how sick I was of the guys I'd been meeting.

"Jack still loves you, you know," she said. Later I wondered how Ann would have known that, but at the time took her comment at face value.

"Trust me, I've been thinking about him a lot lately. He's ten times better than most guys I meet."

"Why don't you call him?"

"How? It's just too scary. Besides, I'm not sure we're right for each other. And you know, I'm planning to study overseas."

"Well, you're coming back, aren't you?"

"Maybe." Had I been unfair to Jack? I mean, who would ever want to hear about something as gross as my bulimia? *What was I thinking?* Maybe Jack was exactly what I needed. Jack wasn't like Brian. He loved me and he was so sexy. He *wanted* to sleep with me, but he wasn't a pig about it like the guy from the previous night. I wanted to call him, but how could I get up the nerve? It felt wrong to even try after our last breakup eight months earlier, yet I couldn't get him off my mind.

I called Jodi and asked her if she would call him for me. I was twenty-one years old, reverting to junior high tactics because I was too frightened to call him myself. "See if he'll meet me in the park to talk things out."

"Are you sure you want to do this? Aren't you considering studying overseas?"

"Yes, but I don't know. I miss him and don't think I'll ever find anyone as good as he is."

❧

When Jack walked up to where I was seated, he took my breath away. He was handsome and tan with the bluest of eyes. He was shaking. My stomach was doing corresponding flips. Some teensy voice in the back of my mind told me not to do it, but I couldn't stop myself. Ann was right—he did love me. And I loved him. One kiss and I knew we were about to pick up where we left off.

A month later, despite our best efforts, Jack and I were back to bickering. He wanted more assurances that I was in the relationship for good, and I wanted more proof that I should be.

"Where were you last night?" he demanded.

"I told you, I was with Julie, and Jodi at CJ's, and I tried calling your house but got no answer."

He stared into my eyes, trying to decide if he believed me.

I reached into our fridge and opened a beer. "Look, it's the truth, so relax, okay? Wanna beer?"

His eyes softened. "Sure, thanks."

That night, Jack and I ate uptown and then walked over to a house party near Millett Hall. Three hours later, Jack stormed off. I wasn't even sure why. Jodi said she thought it was because I was talking to a guy from my Spanish class.

The next day, Jack pretended nothing had happened, and I did the same, chalking it up to too much alcohol, pushing my reservations about our relationship out of my head and readying myself for a week of exams that would require my full attention.

That weekend, Jack and I went to Cleveland for a birthday party Before heading back to Miami, I stopped by to see Gramma, who believed an ancestral Jewish branch of our family had migrated to Spain. While she was excited for me about my trip, the fact that I was in college and no longer a little girl seemed to astound her.

"Oh, my little dolly, you're so tall and beautiful! You're driving!"

Her unconditional love and admiration was just what I needed to hear, and I gave her a hug. I was gloriously happy about my upcoming adventure. So much so, that I was even able to set aside worries about my weight. If I gain weight, I gain weight, I told myself.

Six weeks later on the evening before I left for Spain, Jack came over for dinner. We drove to Lake Erie, and I watched the moon reflect on the cold, still water. We held each other, professing our love and telling each other the next six months would quickly pass.

❧

Madrid! When our plane finished taxiing across Barajas airport, I was one of fifty American students scurrying down the stairs of the plane and onto the tarmac of a country that had been ruled by Francisco Franco for nearly forty years. His death, only seven years earlier, had opened a door to a part of the Old World that was new and thrilling to me. I couldn't wait to see the great art and architecture of Spain, meet the people and hear what they had to say about the world.

It was January; the weather was mild and the sun shone through thin clouds. I was overwhelmed with gratitude. After three days in Madrid, including a trip to the Prado museum, our group headed to Atocha train station for our final destination in Andalucía—Sevilla.

I stayed with two forty-something sisters named Ana and Paqui who shared an apartment with their aunt, a retired nun named Antonia who seemed to be in her early eighties. She was a permanent fixture in her room. She never went outside as far as I knew, but remained perched in her chair, wearing a black skirt, stockings, black shoes, and a black shawl draped over her dark blouse. I loved Antonia's warm and welcoming ways. She wanted to know what was going on in the outside world. She talked about Maradona, the famous Argentinean soccer player who was now playing in Spain. She wondered what was going on in and around Sevilla, the only city she'd ever known.

"*¿Hace frío en la calle?*" she asked.

No, it wasn't cold outside—although sometimes the lack of central heating and the cold ceramic tiles made it easy to see why Antonia thought it might be. Ana and Paqui spoke to her in a dismissive tone. This was a simple and ordinary world with no expectations or claims on me, and therefore what bothered these women at close quarters had no effect on me. I felt only sheer liberation, as if a thousand tiny ropes had released me, and I could stop fretting. I could simply be.

"*No hace frío!* You always ask that!" Ana always answered.

I wasn't sure Antonia noticed their impatience; she seemed content with the life God had given her and told me her only regret was not meeting *El Papa*, The Pope.

Ana and Paqui didn't work, except to care for Antonia and take college students like me into their tiny apartment of no more than seven hundred square feet. I shared a room with another American student from Ohio; a third Spanish student rented the second bedroom. They converted the small TV/dining room into Antonia's bedroom every night, while Ana and Paqui slept in a roll-away bed in the living room.

Neither Ana nor Paqui left any doubt that they were Franco supporters. Franco had given them jobs. Franco held parties at the river. Franco kept the smut off of television and recognized the importance of Family and The Church. They made themselves understood with added hand gestures and asked a lot questions.

A few days after my arrival, Ana followed me into my room. I'd made a trip to *El Corte Inglés*, a department store that far exceeded anything we had in Cleveland in its size and in the quality and diversity of its merchandise. She grabbed the two shirts I had purchased and asked me if they were expensive. Then came questions about a boyfriend and the size of my parents' house. I pictured Ana and Paqui drinking coffee with neighbors, telling them about the new American, relishing any juicy tidbits that might make it all interesting and worthwhile.

At lunch, we always ate with the television on. TV newscasts weirdly juxtaposed images of the dead from wars in Africa and nearly bare women on game shows. Antonia averted her eyes from the death and decadence. I wondered if her eyesight allowed her to notice that Ana and Paqui served her and the students chicken necks, thighs, and wings, saving the breasts for themselves. I pushed the garbanzo beans around my plate and asked for more bread, but I wasn't tempted to binge and therefore didn't need to purge. We sat at a round table in the same room that was used as Antonia's bedroom. Beneath the table, a space heater's hot air stayed trapped under the long tablecloth, keeping our feet warm. For dessert, Ana served us each an apple perched on a white plate with a dinner knife. What was too uncool for my friends at home—sharing simple food with opinionated old women—became something different in Spain. I was having more than a vacation from my problems. I was having an adventure.

I was also about to have one of those spiritual moments that stay with you all your life.

I headed down five flights of stairs, onto the street and down to the corner in Sevilla's oldest neighborhood for a cup of strong *café con leche,* and then up to the *Plaza de Cuba* where the feeling of freedom reminded me of the days when I was a kid in Ohio. I snapped a photo of the Guadalquivir River. Its still waters and Old World serenity carried me into a timelessness where art came alive. Truman Seymour's watercolors captured scenes like this; perhaps Bartolome Murillo learned his vibrancy in this light. Diego Velásquez grew up along its waters, and Columbus returned here from the New World with treasures counted in the *Torre del Oro,* a twelve-sided stone tower I was approaching on the opposite side of the bridge. How my dad would love to be crossing this bridge with me and experiencing the places we'd read about!

On the other side of the river, I headed downtown toward the Cathedral, a huge Gothic structure built after the reconquest of the 1400s. Photos of it and its bell tower, the famous *La Giralda,* couldn't capture the beauty of intricate frescos, carvings, and arches that had weathered hundreds of years. The architects had boldly proclaimed that they wanted to build a cathedral so immense that its viewers would say they'd gone crazy when they first beheld it. I indeed had to stop, stare, and snap more pictures. On its opposite side lay the *Barrio de Santa Cruz,* home to the Jewish community before the Inquisition. I shuddered, despite the warmth of the day. Had my ancestors that Gramma mentioned walked these same streets in grim fear? I imagined the millions of people who had passed at this intersection of so many cultures and religions. A white plaque with black letters near the top of *La Giralda* drew my gaze. I squinted against the bright sun to read: *"The name of the Lord is a strong tower, and them that run to it are safe."*

I had to think for a moment, but then realized it was from Proverbs 18. The thought comforted me so much, I teared up. I felt alive. I felt connected to God and my fellow human beings throughout all time. Goosebumps lifted the hairs on my arms. This, *this* was what the hymn meant about being One in the Spirit. I basked in a sense of well-being. Quivery with gratitude, I went inside the cathedral to thank God for bringing me to Spain.

Enormous columns dwarfed me, and stained glass windows filtered the light through prismatic color. It was glorious, though the altars of gold and alabaster drew me out of that universal moment and back into the world. I couldn't help but wonder if the opulence brought people closer to God or entrenched the power of the Church? I remembered to look for the Gothic *retablo* of forty-five carved scenes from the life of Christ, part of the largest and richest altarpiece in the world and one of the finest examples of Gothic woodcarving anywhere.

Being surrounded by all of the glorious art treasures kept my spirit soaring and reminded me of the days when Dad and I sat at the kitchen table, with dreams of seeing the work of The Masters. I was flooded with a sense of gratitude and good feelings for the world and all it had to offer.

I wanted to savor the good weather, so along with hundreds of *turistas* and Sunday-dressed families with small children, I visited *El Parque de Maria Luisa*, shaded by tall knotted trees and the beautiful architecture of the *Plaza de España*. The *Guardia Civil* loomed, leftovers from the Franco regime. Their machine guns, slung across their bellies, looked a little silly with their shiny hats that reminded me of Mickey Mouse ears. They made me nervous, so I kept walking.

I trekked along by the main campus of the University of Sevilla, hundreds of years old; it had once been the tobacco factory that was the setting for Bizet's *Carmen*. A legless old man begged on the street corner outside a shop that sold orthopedic prostheses, not an uncommon sight with thousands still living who had been maimed during the civil war and its aftermath. A four- or five-year-old, brown-skinned Gypsy girl ran up to me with a carnation, promising me a blessing in return for a few pesetas. I dug into my pocket and pulled out *cinco duros* and told her to keep the flower. Old men played dominoes at a café, two little boys kicked a soccer ball on the sidewalk. A teenage couple held hands and laughed while middle-aged people whizzed by on mopeds. I marveled at it all, listening to the music of my Walkman playing in the background. Hoping to find flamenco music, I turned the dial and heard the name, Karen Carpenter, on a British news broadcast. I stopped, adjusted the headphones, and turned up the volume. Anorexia had killed Karen Carpenter? I couldn't believe it. My heart raced as I pictured Molly's horribly thin hands. She had been doing much better when I left, and I was here in Sevilla, living a healthier lifestyle. Thank God. I was taking it one day at a time, so far succeeding in keeping my promise to myself not to throw up in someone else's home. I knew instinctively that I'd come to Spain to feed my soul's hungers and that I was still hungry.

Twenty-three

Rose Stem Between Teeth at La Feria

KAREN CARPENTER'S DEATH STUCK IN my mind as I hurried to *Avenida Constitución* to meet several American students and friends at *El Coliseo,* a tourist spot near the cathedral.

"Did you hear Karen Carpenter just died?" I said to Teri, a girl my Spanish friends thought looked like Bette Midler. I told them the news, and they agreed it was sad, but it didn't stop their celebration. It set me apart a bit, and I became the observer of loud Americans.

We ordered drinks, and I followed Teri to a booth where we joined four others from our group. They were noisy and sometimes funny. I kept looking over my shoulder to see who was watching us and noticed that other patrons were staring because our group was so loud. Someone mentioned the waiter's gnarly teeth, and they all laughed. I cringed, hoping the man didn't speak English. Flirting with David from Seattle, Teri stood up just when her friend Nina pushed her arm. I watched in horror as Teri's nearly full glass of cold beer spewed onto a young woman seated behind us, who screamed as it hit her in the face and splashed onto her shirt. My drunk friends thought it was funny, but at least Teri apologized. This wasn't what I'd come for, but I didn't want to return to my old ladies either.

Many *cervezas* later, we walked across town to a hopping disco in *Los Remedios.* We stayed for a few hours and then went on to a second club, where we ordered still more drinks. A twenty-something Spaniard approached our group. His handsome features and dark hair attracted me, as did his attire: pressed jeans, a crisp white shirt, and a light blue sweater draped over his shoulders. He introduced himself to me as *Juan Antonio.*

¿Dónde vives en Sevilla?

"I live in La Triana," I told him in Spanish. I'd had enough to drink that I failed to remember that I had a boyfriend.

"Really? That's where I am from." He leaned in.

I didn't pull back. "Well, it's great. I love it."

Juan Antonio and I continued to talk at the bar, and then he grabbed my hand and led me to the dance floor. Fortunately, I had the sense not to go home with him that night. Nevertheless, I was wide awake when I returned to my tiny shared room, hugging myself in the darkness, intoxicated in more ways than one. I suppose I could get all technical and say that I was projecting all my romantic archetypes onto this sojourn, but it felt like the magic of Spain pulsed in my blood. The disco had played modern music, but the sound of flamenco guitars were never far away. They made my heart pound with the flash of a fantasy—me, *me,* raising my arms over my head, proffered rose between my teeth, castanets insistent, drawing a Juan Antonio closer to me. Even though I knew this image was pure *toro* shit, some deep part of me believed it was possible and tingled with anticipation.

Jack... Jack who wanted and loved me. Oh, he'd be furious.

The romance of Spain tugged harder. Handsome men wanted me. Men who might be more sensitive than Jack. Men who wanted an American fling and nothing more. That stopped me. But what about a woman who wanted a Spanish fling and nothing more? Yes. Oh, yes.

No. Oh, no. I lay there, too excited to sleep. I couldn't see Juan Antonio again. I'd thrown Jack away once and was lucky he still cared. Yet, hanging out with just the American group night after night would be a terrible waste of a potentially rich experience. I finally decided I'd go out with him again, but only for a dance or dinner. I would not sleep with any of these ardent Spaniards. And I'd never mention them to Jack.

My dates with Juan Antonio would mark the first of many interested Spaniards and dates over the next several months. Teri called me "The Prize" because of it. Emotionally, the experience made me feel the opposite of how I'd felt in the U.S. In Spain, I felt worthy, exciting, fun, and attractive. I recommend the feeling highly. If only I could make it last.

Feeling good the following Monday, I walked the halls of the university. A student I'd met the night before greeted me.

"You play basketball, no?" She guessed I played because I was a tall American. A stereotype, but not a bad one. "Do you want to play on our team?" she asked.

I couldn't say yes fast enough. The following week I was playing for *Club Náutico* on the Guadalquivir River. I don't remember any other Americans in the league that season. The sheer joy of swishing a shot from outside, driving into the lane, or blocking a shot gave me an adrenalin rush I got nowhere else—well, except at the dinner table or dancing.

During practice, I shot baskets with a teammate named Pilar. She was a center/forward like me, and I was often paired up against her during practice. We had been defending each other for weeks, and I'd been impressed with her playing skills. All of my teammates were good players, and this team was clearly better than my high school team. I laughed along with my teammates when our coach had to call a time-out to carefully and slowly explain some bit of strategy to me.

I fell into bed one night, exhausted from basketball practice and the constant concentration required to think and speak in Spanish. The next day, Ana and Paqui brought me two new letters from Jack and then asked me what he was like. I told them he was handsome and a good person. Although I missed him, I felt a twinge of guilt about dating. I still wasn't sleeping with anyone and reaffirmed my vow to keep it that way.

"Don't expect Spaniards to invite you to their homes," more than one of our professors warned. Under the rule of Franco, people hadn't been allowed to congregate. Though he'd been dead for nearly eight years, the pervasive fear and suspicion still gripped people. Many were very leery of strangers. Despite this, my teammate Pilar invited me to

her house not long after we met. I was thrilled since Pilar was definitely my favorite teammate. On one hand, she was so proper and
polite. She spoke Spanish with a true *castellano* accent, pronouncing
for example, the letter z with a "th" sound. Yet, out of nowhere, she
would say something dizzyingly funny that would throw me off guard
and onto the floor with laughter. She picked me up on her red moped,
and we zipped through traffic to her apartment home near the Maria
Luisa Park. When we reached her apartment, she laughed at the way
my hair was sticking up. And I laughed too when I looked in the mirror. After my unsuccessful attempt to fix my hair, she introduced me
to her parents and seven siblings. I thought they were as charming and
well mannered as any people I had ever met. It was clear, though, that
one of her sisters was sick. She was lying on the couch and looked like
someone who'd recently been released from a concentration camp.

"Can I get you something to drink? *Una cerveza?*" asked Pilar.

"Sure, *gracias.*" We had our own version of Spanglish. Most of
the time, I ended up speaking in English with her and she spoke in
Spanish to me, but sometimes we mixed it up.

We walked to the kitchen, and she pulled two bottles of *Cruzcampo*
and some cheese out of the fridge and arranged it on a tray, adding
olives and bread sticks named *picos*.

"*Mi hermana*, Alicia," she said, pouring beer into my glass. "She
has something called bulimia. *Sabes lo que es?*"

My stomach did a flip. I peeked around the corner for another
glimpse at Alicia. "Do I know what it is? Unfortunately, I do. I've
had it."

"*Verdad?* You have?" She put down her glass and awaited an explanation.

"Yeah, but I'm okay now," I said, eating a *pico* and some cheese,
hoping with all my heart I was telling the truth.

She'd knocked my theory out of the ballpark. I could no longer
claim that bulimia was an American phenomenon brought on solely
by the sickness of our culture's obsession with lithe beauty and fast
food. Alicia had never been to the United States.

When I'd first arrived in Spain, I congratulated myself one day at a time for breaking my addiction to high-calorie food and the need to purge. About three weeks after first meeting Pilar's sister, I happened to wake up at midnight, slightly hungry. I couldn't possibly wake the sisters and Antonia to raid their kitchen. I sipped water instead and realized I hadn't even thought about binging. Was I finally cured?

❧

As always, Antonia greeted me with, *"Hace frío en la calle?"* No, it wasn't cold outside.

What's the word for blanket? "Um... *Quieres una... manta*? Yes, that's it. *Manta?*"

Antonia shook her head. With my knowledge of Spanish in its infancy, I couldn't understand all that she said, but she immediately began telling me stories of wonder and faith. She wanted someone to listen to the ways God had been good to her. Did I know He was watching out for all of us? Yes, I told her, I did. I wished I could have asked her if her faith had ever faltered, like mine, but it seemed too much like prying.

Antonia told me how proud her parents had been when she first told them she planned to become a nun. I stared at the deeply embedded lines on her face, unable to imagine her without them. She was short, no more than five feet tall. Antonia had been in the prime of her life during the Spanish Civil War, but she never mentioned it. Her voice, raspy and weak, sounded as if her heart didn't quite have the pumping power to oxygenate her breath. I pulled my chair in close and listened while she told me how she cried when she left her mother and sisters for the convent. Brushing away a tear, she asked me about my family. I told her that I loved them and missed them, but I would see them soon. For the moment, I was grateful to be in Spain.

"Eres guapa" she said, telling me I was good-looking. "In the days of my youth..." She stopped and took in a breath, put her palm to her forehead, and ran her fingers over the beads of her rosary. What

was she whispering? A prayer or something else? Was that fear on her face? She looked into my eyes. "Where is she? Where's Ana?"

Was she sick? Her heart, maybe. *"Estás bien? El corazón?"*

She didn't answer, so I quickly stood up and nearly ran the short distance to the kitchen for Ana. *Antonia asks for you.* She must have heard the worry in my voice. Ana exhaled loudly and untied her blue and white apron and threw it down on the kitchen counter. I followed her to Antonia's room, the same one that doubled as the dining and TV room. Antonia sat whispering with her rosary.

"¿Que quieres, Tía?" Ana demanded to know what she wanted.

The fear was gone from Antonia's face, but Ana's tone startled her, like she'd just woken up. *"¿Hace frío en la calle?"*

"You asked me to come in here to tell you whether it's cold outside?! *Por Dios, Tía!*"

Antonia looked at me, confused, while Ana continued to berate her.

"No hace frío! Don't bother me with that anymore! Just hold on a minute and I will bring you something to drink." Ana stormed out, shooting me a *CanYouBelieveThisCrap?* look.

I sat down next to her. "Antonia, can I get you anything?"

She looked at me with glimmering eyes, hopeful and child-like. *"¿Hace frío en la calle?"*

Antonia was mostly lucid and even asked me about Sevilla's major event, similar to the Oktoberfest, except in spring: the *Feria de Abril*—a dizzying, week-long festival marking the beginning of bullfight season, with horse shows featuring the proud Andalusians along with their riders in full regalia, and round-the-clock music, food, flamenco dancing, and partying. I told her an American friend named Paul invited some of us to join his Spanish friends at their *caseta*. This was especially exciting to me because most visitors to Seville were limited to the public tents and didn't have access to the thousands of private, green and white striped *casetas* set up on the fairground—each its own party room with bands, food, and a sense of privilege.

Antonia told me to be good. She was no doubt surprised I wasn't already raped and disgraced for running around without a chaperon.

Different every year, the fair's main gateway formed an ornate tower of some 22,000 lights. Public *casetas* sold food and offered exhibits and music, but the private ones enchanted me with their elaborate home-like decor. Framed art graced the fabric walls—so typical of the way Sevillanos included art in everything they did. No celebration was complete without art.

The aroma of food tantalized me. When we found the right *caseta*, I ogled the buffet of paella, *jamón* (the famous Spanish equivalent of prosciutto), *gambas* (shrimp you peeled), Spanish tortillas like omelets with potatoes, hard chorizos, olives, *picos*, cheeses, and an *ensaladilla Rusa* (Russian potato salad).

Though my friend Paul was of Korean ancestry, the Spanish students called him "Pablo." He introduced me to a handsome Spaniard named Manolo and his sister, Rosario.

"Friends call me Magüi." (It sounded like Mow–wee). Magüi was no more than five feet, four inches, but extremely handsome with an air of confidence and fun. I liked the way he patted Paul on the back, laughed easily, and struck a flamenco dance pose when the band played a note for the next song. His sister, Rosario, was beautiful with black hair, olive skin, and deep brown eyes. Their friend Maria Luisa introduced herself, seeming particular happy to meet me, and began to rattle off all of her favorite American singers. She too was striking, with light brown hair and green eyes.

Magüi took Rosario's hand and led her to the dance floor. Paul did the same with Maria Luisa. After that night, I never called my friend *Paul* anymore. He had become *Pablo*. Everyone marveled that a Korean-American could dance so well to the *Sevillanas*. The dancers held a proud stance, chests forward, chins up, arms gracefully reaching for forbidden fruit. They stomped on the wooden floor, clapping to the beat, castanets clicking. All the dancers conveyed desire, a nearly orgasmic look on their faces, clearly confident and comfortable in their own sexuality. Their movements mesmerized and moved me. I was proud and jealous at the same time, wishing I could live with such a connection to history, tradition, and art. Even middle-aged and older people danced with a sense of pride and passion that I had never before witnessed.

As the night went on, they coaxed me to try dancing a *Sevillana*. The experience didn't enact my rose-between-teeth fantasy, and there was no Juan Antonio to inspire me. I was terrible at it, but they appreciated the attempt. We hung out all night, traveling from *caseta* to *caseta,* drinking beer or *Tío Pepe*—Jerez sherry—dancing, eating, and laughing. It just felt right.

At 2:00 A.M., two half-American sisters, Chickie and Dolores, joined us, and we all walked over to *Dianca,* one of the many discos in Los Remedios.

Magüi ran ahead and leapt into the air to tag an awning high above his head. Rosario nearly fell to the pavement in laughter when I passed it and nonchalantly touched it without leaving the flats of my feet. Point taken, Magüi roared when Rosario recounted how funny it had looked. Weeks later, Chickie said, "Too bad there isn't a pill that will make him taller or you shorter." I agreed, but pushed that thought out of my mind, remembering Jack was home waiting for me.

That same night, while the rest of our group danced to "Billie Jean," Magüi and I went to the bar and ordered drinks. He asked me where I was from and what it was like. I told him and tried to explain. Then he asked about my family and I asked about his. We had our own little *intercambio*. Magüi stirred the ice in his drink and then stopped.

"Do you believe in God?" he asked, turning thoughtful.

I realized at that moment that being in Spain, spending time with people who seemed like God's provision for me and seeing people like Antonia with such devout faith, had smoothed a jagged edge somewhere inside me. The pure flow of connection and warmth I felt there, the sense of fulfillment that ended my food addiction empowered me. It was almost as if my strength had returned without my noticing when I read the inscription on the tower, *La Giralda,* that first day. Everything since had strengthened an intimate connection to the Creator. I felt safe and close to the God that had helped my dad return to normal life. It's difficult to explain faith, but I tried.

Magüi listened, but his experiences had been quite different. "Mostly I just remember the nuns making us feel guilty and that some of the priests were pedophiles," he said bitterly.

"Really?"

"Yes, and I remember when I was about six, the nun at my school told me that if I didn't work hard and color my picture with great care, God was going to send me to hell."

We discussed the irony of it all—the way the biggest obstacles to faith could often be the individuals and institutions who proclaimed their dedication to God but didn't show His love. The Jesus I knew, I told him, must weep over the way we humans botch things up in His name.

❦

During my time in Spain, I felt almost as confident as I had in my *Super Susan* days, regaining my footing, my joy. Spring had summoned orange and pomegranate blossoms, and swathes of red and purple bougainvillea. Maria Luisa, the fun-loving and friendly girl I met at the *feria,* invited me to her house on *Calle Monte Olivete* in the barrio of San Pablo, where biblical names graced the neighborhood streets: *Sinai, Gólgota, Monte Olivete.* Rosario's house was named *La Trinidad* and was also situated on *Monte Olivete.* I liked to think this was God winking at me and letting me know these people were His provision for me. Maria Luisa's mother, Loli, welcomed me and offered Spanish tortillas and a glass of cold Cruzcampo beer. I laughed aloud at her father's jokes in Andalusian Spanish I could barely understand. Maria Luisa spent hours trying to teach me the steps of the *Sevillana* flamenco dance, but I couldn't remember the *pasos.* When it was time to go, her little brother, Jesús, sat in a chair and cried.

"*Susan, no te vayas, por favor, no te vayas.*" Susan, don't go, please don't go.

I hugged the seven-year-old and assured him we'd see each other soon. Monte Olivete became my second home—the place where I learned to speak Spanish while enjoying long conversations over Cruzcampo beer or *tinto de verano*, wine coolers.

Dolores and Chickie treated me like family and invited me over for dinner often. Their mother, Carmen, charmed me with her paella and her stories of survival in Civil War Spain. Their father, Lukey, reminded me of my dad. When I wasn't there or at Maria Luisa's, I visited with Rosario and her mother, Trini, who told me her faith was what sustained her through the challenges of life. She too had lived through the civil war, so I knew they'd been significant. I told them about my personal relationship with Jesus, and she looked at me as if I didn't realize Jesus was not a twentieth-century American. *Did she and the others want to tell me that their country knew of Jesus before mine was ever mapped?* Probably, but they were too polite, and like my "unsaved" friends in Cleveland, they were saving me more than I would have ever guessed.

Although I hadn't learned anything more about my family's possible Jewish heritage, it was as if I had traveled 5,000 miles to find a branch of my family I hadn't known before. It was a chord so in tune, it surprised me as well as my Spanish friends. We became so close, so quickly. I had never felt better about myself. Now I really was born again, but not in the way Evangelicals described it. I dreaded leaving all this behind.

When the time came for me to leave Spain, Rosario and Magüi scheduled a taxi to pick them up first and then headed to my apartment in La Triana. I cried the whole way to the train station, holding Rosario's hand as Magüi stroked my hair and hugged me, telling me how much they would miss me. When we arrived, twenty others had come to send me off. I was stunned. They broke into song, clapping their hands and singing as the train pulled away from the station.

Algo se muere en el alma cuando un amigo se va. Something in the soul dies when a friend leaves.

Twenty-four

Mom's Sister

 PUSHED MY FOOD AROUND the plate. No *tapas* here. Mom was hopping around, trying to make things perfect, happy to serve me. I appreciated her efforts and knew that she loved having me home, but I missed Spain and worried about gaining weight again with American food and falling back into bulimia.

With both my family and friends I couldn't stop talking about Spain—their way of life, my friends, the food. How I loved to walk around the whole vibrant city. Loved the way the whole country was so enmeshed with art and history. At first, my Cleveland friends were interested, but interest quickly turned into irritation. MJ, with whom I'd grown especially close, had heard enough.

"Do they *fuck* better in Spain too?"

I laughed, getting her point. The first few days back in Cleveland, I'd held my own and didn't overeat, but I was away from the healthy Mediterranean diet and all of that walking. Exercise seemed like a chore. Where could I walk to? I'd have played basketball if there'd been a team. Sometimes Jack and I played one-on-one.

On the way home from a business law class I took at Cleveland State, I approached a McDonald's restaurant one day. I told myself I didn't need it, and then quickly changed my mind. *Just a small burger.* I walked up to the front counter. I couldn't really have a burger without fries, and if I was going to have fries, I might as well have a vanilla shake. They were running a special—only 99 cents. I'd eat healthy tomorrow. I sat down in a corner booth and dug in, the first bite so satisfying, there must have been a flood of feel-good chemicals hitting my brain. I quickly ordered another hamburger *and* a cheeseburger.

After sucking down the last of my shake, I went into the bathroom and looked in the mirror. Did my face look fatter than yesterday? *Tomorrow I have to start jogging!* Jack and I had shot hoops at the park, but it didn't feel like enough to counter all the food I'd eaten.

I fought the urge to throw up with an internal pep talk, washed my hands, and headed home, unable to simply pass by a Dunkin' Donuts. I'd just have a coffee and chat with the owners who were from Argentina. A cup of coffee turned into two, and before I knew it, I'd eaten two glazed donuts. I was a bloated mess. *No way I can ride a bike now. I just need to get all of this food out of me before I gain even more weight.*

No! The other side of my brain argued. *You can't do that. It will be like a second death after a resurrection in Spain!* Somehow, that side won out—but I needed help.

Within two weeks, I was purging and binging as regularly as ever. Jack was so happy to have me home, I felt bad bringing up the sick topic of my bulimia. He was conventional and predictable. The real me had returned in Spain. I wasn't sure I could bear going back to the old, insecure/scared/bulimic one. I wanted to explain it all to him, but it seemed nearly impossible to know how to start, especially after the fiasco of my last attempt. So I just kept going and buried the idea of asking for help again. Food was the only thing that made me feel better. I knew that was the trap, but I refused to think about the consequences of binging until they appeared as ten pounds of fat, all gained in the thirty days since I had been back.

One afternoon, I planned for a bike ride and noticed my white sleeveless shirt and baby blue knit basketball shorts were feeling tighter than I had remembered them just a few days before. I glared at myself in the bathroom mirror in total disgust. *You are a cow!* I looked at the fat hanging onto my backside, thighs jiggling. After leaving the bathroom, I passed Mom, who shot me a look in between the spray of furniture polish and a swipe of her dust rag.

"Oh my, you really have put on some weight. Please don't tell me you're going to wear those anywhere."

"Leave me alone," I replied, unable to explain I was in a fight for my life.

"Jean, get off of her back," Dad very uncharacteristically told her as I ran out the door and hopped on my bike. I pumped the pedals as fast as I could...*fat...ass...fat...ass...fat ass....*

Was I hearing a voice? Was it my own or someone else's? I wasn't sure and *that* scared me. "*You* are such a *loser,*" it said. "How could you have let this happen again? Look at the fat on your thighs! You can't wear that outfit! What are you thinking?"

An hour later, I sat in my room and stared out the window like Mary Beth and I used to, only I wasn't singing pop tunes. I watched a spider spin a web in the track of my sliding window. *I'm with Jack,* I thought. *I should just be grateful. He's sometimes controlling, but that's because he loves me. He's a good guy, and maybe it's just as good as it gets. The guy's cute too, and I love him. I just need to buckle down, find a job, and start saving money.*

⌘

The economy wasn't good when I graduated from college in 1984. Job opportunities were not as I had imagined them. Tool and die manufacturers that dotted the Cleveland landscape needed salespeople. There were opportunities to sell insurance or fax machines. None of it sounded appealing, not even the position I eventually accepted as a sales representative for a distributor of memory typewriters in the days just before the advent of the personal computer.

One of my first official meetings with my new boss resulted in a conversation about my sales activities.

"I have some good prospects, but I need to speak to you about some other issues."

"Issues? There should be no other issues. No other priorities."

I felt my stomach churn and scribbled on my note pad. He stood up and headed for the door and then turned toward me.

"Fuck the customer. Go out and sell something, you're behind this month."

The impact of his words was like a hard tackle during one of our neighborhood football games. It knocked the wind out of me. I wanted to tell him to fuck off, but I owed my parents rent, had charged clothes, and had to pay a car payment and insurance.

"I want one hundred cold calls per week. No exceptions."

A month later, I drove to Broadview Heights to deliver a memory typewriter to a Ukrainian credit union. (*Sooo Cleveland.*) After the long back-order, I was only too happy to deliver it. I parked my car and got out, then bent down to reach into the backseat for the cumbersome box. I knew that carrying it in high-heels would be a chore, but was able to make it across the black asphalt to the heavy front door. I pulled on its long handle while juggling the cumbersome box. Just as I went to step onto the marble floor, I lost my grip on the box, and the $2,000 typewriter crashed to the floor. Customers stared, a baby cried. I wished I could die.

⚘

I needed a distraction from the job I hated and was happy to find it in the form of my dear friend Pilar, from Spain, who'd arrived for a month-long visit. Mom invited Aunt Joy over for dinner, knowing she would enjoy hearing about life and art in Sevilla.

Joy had been through some tough times, but she looked good and seemed upbeat. We talked for hours over Mom's lasagna and a few bottles of Chianti. At the end of the evening, Aunt Joy squeezed me as though she were going away for a long, long time. It surprised me and seemed a little odd. I could feel her loneliness, and although I could have used some propping up by my family, I felt compelled to help her if only I knew how. I didn't know what to say … or what to offer.

Pilar's return to Sevilla, the impossibility of going with her, the drudgery of my job, the pain of looking for a one, all combined to depress me for weeks. I grew increasingly worried that I would never find a job I liked. I had no idea where I fit in. My chest tightened with a familiar response to panic. Inside my head, a voice whispered, *You'll end up like your father, always hating your job and feeling like a nervous wreck all the time.*

Absorbed in my own problems, I didn't see the next train wreck coming. It was a cold Sunday night in March of 1985, and I escaped to the basement rec room to watch a spring training program about the 1985 Indians on TV. As I chomped the first satisfying bite of my sandwich, the phone rang. Annoyed at the interruption, I picked up the receiver, still glued to the tube. *Loved* the crack of the bat hitting the ball as Joe Tait commented on the beauty of the Florida day.

Someone was screaming, "Joy is dead, Joy is dead! She shot herself."

"What?"

"She's gone, she's gone. . . ." Gramma wailed.

My legs were frozen in the chair; I couldn't speak. The ball popped into Chris Bando's mitt while the garbled sounds of Joe Tait mixed with what I was hearing through the phone.

Images of Aunt Joy's face flashed in my head—the way she looked the last time I saw her, those shoes she wore that enhanced her long legs, the warmth in her eyes when she squeezed me good-bye.

Finally, I yelled upstairs.

"Dad, pick up the phone! It's bad!" It was the best I could do.

Dad broke the news to Mom upstairs while I sat frozen in the basement. After a few minutes, I ordered my legs to carry me upstairs; Mom's face was streaked with mascara. She heaved a long sigh.

I robotically told them I would follow them in my own car. We stood there blinking, running our hands through our hair, and then shuffled to the closet for our coats. In my car, my hands clutched the steering wheel like a vice while my mind worked the disaster over and over in my head. *How could she be gone?* Anger at Joy chased my grief. *Don't you know what your suicide is doing to us? What could be more selfish?*

We drove down I-71, the brown and gray landscape becoming the scene of yet another suicide movie that took residence in my head. I waited in my car until my parents went up the walkway toward the house in a freeze-frame mirage. When they reached the front door, I unbuckled my seat belt, took a deep breath, exhaled, and headed toward the house.

My cousin, Sam, was seated on the dryer in the laundry room, his head down and his girlfriend holding his hand. Dad asked him where to find Aunt Joy's body and then took a deep breath and walked up the stairs.

On his way back downstairs, he gripped the railing, his face pale and stretched in a grimace. I dared not speak as he walked to the phone and made the call to the police.

When he'd finished, his face was white, hands shaking so hard I thought I heard bones rattling. He hung up the phone and shook his head.

Mom was as white as the painted wall behind her. Limp. I had to close my eyes because I knew if I looked at her for one second more, I would collapse. She, more than I, had been forced to fight flood tides of mental illness. It made me feel faint to think about it.

"Did you see a note?" she asked in a near breathless voice.

"No, there was nothing."

Later we discovered Joy had cleaned out her desk at work, and just the night before had dinner with her ex-husband. He said that she seemed happier than ever. I know now that that's what happens sometimes. Life has become so miserable for the person considering suicide, that when the decision to end it all is finally made, they feel a sense of peace and happiness.

I wondered what had tormented her. I knew that Joy's divorce had been painful and that she seemed bored with a world that wasn't as beautifully colored as her paintings. Maybe mundane truths had zapped her spirit beyond repair, and her chemically imbalanced brain couldn't convince her body and soul to stay on the planet.

I could only imagine how Gramma and Poppy felt. And then there was Sam. Old fears, long abandoned, crawled from the crevices of my mind. Joy's death brought back feelings I had tried to stuff, hide, shellac, or outrun. I can't say that I remember much of anything about Joy's funeral. Did Jack go with me? I'm sure that he did, but I don't recall a thing. It was a solitary experience, blank and disconnected.

Gramma and Poppy grieved openly about Joy's death at first, but not long afterwards, they barely mentioned it. Mom did the same. At first, Sam cried, but it was so much easier to talk about other things, like the new girl he was dating. It was like having a Plexiglas wall between our true feelings and the pragmatic world. Sometimes, I wanted to crash it, those walls of denial. At other times, I stayed away from them, exhausted from so many run-ins with realities I never wanted to think about. Maybe this was how my parents felt: exhausted by calamities over which they had no control, perhaps they decided to focus on prayers, hymns, and church fellowship.

Joy began to show up in my dreams. We're always on our way to another city or the park or some campground somewhere. In the dream, I'm planning to try to talk her out of killing herself, but when I search for her, Gramma tells me she's gone. I tell Gramma that it just can't be, that all she needs is medication. Gramma just shakes her head, and I realize it's too late.

I loved Sam almost as much as I loved Aunt Joy, but he didn't seem to want to talk about his mother, and I didn't press him. Instead, we talked around her, as if she had never existed. Then we talked about the car he bought, pretending that neither of us remembered that it was purchased with the insurance money from Joy's death. Sam said he planned to join the Air Force, and I didn't ask any more questions. Without realizing it, I had become like others in our family. I was afraid to deal with the difficulties facing my family members, worried *I* might not be able to handle it all.

My job continued to stress me out. I worried constantly that I wouldn't sell enough and would ultimately fail. I snapped at my sister one morning as I waited for the bathroom. "Look, I'm sorry, I don't want to be late for an appointment, and I'm just really stressed about work."

"God, relax. or you'll end up like Dad."

She was right. I was becoming like him, pacing and retreating. I didn't know what to do about it, or whom to talk to. I was more than stressed. I felt desperate and sometimes frantic. I wished I could talk to my fiancé, but what if I got a clichéd reaction like his beans-to-spill speech? Plus, Jack had other things on his mind.

"Us," he said gravely. We were sitting in his car in my parents' driveway after going to a baseball game. "I was, you know, kinda wondering your thoughts."

"Well, I mean, of course, I've thought of us," I said. "You know I love you . It's just that sometimes I worry that you're not a Christian."

He stared and blinked as if I'd just called him a blue Martian. "And *you* are?"

My turn to be stunned. He was right. There was nothing so damn different or better about my behavior that gave me the right to question his faith. I had to admit to myself that my response was classic, knee-jerk "Christian." My bulimic self wanted to admire my lovely Christian cake, calling myself *saved,* assuming I had the right to preach, and feeling the "purity" of purging. Yet, I was devouring those frosted layers too. I was pigging out, partying, having a sex life, and ignoring consequences I was supposed to be facing. I assumed Jack was *lost* and then had the nerve to say he wasn't worthy because of it. Deep down I knew I wasn't any better a Christian than he was. It would be foolish to let him get away.

"Marry me, Susan," he said.

I said yes.

Part Four

Forty-one

Twenty-five

The Big Escape

HAVE FINALLY FIGURED OUT I can't fix everything. In fact, I can't seem to fix anything at all. Maybe what brought on my dad's suicidal despair was the wall of utter powerlessness he ran into when he most needed to fix things. Maybe Aunt Mary Ellen and Aunt Joy got to the point where everything seemed futile. Dad was forty-one when he tried to kill himself. Aunt Mary Ellen was forty-one when she jumped off the overpass. Aunt Joy was forty-one when she shot herself in the head.

Sunlight streamed through one of the many windows in my bedroom. I lie in bed in my home in Houston, Texas, and *I'm* forty-one. I have two great kids, a perfect house, great friends, and so many blessings. Yet, I feel like air in a balloon, pushing at the walls of this *be-who-others-wanted-me-to-be self* until the inevitable bang. I've been holding back the truth and telling lies to cover it up, but it's not working. I hate myself and can't think of any way to be except miserable. Death seems preferable to the pain I can't stop. Am I cursed with some sort of family *sickness*? I feel like I've been fighting it all my life, running and looking back over my shoulder, only to crash into the wall of its inevitability.

My marriage is over.

This I say out loud even though I'm alone. The kids are asleep in their rooms. I'm weeping as I stare at my bedroom ceiling, gripping my hair. The sniffling gets to me. *Where's a goddamn tissue?* The box is empty, so I get up and walk to the bathroom, stepping over clothes I wore the day before. No tissues there either, so I settle for a roll of toilet paper. I return to my bedroom with its vaulted ceiling and earth-tone walls, pondering the fact that the only man who ever loved me is gone. I told him to go. Jack and I are in that awful place of maneuvering through a divorce—one he doesn't want and one I need. For years I begged him to be authentic, although *I* sure as hell was not. I so badly wanted to connect with him. We were two wildly different people, like ice cream and spaghetti—that's what I told the kids—good on their own, but not anything you'd want to see in the same bowl.

I should stay up, but I've gotten so little sleep, and it's chilly. I crawl back between the thin, faded sheets that need changing. I haven't done laundry in such a long time. These sheets arrived as a wedding present sixteen years earlier; they have withstood our passion, stretched between our silences, and endured, growing ever more frayed at the edges, like me. I didn't know what marriage meant when I said, "I do." Does anyone? I paid far more attention to wedding plans than the actual act of sharing my life and soul with someone.

I almost doze, and the ghastly man in the fedora hat appears—my recurring dream. I jolt awake rather than face him again. A fly is pestering, having somehow found its way into my bedroom at dawn. I sigh and sit up, swatting. Winter doesn't stop the bugs in Houston. Cursing, I drag myself up off the mattress, turn to tug at the blankets in a half-assed attempt to make the bed, bump my shin on the side of the bed, and curse again. I hate this early-American bedroom set, a relic of my past. One way or another, I won't be seeing it much longer. It hits me. Today is the day I said I'd meet Jack.

He wants me to bring my tax deduction information since we're filing jointly one last time. Putting affairs in order is the least I can do before walking out of everyone's life forever. He'll want to discuss the divorce, though, and the kids. He needs to go over and over all of the reasons why this marriage doesn't work. He wants to rub it in that breaking-up is hell, as if I'd missed that fact and was breezing through. I face moments of regret and seasons of guilt, moments when I look at his handsome face across the dark-stained table at Starbucks, when we meet to discuss the state of our relationship, wishing we could understand each other and *connect*. I hate the thought of a family break-up, but continuing what we now call our marriage feels even worse. My poor kids…

My heart starts racing, my nerves ragged. Yesterday I screamed at them after their horseplay spilled into the living room and knocked over a small vase my friend Charlotte had given me. I watched in horror as it hit the ceramic tile floor and shattered. It seemed an omen, an obvious metaphor for the relationship. Their game suddenly ended, a silence before the storm of my reaction.

"What the *hell* are you thinking? You broke it. You broke it! How could you have done that?"

"Mom, I'm sorry," Eric said. "It was a mistake. I'll get you another one."

Allison cowered in the corner at my rage.

"There *is* no other one! Oh my God, just get out of here, please! Go to your rooms! You kids are driving me nuts!"

Guilt is a steam iron that flattens me now as I walk to Eric's room at the far end of the hall. I find him sleeping peacefully. Looks so much like his father, his eyelids only half-closed over blue eyes, mouth open. I brush the hair off of his forehead and kiss him; it's one I have to steal now that he's thirteen.

"I'm so sorry, honey," I whisper, knowing it's not enough. Not for yesterday and not for all of it. I move slowly, brushing fresh tears from my face, overwhelmed with my love for this beautiful boy, wishing I could make everything right. I toss a prayer up to heaven, not knowing if God even listens to me anymore.

"Please help me." It's all I can think of.

Lady, our Wheaten Terrier, wakes and sees me, thumps her tiny tail against Eric, still deep in slumber. She jumps down from the bed and follows me as I pad down the hall to Allison's room, all pink and green with Barbies and Beanie Babies that I couldn't stop buying. A few months earlier, my eight-year-old daughter astonished me. I told her that her father and I were separating. She leaned back on my bed, folded her hands behind her head, and said, "I saw *that one* coming a long time ago." Funny if not so tragic. I kneel beside her bed now and trace the outline of her profile with my finger, her features and coloring even more like her father's than Eric's are. "Forgive me, sweetie. I love you."

I'm amazed at how much you can love two someones. One day they'll realize they are better off without me. I head downstairs, let the dog out, and traipse over to my study. Jack wants a nice neat accounting of what I've spent on deductions and charity. Somehow I have to figure out how to make up a spreadsheet of sensible numbers from a box of tattered receipts and my incomplete records and memory. Dammit!

I log on to my laptop and, instead of bringing up TurboTax, I open Outlook like some sort of addict. E-mail. Lately, I've been using it as a flame-thrower when fighting with both Jack and Charlotte. The embarrassing evidence floating in cyberspace somehow doesn't prevent me from using it again and again. It's a talent and defect Jack shares. Before I open his latest, I take a few deep breaths.

Have you done the tax list I asked for? So what goes on in that house now that you're running things? What lies are you telling my kids? You know, you really should check yourself into a facility. I've lost all control over my kids. Has your lesbo lawyer come up with any new requests?

Jack still doesn't call me a "lesbo." No doubt it's crossed his mind. Does he know about my best friend, Charlotte? Surely he can tell that I love her. The way I look at her is the way he wishes I would look at him. He doesn't realize that she doesn't want anything to do with me anymore. Tired of my emotions, my desire for something more, she finished with me before we started. Ironically, Jack doesn't realize I understand *exactly* how it feels to love someone who won't love you.

Charlotte doesn't play the e-mail game the way Jack and I do. She just uses it as another way to ignore me. Somehow though, I still check my inbox carefully for a message from her. There they go again. My eyes. Drippy things. I dab them with the toilet paper wadded in my hand. I want... *need*... her to tell me what happened to us.

I click through ads and unwanted jokes. Nothing from her. I grab the phone. Don't give a shit that it's 7:00 A.M. on a Saturday. I'm going to give her a piece of my mind.

"Hey, um, look... I need to talk to you because, well I mean, damn it, you said you'd talk to me last night and the night before and the night before that. We still haven't talked. I thought you loved me. I'm goin' crazy. Call me, *please.*"

Part pathetic, part angry, and 100 percent ineffectual. I head toward the bathroom next to the laundry room. The mirror gives me the bad news: I look like shit. My hair is sticking up in four separate directions, the Houston humidity wreaking its usual havoc. It could also have something to do with the fact I haven't washed, dried, or straightened my hair in three days. A shower? Harder still. I stumble to the kitchen for my Zoloft, thinking I should ask for a larger dose the next time I see my therapist, Dr. Looney. Yeah, Looney. Perfect. And there probably won't be a next time.

In the same way that some people see their life flash before them before they die, images from my past are now showing in my mind's cinema. I'm so desperate and unfocused, I grab at them as if they were capable of keeping me from going under like the flotsam of a shipwreck. Maybe I still want to hold onto something.

Rosario. I picture her smiling at me. How I wish I could sit at a sidewalk café and talk to her about this bend in my life's path, or let her sister-in-law, Carmen, who's become like a sister to me, soothe my nerves with her "this is how it is" wisdom. It scares me to think about telling the others, my Spanish "family." Will they disown me like my American one surely will? I reach for a photo album and flip through its pages, tapping my fingers over years of memories. Here's one of the kids with Carmen and her family. Another with the whole group of fifteen Spaniards who met us at the airport two summers ago. Adolfo, Carmen, Fito, Magui, Rosario, Maria Luisa,

Pilar, Damaso, Clara, Pepe, Dolores, Chickie, and the rest. In this moment, their love keeps me afloat, reminding me of my gratitude and appreciation for what they have done for my kids and me.

"What did you learn while we were in Spain?" I asked Eric.

"I learned a few more Spanish words. That they have a lot more free time than we do…and, well, that Carmen is like my second mom."

I smiled. "Anything else?"

"Yeah." He added an exclamation point with his finger like he'd made an unexpected discovery. "I wish I'd been born there."

Allison, then just seven, smiled to herself.

"What're ya smilin' about, sweets?" I asked.

"Oh, I was just thinkin' that before we went to Spain, I used to think that *this* was all there was." She motioned her arms in a circle around the room. "And now, now I know there's so much *more!*"

Here's a picture of Jack, laughing with my friends in Sevilla, laughing in a way I haven't seen in years. We'd arrived in Sevilla that January, and on the flight over, he'd asked me to teach him how to say *Happy New Year* in Spanish.

"*Feliz Año Nuevo.*"

"Fay-lease An-Yo Nu wave-o," he repeated.

"Perfect."

By the time we arrived in Sevilla, we were tired but ready for the partying that wouldn't end until we'd spent hours talking, drinking, and laughing with everyone.

We sat in Trini's living room with two of her other daughters. Rosario was there, and her boyfriend, Antonio, and her brother, Magui. We were soon joined by Pilar, her siblings Adrian and Clara, as well as Maria Luisa, Dolores, and Chickie. Basically, a cast of thousands.

Jack was feeling good and interacting well with everyone, alcohol burning down the language barrier. He raised his glass and said, "*Feliz Ano Nuevo!*" (Fay-lease Ano Nu-wave-o)

I gasped. The rest were silent, which is no small feat for them. Then, like air being let slowly out of a balloon, repressed laughter began escaping, and we rolled on the floor.

Jack asked, "What'd I say? What'd I say?"

Chickie, the sweet one, looked at me with big eyes. "Should you tell him, or should I?"

"Tell me what?"

"You said, 'Happy New Anus.'"

Jack couldn't believe it. And really, he was right. Why in the world would any language have such a small difference—a little squiggly tilde over a consonant for such a big difference in meaning?

The thought of that joyful trip now brings feelings of regret. Guilt. He tried to make our marriage work in the ways that he knew how. Tried to adapt and accommodate. And yet, in other ways, he failed. It hits me that we are alike that way. Both wanting to fix things in some way, but never finding the key. I have failed him as much or more than he has failed me. The here and now sets in, and before my eyes, Jack's smile becomes a squinty frown. I haven't even started my taxes. My hands ache as my fibromyalgia flares. I have to face him, get this over with. He's going to quiz me on why I won't go to yet another therapy session that will make absolutely no difference. The man doesn't want our marriage to end, but he also doesn't want to do anything different. So, it's me who's breaking up our family. Why shouldn't he get custody, he will ask insistently.

I can't live without them, I want to scream, but it's more than that. They belong with me; they need me. *You don't even know them.* At this point, none of his bullshit can hurt me anymore, not even the part where he wanted to control everything even though he didn't listen, didn't care, and didn't want to spend any money on any of us. I always paid for upgrades to the house, the kids' private education, and trips back to Cleveland for the holidays.

"Let's not get each other Christmas gifts," he said every year, despite the fact that I always got him one. None of that matters now.

If I am to meet my maker soon, I must be honest. I exhale my anger and *admit that some of this is my fault too.* Maybe his need for more control grew steadily because he couldn't control my feelings for him, could sense me focusing on someone else. *But what did he expect?* The other side of my brain pipes in to my defense. His cheap ass showed up to our marriage like a man going to work, doing very little, and expecting a raise. Yet I know my choices don't look good. Society says I am the one to blame. The judges in our conservative county would dwell on my relationship with the "other woman." I can't face Jack standing up in court and spinning it so that I am the wanton woman, the lesbian whore who doesn't care about her family, especially when all I've really done is *love* someone. How could hunger for a deeper and more loving human connection lead to such disaster?

The whole mess has wreaked havoc on my health. I'm depressed, in pain, and exhausted. I walk through the family room and into the kitchen. Damn it! My Zoloft is not here. *Best not to start the day without that.* I head back upstairs and pass family photos and children's artwork, including the colorful rocket Eric drew as a kindergartner and the Cubist clown Allison painted when she was four. I smile for a brief second, remembering how she made sure I understood what she was going for. "See, Mommy, it's a clown. You can see he doesn't really have two faces, that's just the way I drew him." I choke in a cry at the thought of leaving her. A few more steps and I stop to pick up the *Junie B. Jones* book she left on the hall desk, remembering the many times we've read the series together, Allison rolling on the floor in laughter. What's best for my two wonderful kids?

Oh, how I want them to always be happy and safe! Never feel the way I do right now. I brush away still more of my nonstop waterworks and pick up the stuffed teddy bear I won shooting hoops at Cedar Point the previous year. I kiss it, knowing the days of loving such playthings are gone for Eric and dwindling for Allison. I don't want to let my children down, but guilt and loneliness isolate me. I can't make this misery end. It continues to wall me off from blessings so many would fall on their knees and thank heaven for if such gifts were bestowed onto them. Maybe I'm unworthy of my children's custody. I just want to lie down and quit.

And face eternity. I see myself as going to heaven.

People who kill themselves go to hell. Wasn't that a headline straight from the Bible? The pope? I again remembered little Holly Adams and her certainty that this fact was indisputable. Do I believe that, or not? And what about people whose sexuality is not "normal"? Equally damnable. So, God can you hear me? Or do *you* hate me too?

I can't tell if I'm praying or making snide remarks to God.

Back in my bathroom, I grab my prescription bottle and think of my father and his suicide night. He popped sleeping pills. I, on the other hand, need "happy pills." Lately, I find they mostly don't work, but I take them anyway, as I have been for the last four years, ever since I admitted to Dr. Looney that I was in love with Charlotte. Saying it out loud had made it real, and it both horrified and delighted me. I didn't feel crazy at all—just sinful. And scared.

In the past, I was always able to discuss my fears with Charlotte, the person who had become my lifeline, my dearest friend. Without another thought, I comb my hair and grab my keys off the hook in the laundry room. It's Saturday, meaning the kids won't be up for a few more hours. I'm almost sure I'll be back before they wake, but write them a quick note anyway, reminding them of my love and my need to run an errand or two. *Call my cell if you need me.*

I've ignored Lady out on our screened-in back porch. She has food, water, a doggie door. It isn't enough. Even dogs aren't really content with the mere basics. I step into the car, blasting the stereo. My well-worn Eric Clapton CD skips over an occasional scratch as he croaks out "I Can't Stand It." Not exactly what I need to hear right now. The ten minutes to Charlotte's house take *forever.* The closer I get, the more my stomach flips. I guess this qualifies me as some sort of a stalker. I slow as I near her house and look for signs of life, but it's as silent as my phone. My legs turn to rubber at the thought of walking up to her house. Charlotte used to *love* to see me come to her door. After years of knowing her, I learned that she also enjoyed seeing me walk away. "Do that again," she'd say seductively, challenging me to turn back around and walk away for a second viewing, eyes on my ass. The first time it happened, I was stunned and stammered something stupid.

"Oh, well, okay... I was just, yeah, okay then." Secretly, I was excited about having someone show so much interest.

Now I'm outside her house, here to beg her to explain how it all went wrong, demand that she keep loving me. I set the parking brake and imagine the scent of her favorite perfume—*Happy*. "If you can't be Happy, you might as well wear it," she'd say, half-joking. But me, I want to actually be Happy, and the only way I can see that happening is with her.

What's wrong with me? I've never needed anyone like this. My right leg shakes. I glance in the mirror to see the whites of my eyes lined with red, my father's daughter looking back at me. I reach for the door handle and let my left leg hit the pavement. Heavy. Charlotte's house is only a few steps away, but it feels like more work than my legs can handle. Heart racing, I walk up and knock.

Nothing. I try once more and notice a slight movement in her family room. I ring the doorbell three times to signal I won't be going away. As she walks toward the door, I feel even more afraid, but I must settle things. The door opens, and she turns and walks away without a greeting of any kind—a tactic of hers. Passing through her well decorated home, I follow her mood into the kitchen, mentally rehearsing the right way to start, my raw emotions likely to overthrow reason.

"Why haven't you called me back?" My tone seems harsh, even to me, but my anger is a freight train. "For the last four days, you've been telling me we'd talk, but you never call me. After all this time, after everything, you can't even call me back?"

Her brown eyes look blank. "I have a lot going on with the kids and I—"

"I know that, but aren't I important enough for even a conversation? You're closing me out and I can't take it."

She adjusts her glasses, exhales. "I can only do what I can do."

I hate that answer and pull her house key off my chain. "Why do I even care? You don't!" I throw her key down on the kitchen floor and scream at her. "When was I ever important? When was it ever about *us*?"

Charlotte's eyes are wide, like a scared animal. I slam my hand on the counter and she jumps. Her teenage son flushes the toilet in the upstairs bathroom, reminding me we are not alone. A deep breath and one last look at her cowering in the corner of the kitchen. I've gotta get out of here. I storm out of the house, jump into the car, drive a few blocks away, stop the car, and burst into tears. My fist hits the dashboard. I have done the exact thing I never wanted to do. I have frightened her.

※

I can't let the kids see me like this, don't want them to watch me and worry the way I used to watch my father. I sort through my CD holder and pop in Stevie Ray Vaughn.

> Well there's floodin' down in Texas
> All of the telephone lines are down

I pull into a local car wash, wishing I could just stand in it and wash away the mess of my life the way my car sheds the dust and debris from hundreds of miles of Houston traffic. The melodic rat-tat-tat of the water gives way to the rhythmic bump-bump of blue, brushless foam strips scrubbing back and forth. Eric and Allison, Eric and Allison. I wish I knew the best way to protect them and do what's right for them.

Car clean, I drive over to the local Wendy's to appease the kids with breakfast sandwiches and Frosties. I fight the urge to order three for myself. Food continues to be my vice and my comfort. I wanted my kids to have every advantage in life—not come from a divorced home or be stuck with a freak of a mother who falls in love with a woman. I wish I could fix things, give them some magical gift that would ensure their safety and happiness.

In the parking lot, I try to get control over myself. I sip Wendy's coffee and think about a nice efficient gun as the only way to truly stop the storm-spin in my mind. A sparrow is pecking around in a nearby trash can. Scriptures say that God knows when even one sparrow falls from the sky. *Was I at least as worthy as a sparrow?* A bird would probably never qualify as an abomination, of course, but then sparrows probably got their little wings ripped apart in hurricanes on God's watch.

A man in a black windbreaker stares at me as he passes, probably because of the red eyes and tear-streaks of a woman losing her mind, but I turn him instantly into the guy in the recurring nightmare I've had over the years. A man in a gray trench coat and black fedora hat waits for me outside a convenience store, his back to the wall. It's dark and I walk by him, but I can't see his face, though it's clear that his intentions aren't good. On my way in, I feel his eyes staring at me. He never says a word, but as I walk by, he tries to grab me. I duck and escape, and always at that moment, I wake up, my heart racing, my sweat cold.

The Bible teaches that Satan comes like a thief in the night. Maybe the man in the fedora is Satan, trying to claim me as one of hell's own. He stands in the shadows, avoiding Jesus who died to save those who repeat the Sinner's Prayer, those who don't kill themselves, and those who aren't gay.

I shift my car into reverse and then head out of the parking lot. Fifteen minutes later, I'm home, listening for signs of life. The kids are still asleep, so I put their breakfast in the oven set on *warm*, Frosties in the fridge, and try to force myself to do the damn taxes.

Instead, all the experiences I've ever had are bumping into each other inside my body and brain. I can't sit still. The food I bought the kids smells good, and I'm tempted, but, *no*, I will not do that. My feet carry me to the fridge though, my unfailing source of comfort. I open the door and stare. Beer. Cold pizza. My stomach clutches.

With the opening of the refrigerator, my cat Cleveland material-izes, meows incessantly and paws at me. *Hang on, you food addict!* In the laundry room leading to the garage, I lift the bag of cat food and just stand there, obsessing on my scene with Charlotte. My cat winds in and out between my ankles, purring, more meowing, wondering at the holdup. God! I can't even concentrate enough to scoop out kibble. I pace in the garage, my steps a tempo for the thoughts racing in my head—the most comforting being one of escape. The Big Escape.

Without warning, I think about the cool barrel of a gun in my mouth. I rub my tongue over my teeth and can almost taste the metal-lic flavor. A wind of peace sweeps over me at this thought, as if I've come up out of the murky deep end and can finally breathe again. I try to shake the images out of my head, but still they keep coming.

Twenty-six

What I Should Want

IMAGINING MY DEMISE CLASHES WITH only one opposing thought—my children.

Asleep upstairs, they are my loves and my life. I cannot imagine leaving them. Their father and I built our world around them, one filled with the lovely small things that bestow a profound sense of privilege: hand-made Halloween costumes, neighborhood parties, birthday sleepovers with a houseful of giggling children, and red-white-and-blue July nights filled with Jack's insistence that he really *does* know what he's doing with firecrackers. I miss those days. But I can't go on being who I'm *supposed* to be. It's far too late for that. I managed to torch my bridges months ago. It occurs to me that if my children walked in now, they'd see a zombie staring into the depths, as if they were watching me through a window into one of those aquariums at Sea World. I would be close, but not really reachable. Like my dad had been. This thought jolts me. I just can't be like he was. I can't do this to my kids.

The tax shit. *Just focus on that.* I drag myself toward my study, rubbing my hands together to soothe the pain that bolts through the muscles in my hands and forearms from my fibromyalgia, my recent diagnosis. I stretch my back and neck, hoping it will help. My jaw begins to feel numb, and a shock of pain runs from my legs into my feet.

I rub my face and try to exhale some of the tension. It's no use. Stacks of unopened bills await me. Allison's school project sits unfinished, requiring a trip to the hardware store.

The hell with it.

Lady whines out on the porch. I go to her, and she licks my hand, happy to console me.

"We don't need a dog," Jack had argued two years earlier. "It would create more of a mess in the house than we already have." This verdict, blamed on my housekeeping skills, preceded a great swig of Bud. We were sitting on a dock outside the lake house of a neighbor with three other couples on a warm Texas evening, the sky orange just before sundown. I looked across the sparkling water and thought of the puppy we'd stopped to cuddle.

"You should have seen this cute litter of puppies at the mall," I said to Bonnie.

"What kind were they?"

"Adorable Wheaten Terriers. I wanted to get one, but Jack won't let me. He can be a stick-in-the-mud about those kinds of things."

Bonnie laughed.

And then a wet and cold stream poured onto me. Stunned, I watched as amber liquid pooled in my lap and then dripped to the red-stained deck. In slow motion, I looked up to see Jack, standing over me, emptying the last drop of his beer, hatred on his face.

I didn't wait for the reaction of the others; I stood up quickly, snapping off the green plastic chair that stuck to the back of my legs, beer running down my front. I turned and walked toward the house, grabbed my purse and keys, and drove home.

I made sure the Wheaten Terrier moved in the following week.

❧

Now, I lavish attention on Lady, appreciating the morning sun on our lush banana and sago palms, the tall southern pines, all standing firm like old friends who make no comments. Sated with my love, Lady runs out into the greenery along the back fence, as joyfully as if she were running free in a subtropical forest. Watching her from the door, I long to stay here, suspended for a time. Right this second, I ache with a love for this world, a love bordering on bliss.

Yet I can't live in my backyard. Even if I could, the perfection of this moment would fade, and the love that fills me has a human context. Except for my children, the dear ones in my life would find me somehow *less than*, maybe even subhuman, if they knew the full reason my marriage is over.

The buzz of a leaf blower punctuates my solitude. It must be 9:30. I could have accomplished so much while the kids were still asleep if I hadn't been wallowing in my self-pity. *Enough*. Back in the family room, I turn on the TV for background noise to stop my mind from racing long enough for me to get the goddamn tax info together, the bills paid, the laundry done, and—oh jeez—the kitchen...

Sorting receipts, I flip through the channels, the *Bible-Belt* selections dizzying with at least a dozen TV preachers hawking their wares. I'm too drained even to get angry at oddballs like white-haired, pancake-make-up faced Jesse Duplantis, the TV preacher who tells me my problems will be solved if I just send him money—or something like that. It's not hard to dismiss people like Swaggart, Duplantis, Benny Hinn, or Jan and Paul Crouch and others, the hair-sprayed men and women who distill life and faith into a simple little formula, staging an emotional appeal for our trust and funds. They tell us all how it *really is*.

A famous radio pastor says that God doesn't hear the prayers of those who aren't *believers*. What a snot his God is. Vote Democrat or Pro Choice, another says, and you can't be a Christian, because Christ, of course, ran a very exclusive country club. Okay, I can dismiss idiots like Pastor Fred Phelps from Kansas who *picketed* Matthew Shepherd's funeral with signs that read "God Hates Fags," but did any of the more respected church leaders protest in outrage? No. Their silence affirmed an acceptance that cut through me and accused me at the same time.

As I sort through the cancelled checks for the thousands of dollars we gave to churches, I get angrier, though I still want to believe in the good parts of my faith, those parts that outweigh the hypocrisy and marketing mania that has so often dominated the high-profile "believers." My own positive experiences have sustained me. For most of my life, my faith has been a fence around my behavior, a dam holding back my feelings, and a border surrounding my feverish mind. It should be enough. Yet now I face the supposed sacrilege that questions whether having all of this "American, twenty-first-century-style, *come-to-Jesus* faith" has been helpful or destructive.

Doubts are normal, I argue. The only people who don't seem to have them are those who pontificate about their *certainty* in order to keep their coffers full. *Real people* have doubts that sometimes gnaw sharply at the soul. My own ragged edges make me feel foolish and small sometimes for believing a higher power cares about the mundane details of anyone's life.

Somehow though, those doubts recede, and their existence doesn't negate the *something* that is full of love and hope, the something deep inside I know to be true.

Jack and I were always so involved at church, leading the youth group and volunteering downtown, getting to hear what the teens in the various programs were going through. It brought us closer at the time, and I could see that he, too, was trying to be more real. He loved me, and he was trying. I loved him for that.

Dear God in heaven, why couldn't it have been enough?

⚜

In 1985, jack and I planned our wedding. It seemed like the thing to do. He was a good guy, steady and reliable. St. Richard's seemed like the logical site for the ceremony since both Jack and his parents were Catholic and my family used to be as well. This choice would be less problematic all around.

We showed up for the premarital counseling that the Catholic Church provides for engaged couples. The priest asked us questions like, "How will you settle differences over finances?" And, "Are you willing to compromise and listen to your partner's side of the story during an argument?" Our answers all began with, "Uh..," or "Well...um..." He looked almost amused by our ignorance of the institution of marriage. I wondered how it was that he seemed to know so much about it.

"So, you're the Parker family on Stelay Lane?" he asked me. "The ones who haven't given any offerings to the church since 1975?"

Since tithing was a topic my parents practiced better than anyone I had ever known, I thought the priest seemed way out of line. Mom and Dad knew that to give was to do more than just add to the church coffers for the Pope or some TV preacher. Oftentimes, they invited people over, gave them money, bought them new clothes, or let them live at our house for a few months. While this priest judged them for not giving money to the Roman Catholic Church, they had given more than their share to the Protestant churches in which they felt more comfortable, as well as to a host of people for whom they prayed, helped, and hosted. I doubted that the smug priest had as much charity in his heart.

"Sir, my parents are the most generous people I know and have always tithed. Maybe just not to the Catholic Church."

The conversation deteriorated. The following week, we returned to find that our Pre-Canna Compatibility test showed that Jack was a good and compliant Catholic, and I was not. I tried to ignore it, but that became impossible when the priest asked how we would raise any future children.

"Well, we aren't sure about that."

"It would be best if you would just tell me that you'll raise them to be Catholics."

"Well, but if that turns out to be not true—and I suspect that's the case—that would be a lie, and why would we want to start our marriage off on a lie?"

He didn't seem to see my point, so the next weekend we did some church shopping. I stumbled on an Episcopal church that was minutes from Mom and Dad's house. It was a denomination I hadn't previously tried, but I found it to be just right for the mix of our Catholic and Protestant backgrounds.

Jack and I settled on a June wedding. I didn't know much about things like music and dinner and cake, but Mom was up for it, so I let her take the reins, showing up when and where she asked me to. What was I doing? Did I even want this? I had no idea. I had turned off whatever switch a person has that allows us to discern what *we* want from what others tell us we should want.

I walked down the aisle into married life, matching Dad's stilted steps until I reached the altar and my beaming, tan, handsome new husband.

⁂

During the first few years of our marriage, I came to understand what my parents saw in the whole Christian community thing. Jack and I were stamped with the approval of Marriage. We were the young, good-looking couple who got involved in the church community and actually enjoyed it. There were long lists of prayer partners and helpers. *Need help moving? Give us a call. Need a babysitter? No problem.* It was easy to have a social life because a social function or some type of service or class took place almost every day of the week.

I lost touch with what was going on in the world of music and literature during the mid to late 1980s. I did continue to travel to Spain every year to see my friends for a few weeks, always wishing I had more time there, or better yet, could move there. For the most part, though, Jack and I spent our twenties happily leading the Youth Group, attending church socials and Bible studies, and listening to Amy Grant, Sandi Patti, Steven Curtis Chapman, and other contemporary Christian artists. If I wasn't reading the Bible, I was underlining chapters of the latest books from Charles Stanley or Chuck Swindoll. Some of my friends probably thought it was weird, but they could see I was happy. I lived in two environments, the party/bar scene with my friends and the Christian church world. I didn't feel the need to act differently in either environment—accidentally swearing during Bible studies or purposely talking about Biblical truths at bars. Always searching for truth, however, I began to see the walled-off passageways and locked iron doors where orthodoxy not only had no answers, but offered mind-bending diversions and cattle-prod voltage to anyone, especially a woman, ballsy enough to want honest, consistent beliefs.

An inexorable new direction began for me in 1987, when I heard about a weekend church retreat program called CRHP, nicknamed "Chirp," that stood for *Christ Renews His Parish*. Designed by a Catholic priest, it offered the opportunity to get beyond the usual small talk at church functions and go deeper. The idea of hearing the stories behind the pleasant faces at church intrigued me.

As people opened up about their struggles and doubts, I nurtured the feeling that this intimate soul connection was more like the fellowship that Christ's early church intended. Jesus and his disciples met in small gatherings on grassy fields or rocky hills under blue sky. Where did we get the idea for a church with doors and a steeple?

At that first meeting, we sat in a circle around the table of one of the Sunday school classrooms, as diverse a group as fifteen white women could be. Marilyn, originally from Germany, told us that when she was five, the Americans bombed her town. She remembered the pattern of the ceiling cracking when their house was hit. Seventy-eight-year-old Mary Alice started her introduction to the story of her faith with, "When I was four…" I knew we were in for a long night, but it was good to imagine her as a young girl and hear the struggles she'd faced as a female in the early part of the twentieth century.

A tall, thin woman spoke next. Cheryl was just a few years older than I was. She had struggled with Hodgkin's disease for seven years, gotten married, and even had a baby, then eighteen months old. Her cancer was in remission, but she lived every day knowing that if it returned, she would die because the doctors had exhausted all treatment options.

No one moved or cleared her throat or even breathed audibly as Cheryl admitted she had been angry at God and angrier still with "church people" who suggested she wasn't healed because of her lack of faith. She believed all along that whatever the outcome of her disease,

God was walking with her. While she spoke, I watched the power of honesty wash over our group as we listened to the stories behind our nodding acquaintances.

When Cheryl finished, someone whispered, "Thank you." I nodded and said it aloud. "Yes, thank you." When it was my turn, I didn't think to share about my childhood. By then, those nightmares lay buried so deeply under layers of "I'm Fines," I had forgotten they were there. Inspired by the others, I shared my struggle with bulimia, dalliances into pot and alcohol, and my quest to reconcile my faith in a world of doubts. I hated myself for having such "weird" problems. "I mean, bulimia is not as 'cool' as a cocaine addiction or as common as a serious drinking problem."

Wait, do you hear what you are saying?

The look on the women's faces suggested that they were thinking the same thing.

I confessed that I had puked over 6,000 times during the six years that I was bulimic. "Just thinking about that makes me want to take a shower. I somehow managed to stop over a period of time. All I knew was that I was hungry for something that food, alcohol, and pot just couldn't fix, and I'd had to purge away my unworthiness."

I wasn't sure what to expect when I finished. A quiet, pretty woman with prematurely gray hair named Carrie put her arm around me and whispered, "Thank you." I looked up; others were nodding, and a woman named Sally wiped away a tear. The experience left me feeling as if I'd stepped into a room full of mountain fresh air. I could breathe deeply at long last.

Over the course of the many weeks, we met in preparation for our task of delivering the next retreat. I was selected to be the director of the group. My official title was "Lay Director," and I made sure to tell Jodi and the gang about that one, laughing along with them at the title that invited their terrible puns.

As time went on, the Chirp group found that we laughed as much as we cried, creating a safe place to share our fears, doubts, and gratitude for a God we couldn't quite explain. These women healed me in a way my husband could not. However, instead of thinking, *oh, this is great; now I can bring "wholeness" to my partnership with Jack*, I blamed him for not being able to listen the way my Chirp friends did, for being unable to heal me in the way their love and attention seemed to.

Carrie became my closest friend in the group, but I also felt close to Cheryl and Sally. We attended church events together and often met for lunch or dinner with and without our husbands. Other than occasional get-togethers with Julie, Jodi, and my other college and high school friends, the rest of the world of popular culture faded further away. Jodi sometimes gave me grief for it, but I didn't care. My evolving faith and spiritual intimacy soothed me and chased the dark fears that lurked in my past. I felt cared for and fulfilled. I probably should have noticed even then that I'd stopped searching for life's profound connections through partnership with my husband. And that I found them through women.

※

My new focus on our discipleship group and its intimate friendships kept me upbeat. I felt well prepared for any hard times that just might be headed our way. Over that following summer, the group took some time off for vacations. Jack and I were both excited to go backpacking in Europe, and Jack had agreed to meet my friends in Spain. Bless him, he even tried Flamenco dancing with me—less than sober, of course. He was trying, in his way, to connect with me, but as much as he enjoyed the beauty and lifestyle of Spain, he didn't speak Spanish, and he probably felt a little threatened by my flirty, party-going friends. Still, it was a high point in our marriage. If only we could have figured out a way to keep it going.

In late July, we returned, and the phone rang almost as soon as I put my bags down. I was too tired to answer, but checked the clock and picked up anyway. It might be my mother, making sure we'd arrived home safely.

"Susan, it's me, Cheryl." Her voice was shaky. Tired. Old. "How was your trip?"

"It was terrific. Spain was great, as always. I have the best friends in the world there— they're family. But what's going on with you?"

She muffled a cry and put the phone down for a few seconds. Time slowed. I looked at the tangled phone cord, and "Oh no" shrieked in my head.

"It's back."

Twenty-seven

The Father's Loving Care

IT'S BEEN FIFTEEN YEARS SINCE I watched Cheryl be eaten alive by Hodgkin's disease, and it still hurts.

I get my ass up off the sofa, set the piles of tax receipts aside. The desperation I feel about my own problems should be nothing when compared to Cheryl's struggle. How dare I consider throwing away what she fought so hard to keep? And yet her battle lies at—or at least near—the heart of why I want to chuck the whole mess right now.

Cheryl's death assaulted my beliefs and marked what would become an avalanche of tragedies that would make me wonder if God was napping through my prayers and pleas. *Do you not hear me God? Or worse yet, do you hear me and still do nothing?*

The kids are bumping around upstairs. They'll be down soon and see the depressing turmoil the kitchen has become. I force myself to load the dishwasher, memories of Cheryl still disturbing me as I chip away at spaghetti sauce I should have washed last night. While Cheryl was sick, Carrie and I often went to her house for visits or to help out around the house. One Thursday, I called Cheryl and told her I was leaving work early.

"Want anything? Ice cream maybe?"

"No thanks. My mom is at the grocery store now. Just come by. The door's unlocked."

When I arrived, she was lying on the couch under a green blanket and propped up with a pillow, a captive audience to my random chatter.

"Come on in. So glad you came."

I reached down to hug her and could feel every bone of her rib cage.

"Want any tea? Mom just made some. Help yourself; it's in the fridge."

As I walked back from the kitchen with my iced tea, she said, "Did you know you can catch cancer?"

I set the tea on the coffee table and sat close beside her. "What are you talking about?"

"You know Brandi. She seems to think so." Cheryl sighed. "She was here the other day and acted like the glass I had used was radio-active. Picked it up, making sure to avoid the rim. When I asked her why, she said she just wanted to be sure. 'You know,' she said, 'I have kids and all.'" Cheryl brushed away a tear.

I knew Brandi from Chirp. That this was particularly painful since she was Cheryl's best friend. It was the kind of behavior that seemed to hurt her more than anything—that and the judgment from finger-waggers who implied that she and her husband just didn't have enough faith for her healing.

"Ugh, I'm so sorry."

"Yeah, well, it's okay. I guess it's just fear."

"Yeah, for sure. And ignorance."

"So how are things going with the Chirp group? It must be really boring without me at the regular meetings." She managed a smile.

"Absolutely, I'm thinking about bringing vodka to the next one to pep things up a bit."

She laughed. I loved making her laugh. I could read in her face, the thoughts that must be crossing her mind, the ones that wished this weren't happening, and then the ones that told her to "deal with it." The subject of our Chirp speeches came up.

"You're not still planning…?" I let the words drop.

Cheryl put her glass down. "I take my commitments seriously, and I said I'd do the one for 'The Father's Loving Care.' I feel that God is loving me and taking care of me even now, but I'm worried it won't come across that way."

"Explain." I was afraid I knew where this was going.

"Well, I worry I'll get too emotional, and it'll end up sounding like I feel sorry for myself, or that people will hear it and come up with the opposite conclusion."

"You mean, that people will think God is really screwing you over because you're dying?"

Her head jerked back a bit with my blunt question. "Yeah, I do. And maybe the truth is, there's a part of me that feels that way too."

"Well, I think that's totally understandable. And who knows? Maybe that's worth mentioning somehow. Maybe people need to hear that doubts are okay, that everything isn't so neat and clean and easy."

Cheryl and I talked for a long time that day. We turned on the tube, fascinated with current sagas of the televangelists as they made money and burned up the airwaves with never-ending sermons, theatrics, and promotion for their theme parks. Those swindlers, those great crying preachers, begged on air—live—for forgiveness from flocks who'd outfitted them in mansions, private planes, and air-conditioned abodes for their pets. People like Jimmy Swaggart tattled on fellow preachers Marvin Gorman and Jim Bakker, bathing in his own self-righteousness until it became apparent that he liked the "ladies of the night" (or of the congregations) as much as they did. Cheryl and I had rolled our eyes over Swaggart's tear-streaked "I have sinned against you, my Lord" speech. If the dramas were bad, however, the televangelical sermons were even worse, we both agreed.

I gained so much from those afternoons keeping Cheryl company that I felt like she was there for me more than I for her, as she tried to keep breathing long enough to make sure her two-year-old daughter would have a mother on planet Earth one more day.

"I want her to remember me," she told me later that afternoon.

Near the end, Cheryl looked like a concentration camp victim left on the floor of her living room to die.

"I can't find a way to make her feel comfortable," her mother told me. She's mostly out of it, but when she's lucid, she tells me she wants to be on the floor. I have no idea why."

I remember looking at Cheryl's sunken eyes and her gaunt, gray, nearly lifeless skin. Her mouth hung partially open because there just wasn't enough flesh left to cover her skull. I wished I could kill the cancer that was murdering her. Instead, I hugged her mother, wishing there were words that made a difference, knowing there were not.

In late January, two days after I'd seen her despondent and on the floor in the fetal position, I got the call. Cheryl was gone.

Jack and I sat with Carrie at her funeral. Cheryl's husband, Stan, was uncharacteristically dressed in a suit. Their two-year-old wasn't quite sure what was going on. Stan spoke.

"If Cheryl were here, she'd tell you to live life to the fullest. To enjoy every day and be thankful. That none of us knows how much time we have. She has known since she was twenty-two that death could claim her too soon. For eight years she faced it down. It wasn't easy, but she stayed strong mostly. She lived and loved; she laughed and cried. Before she died, she asked me to play this at her funeral. Her testimony to *The Father's Loving Care*."

It was strange yet sweet to hear Cheryl's voice in the stillness of the sanctuary. I sat there with Carrie and Jack, sobbing silently, knowing that she would have wanted me to hold it together, to really listen to what she had to say. Through it all, Cheryl had learned to trust in a Father that didn't always give her the answers she wanted.

❧

My hand throbs with a spasm of pain, and I drop a glass that shatters on the floor. I stare at an especially wicked shard and pick it up, fascinated by the instant vision of a quick slash at my wrists.

Upstairs, Allison and Eric are thumping around. I set the glass in the trash, close my eyes, and remind myself of the courage Cheryl had to muster to overcome her exhaustion and read a story to her daughter. She would be forty-five now, but she is frozen in my mind as a thirty-year-old, smiling through her tears.

"Good morning, sweethearts!" I yell upstairs. "Come get your breakfast when you're ready!"

No reply. I sweep up the broken pieces, finish the dishes, dry my hands, and put on a pot of coffee, though I'm a little wired from the strong brew at Wendy's.

Would my life have been better if I hadn't known Cheryl and therefore could have been spared the devastation and sense of God's injustice? The answer is obvious. No. I'm grateful for her, and despite how corny it sounds, I want to believe God sent Cheryl and others to me, each with the gift of a different perspective that helped me muddle through. I hope that God intended for me to do the same for others.

Or is that something I just want to believe? I feel so confused and alone here in the Bible Belt of the Lone Star State, that my faith has taken another turn, one I can't seem to steer away from the long road off of a short pier.

⚘

I turn the damn TV off, unable to handle even the weather station. It occurs to me that what I want to listen to—*need to listen to*—is that tape of Cheryl talking about *The Father's Loving Care.* I sip hot coffee against the morning chill and let her words comfort me.

> You might not receive the answer you want, but I've found that through it all, God is faithful. He never leaves us. Like the bright Morning Star, just when things get the darkest, He shows Himself. Sometimes it's in the quiet whisper of encouragement from a friend, a smile of a stranger, or the prayers of friends and family. In the end, I've found that it's enough. In the Father's loving care, I find my ultimate destination and purpose.

It was poignant and simple, yet powerful. If someone as damaged as Cheryl could still feel that loving connection, couldn't I also feel it?

I'm terrified that the answer is that my damage is of a different kind—the kind I should be able to repair myself. And can't. I think the definition of hell is when you are in that place where you can't even imagine any connection to God's love.

Twenty-eight

Abomination

IMAGINE A PHONE CONVERSATION with my mother during which I blurt the truth.

"Hi, Mom. I'm gay."

"What are you talking about?" she would say. "You're a woman—you can't love a woman. I don't want to hear about your sexual relations. That's sick! You're sick!"

"I'm in love with Charlotte. It's not about the sex. I don't want you to call it an abomination."

"Well, *homosexuals* themselves aren't an abomination—but *homosexuality* is. You go any further with this, and you're going to hell."

I used to believe that if I accepted Jesus as my Lord and Savior, my name would be written in the Book of Life. I used to picture that book, its parchment pages edged in gold like Grandma Marie's Bible. I *knew* I was among the saved, my name written in golden ink with the quill of a feather from an angel's wing, loved by Christ, my Savior. If He could love me, then I could love me too.

I still accept Jesus, but it may not be mutual. I can't seem to get the pointing finger of the evangelists out of my mind. Some sort of heavenly eraser is obliterating my name from the beautiful book. Yet if God really wants only the cookie-cutter Christians, he certainly went way out of his way to create a plethora of human variety and individual uniqueness.

God made me the way I am, didn't He? I'd always felt different from other women. I never sought the attention, compliments, and security from a man the way many of my friends and acquaintances did. Travel, adventure, and competition interested me far more. For so many years, I'd loved the women's Bible studies, the discussions and the people, but I felt out of place, especially during introductions. Tell us what your hobbies are, they said. They mentioned needlepoint, knitting, or scrap-booking. I said "basketball" and watched the smiles fade into polite distance. "So, there you have it. I guess this means you know who *not* to call for the bake sale. Heh-heh." These church women, who probably hadn't played a team sport since eighth-grade gym class, sat in silence, trying to figure out if there was a punch line.

✜

It's 10:15, less than three hours before I have to see Jack. My stomach does a flip. Not only are the taxes still unfinished, my hair is a mess. I can't let him see me looking like this. He'd start commitment proceedings.

A third cup of coffee has left me so jittery I dare not pick up sharp objects if I'm to get through this day. In the kitchen of my husbandless house, I'm so exhausted I can't imagine finding the strength to continue. What happened to my competence? My independence? I hate to admit it, but I'm afraid to be alone. *I don't know if I can pay the bills, manage the house, keep things going for the kids. I'm afraid to keep living.*

What I need is a shower.

I set my coffee cup in the sink and head upstairs to try to rinse away all of these thoughts. I caress the banister and pause to admire the elegant archways of my four-bedroom house, the twenty-foot ceilings, the warm walls in tan, chocolate, and burgundy, the silk plants and framed art prints. Tiles cover the same steps that bore Jack and me as we carried the kids to bed at night. Inside the bedroom that is no longer "ours," I see one of Jack's old slippers we'd both missed, poking out from under the dresser.

Those last few months before Jack moved out, I went to bed early. I'd lie there, searching my mind for a solution. Later, I'd listen to his breathing, wondering if he was faking sleep as I was. By then, we had passed the point of meaningful dialogue and obliterated any chance we had of intimacy. The air hung heavy above us, charged with grief, anger, misunderstanding, and the overwhelming feeling that I wanted to bolt. Sex had mostly evaporated because having physical intimacy with someone with whom I couldn't share emotional intimacy seemed dishonest. Wrong. How could I connect with him if I couldn't talk to him the way I bonded with women friends, sharing the secrets of our innermost souls? He could never open up that way to me and couldn't deal with it when I tried to open up to him.

I turn on the water in the shower and sit next to my bathtub, wishing there was someone who could help me. My mother isn't an option. Would my father be any help? *I miss you, Daddy. What would you say about all of this?* Oh, God, I can't bear the thought of his judgment, his certain rejection.

Yet, if I could bring him back, I would. Six short weeks after Cheryl's death, I received the Sunday night phone call from Mom that blindsided me. As with Cheryl's death, this painful memory is never far from my thoughts, another sorrow on a replay loop.

I remember the beagles living in the first-floor apartment of our Cleveland duplex started baying, just as my mom said Dad was going in for some tests at the hospital. I pushed the phone closer to my ear. Mom explained that Dad's diarrhea had been going on too long.

I stamped my foot, the same thing Jack always did to get the stupid hounds to stop their racket, but it was more like a child having a tantrum. I knew this was serious. An anxiety rooted deep in my childhood sent me into a panic. *I have to save Dad!*

It was two years into our marriage and Jack was immediately supportive at the time. After work the next day, we hustled to Fairview Hospital for visiting hours. Draped in a white hospital gown, Dad seemed in good spirits, trying to pretend nothing at all bad was happening.

"Your dad is gonna be all right," Jack said later in the parking lot. "He's a big and strong guy. Don't you think he looked healthy?"

On Wednesday morning, two days later, he was still in the hospital. I couldn't bear to go to the office that morning and worked from home, staring at my sales reports for the week, trying to prepare myself to make some cold calls. I jumped when the phone rang.

"Hi, sweets. It's me." He breathed in as if to ready himself, and then he cleared his throat. "Well, honey, they tell me I'm sick. Turns out, I have colon cancer that has metastasized to my liver. I'm afraid it's terminal, honey, but God is good; I'm not afraid to die. Whatever happens, it will be okay and—"

"Okay? Well you're not okay, and it's not okay with me! I mean, let's get a second opinion." My heart raced like I'd just run a few miles. The blue wallpaper Jack and I had hung that winter blurred as tears filled my eyes.

"Well, I'm going to the Cleveland Clinic in May—"

"May? That's in six weeks! Can't they take you any sooner than that?"

"No. Try not to worry, we'll call you when we know more."

It all felt unreal, like I was floating in a dream, and his voice sounded further and further away. I wanted to hug him, let his strong arms reassure me, and feel the scratch of his mustache on my cheek. The line was dead, and I slammed the phone down, wishing I could blame this on someone, but there was only God. *God damn it. Why is this happening?*

I threw myself onto the gold couch that Mom and I had found in a yard sale right after graduation and sobbed into the pillow. The phone rang. The dogs downstairs bayed some more. I grabbed the phone.

"Hey, it's me, Jodi."

"Listen, Jodi, I really can't talk now." I choked back a sob. "I just found out that my dad is dying of cancer—I can't talk. It's bad."

"Oh my God, I'm so sorry, but I really need to tell you something."

"Can't it—?"

"I'm gay."

What? The room was spinning like Dorothy's house ascending to Oz. What was she saying? I got up and then sat back down. This was inappropriate. Life was inappropriate.

"Why are you telling me this? My dad is *dying*! I can't talk to you now!" I slammed the receiver down. At this rate, the phone wouldn't last the week. At that point, I didn't realize that I was gay and thought that if she was gay, we had nothing in common anymore.

Now, that ironic moment haunts me. I leave the bathroom, only vaguely noticing the hot cloud of steam, the shower still running as I remember hurting my sister then as well. Unfortunately, Ann, twenty-one and on spring break in Florida, got left out of the turmoil. We all thought we had more time to tell her about Dad's illness, which proved to be an unforgivable mistake.

That next morning, I arrived at my parents' house by 9:00 A.M. and found Dad coughing and shuffling along like someone in his seventies instead of a man of fifty-seven years. How had the change happened overnight? It didn't seem to faze him. He was certain about an afterlife in heaven. Jesus had paid his way to the Promised Land. *Was he looking forward to his own death?*

That evening, Jack told me that miracles happen, that we needed to keep praying. Maybe the Cleveland Clinic might be able to help him. I wanted to believe him, but the voice in my head just kept repeating *Oh, no... oh, no.*

"Just go lie down and relax. Try not to think about it anymore."

"I don't feel like lying down."

"Just do it. I'll bring you the paper."

"I want food."

If I didn't eat publicly, I might binge privately and risk a bulimic episode—something I hadn't done in almost three years.

Jack nodded, put his arm around me, and we headed to Johnny's for lasagna.

The next morning, I awoke to a 6:00 A.M. phone call. Mom's voice was measured, in control. *"He's collapsed. Meet me at the hospital."*

Quickly, Jack and I got dressed and rushed to the emergency room. I ran to the nurses' station, but before I could open my mouth, Mom grabbed me.

"He's gone."

Three days after his diagnosis, he was dead.

❧

I'm shocked to realize the shower is still running. The steam has died away because I've used all the hot water in the tank. Not that it matters. Taking a shower is too much work. It means I'd have to dry my hair and then straighten it. I can't do this. Can't cope. Can't function. I shut off the water and go downstairs for more coffee.

Twenty-nine

The Strong Tower

𝔘NSHOWERED, I'M STILL IN MY sweats. The Wendy's sack still sits in the warm oven, but the Frosties have disappeared from the refrigerator, so the kids have made a foray. They're fine without me.

My sweethearts. How can I possibly be the mother they need? My parents did their best, and it wasn't enough. I feel like a total failure for not fitting the mold of the perfect mother who bakes home-made cookies, adores her husband, and sings in the church choir. I resent the mold, yet I keep crashing into it as I try to see myself as something other than a pitiful misfit. I can't seem to tear myself away from a marriage—which my family considers the most worthy contribution I'll ever make—without feeling like I'm severing a limb, without severing my children from their roots as well.

The Easy Exit is so attractive, but I shudder and think of Aunt Joy's death. Is *she* at peace up in the great by and by, even though she killed herself? My own special dream man makes a sudden cameo appearance in my mind—the man in the fedora hat, trying to grab me. It dawns on me that he is Death, stalking me the same way he stalked Aunt Mary Ellen and Aunt Joy, a mugger who wants to snatch God's gift of life away from us.

I slosh coffee from a fourth cup as the sprinklers out back click on. Like a zombie, I pace between the kitchen, the family room, the study, and dining room.

I could never leave my body for Eric or Allison to find the way Aunt Joy did to Sam. The way Dad almost did to me. If I do the deed, it will have to be when they are staying with Jack. He would protect them from the sight of anything grim. Reliable Jack. Aunt Joy felt so peaceful once she'd made her decision. I must not have made my mind up yet, because I keep stepping back out into the storm.

I set the Wendy's sacks out, intending to summon the troops, but I pick up my Bible instead and open it, hoping that it will lead me to a passage that provides comfort or direction. I've heard others call it "Bible-dipping," and I've always thought it was weird, even though I secretly did it too.

> "In the first year of King Cyrus's reign, a decree was sent out concerning the Temple of God at Jerusalem. It must be rebuilt on the site where Jews used to offer their sacrifices. . . ."

That makes no sense. Oh my God. What am I doing? What a pathetic practice. I just want so badly to believe that God will communicate with me and has not abandoned me.

Beside the Bible's place on the shelf, stands a folder of old cards and letters, crammed with loving messages from people who love me. This is what I should dip into. Hungrily, I reread them, each word a strong link in a chain that just might help haul me back from the edge. I caress one card in particular, congratulating me on the birth of our son—this one from my high school friend Carol. She and I were pregnant at the same time. I turn it over again and again, reminding myself that there were plenty of times when I felt God's help and presence, never more than when Eric was born, thirteen years ago. It was early December of 1989; with the due date Christmas Eve, I was nearly nine months along. I had a scheduled appointment with my obstetrician, a stout, cold woman who'd never had kids of her own. I picked her solely on her reputation as a good clinician. Personality and compassion weren't part of the program.

"Have a seat. The results from your last ultrasound were misfiled, and I have only just learned that we're probably looking at something called Polycystic Kidney Disease."

Misfiled? I couldn't process what she was saying. Some other baby had a disease?

Dr. Maltz leaned back in her chair. I watched her mouth move and the fat quiver underneath her chin as she spoke—words even, unemotional, matter-of-fact. "If anything, it will be a long-term medical problem that may require kidney dialysis and/or transplantation."

I gripped the arms of the blue plaid chair; my stomach hurt. "Okay, well what now?"

"Let's do a non-stress test and see how the baby is doing and go from there."

By the time I stumbled out of Dr. Maltz's office and down to the garage, I felt like I'd been dropped on my head. *Where did I park my car? Which floor?* I couldn't think. I exited on the second floor and dragged myself along. My blue Celica. It was nowhere. *God, can you at least help me find my damn car, please?* I guess He did.

Jack hurried home and was there to hug me when I walked through the door. Some men who don't do words well can convey profound messages with the way they hold a woman. The hug I needed would press me close, encircling and assuring me that we were in this together and would somehow see things through. A hand might cup the back of my hair and stroke it a time or two. A sandpaper-y cheek would mesh into mine, and I'd hear a murmured, "Sweetie...oh, sweetie." Like that. But that didn't happen. Instead, Jack's hug lasted a full second longer than normal. "Just try not to worry," he said.

Would he ever stop telling me this? Life was dripping with reasons to worry. I wanted something that felt real, just a few words that showed he was more than a looks-good-on-paper guy. I lacked the ability to see past whatever stopped him from being the loving human being I *needed* him to be, especially in that moment.

And yet...That evening, I lumbered downstairs after a bath, and Jack was singing along to a Christian tape by Leon Patillo.

"The name of the Lord is a Strong Tower. Them that run to it are safe...."

I tried to let the music wash over me. Oh, to know that strong tower was within running distance. *Please God, watch over this baby.*

Two days later, after bad news from the non-stress test, I was scheduled for a C-section. We awoke to several inches of powdered snow and winds that could knock you off your feet. The radio reported we were in for near record-breaking, below-zero temperatures. Jack held my hand as I waddled to the car, and we headed to the hospital like two soldiers going to battle.

"You okay?" Jack asked.

Of course not. I nodded.

We checked in, and a nurse began my pitocin drip. Because it was December 18th, I asked Jack to read me Psalm and Proverbs 18. Jack looked nervous, cleared his throat, picked up the black, leather-bound Bible I had packed in my overnight bag, and started with the Psalms:

> Though the cords of death entangle me, my God delivers me . . .

Did he picture, as I did, our baby's own umbilical cord and a description of his deliverance?

Jack squeezed my hand and then read Proverbs 18.

> "The name of the Lord is a strong tower, and them that run to it will be safe—"

"Hey, that's the scripture from the Leon Patillo song you were singing!" I said. "I forgot it was from that proverb. I should've remembered, since that was the verse on the Giralda tower in Sevilla." A sense of calm filled me as I remembered that moment of timeless connection to all of creation.

A new sense of calm filled me as Jack and I continued to pray, searching for the right mix of piety and deal making. Hours later, it was clear that the pitosin wasn't working. Eric's vital signs were not good, and my doctor let us know her plans.

Dr. Maltz spoke with the same even, empty tone as always. "I'll be performing the C-section, but before we begin, both the anesthesiologist and neonatologist will be coming in to speak with you. We're scheduled for a 2:00 P.M. delivery time."

The anesthesiologist entered the room with his plan. "We'll be giving you a spinal, and I want you to remember to just try to relax."

Yeah right. I gave myself my own internal pep talk. *Stay calm, God said He would never leave us or forsake us.* The neonatologist arrived, and he too was emotionless, his hair greasy and disheveled, like he'd been asleep in the room next door.

He said, "Your son will probably expire in the delivery room." He might have said in the same tone that the Browns lost yet another big game in the snowy cold of Cleveland Stadium.

Did the oxygen just leave the room? While I tried to catch my breath, Jack asked him to explain what was happening.

"This is a very rare genetic condition. You have a one in four chance of this occurring in subsequent pregnancies, but since we know to be looking for it, depending on your religion, you can abort affected fetuses."

Abort future fetuses? I couldn't breathe. Why was this guy telling me this right before I was to go under the knife? As they wheeled me into the operation room, I watched the drab green walls pass and looked at the blank faces of doctors and staff. Another day at the office for them. Would my baby die in the O.R.? My inner voice had told me everything would be okay, but the doctors' certainty was frightening, and I lost faith in it. I could smell the Betadine solution and whatever else hospitals use to disinfect patients and floors, walls, and the metal tools that would be tearing open my flesh.

Dr. Maltz greeted Jack and soon got to work. I could feel her tugging at my now open abdomen. Jack held my hand as he sat near my head and behind the surgical screen. An hour later, amidst our tears and prayers, Eric was lifted into this world in the hands of my doctor. When we heard his strong cry, our hope grew.

"I have him; now they'll be giving him the APGAR test."

I could feel my doctor tugging on the sutures to close me up as I watched the Labor & Delivery team poke and prod Eric.

I offered up some deal with God to adopt a Chinese girl if He would just make sure our son was okay. I had a lifetime of thoughts in those moments about my tiny baby. Did he look like me? Jack? Would he like basketball and Spain or poker and camping?

"His numbers look good," I heard the neonatologist say.

"We're going to send him to the NICU while you're in recovery. I'll check back with you once we monitor his progress."

A few hours later, the doctor returned to tell me that he couldn't find anything wrong with Eric. I had no way of knowing if the tests were wrong or if God had given us a miracle.

Nothing?

"Nothing I can find right now." He seemed disappointed. Like maybe we were mutated subjects of an experiment gone awry. The human element of the whole equation seemed completely lost on him.

If not for my gratitude, I would have lashed out at him. Instead, Jack and I thanked God for the miracle of Eric's birth, not really sure why our baby was spared when others were not. I wasn't about to question God on that one.

At least, not then. Of course, if I hadn't questioned all along, I might have saved myself nightmarish fears and depression. This time, God had delivered a miracle. I wanted more than anything to trust this God again. And I did. Oh, I did. Only to have my faith come back and slam me into the dirt. Thinking back on the three years that followed Eric's birth, it was as if they were intended to test every shred of faith I had—to stretch, bend, bake, and fry what I thought faith even was.

Thirty

Daniel and Carrie

NEXT TO ERIC'S SOCCER PORTRAIT on my desk, I place the congratulatory card that Carol gave me. It is also in front of a few of my favorite books by some of my favorite authors. Maya Angelou, Toni Morison, Truman Capote. I hear a giggle and stick my head out just in time to see Allison flying up the stairs with the breakfast bag from Wendy's under her arm like a football. Her flat feet smack the stairs as she readies herself to dodge Eric at the top.

"Hi, Mom, thanks for the breakfast!" she shouts from above, laughing before Eric makes a grab for the grease-stained bag. "Too bad Mom didn't get anything for you," she tells him.

Seconds later, I hear more laughter. The fact that they laugh so much when they're together gives me comfort.

"Allie! Give me my breakfast!" Eric demands through his laughter.

"Sorry, but like I told you, Mom didn't get you any."

He laughs. For a second I forget all my troubles and feel complete gratitude and joy for these children of mine.

"C'mon—give me mine."

I could picture Allie's little face, green eyes flashing. Eric half amused, half irritated, chuckling.

"Well, then we're gonna watch what I want to watch. No more *SpongeBob* for you."

"Mo-om!" she shouts, dragging the one syllable into two. "Eric won't let me watch *SpongeBob*."

I know I should go upstairs to settle it, but instead I shout back, "Allie, give Eric his breakfast. Eric, let her watch *SpongeBob*, and then you pick the next show."

"That's not fair! I—"

"Then, honey, come downstairs and watch TV down here."

"Allie!" Eric laughs, trying to stay angry. She is no doubt making a face or some comment that he can't help but admit is funny—their happy voices so different from the days when they got caught in the crossfire of my war with their father, like the time six months earlier when Jack chastised twelve-year-old Eric for his inability to start the lawn mower. It escalated when an embarrassed Eric refused to try any more.

"Get over here before I pound you one," Jack snarled.

I stood between him and Eric and grabbed Jack's white T-shirt, begging him to calm down. He pushed me aside, and before it was all over, threw a full water bottle at Eric point blank. To my great relief, he missed somehow.

Later in his bedroom, Eric looked at me through teary eyes and sighed. "Sometimes it's like he doesn't even *like* me."

I choked in my own sadness and tried to explain that it was *me* his father didn't like; mostly, I just hugged him and assured him that he was loved.

Four months later, Jack pounded on the bathroom door while Eric was inside. "What's taking him so long?"

Before I could stop him, he picked the lock and burst into the room while Eric was on the toilet, pants to his ankles. Allison was watching *The Cosby Show*, and when it was over, she looked at me and asked why she couldn't have a dad like Dr. Huxtable.

That was it. I was done. Charlotte was no longer an option, but I couldn't stay with Jack.

※

I have to face him in two hours because he thinks an explanation is necessary. And truthfully, for some of it, he's right. I should have been honest about my love for Charlotte, but for fear of losing the kids, I chickened out. Now I can't help but feel angry with myself and God. I really need my Maker to help me figure things out, but He is nowhere to be found. I just want some sort of can't-miss sign, so I know what to do. Yet He remains silent. I have moved out of His earshot, and He left me in this soundproof room of a life. He seemed to listen and help with the birth of Eric, but He didn't help Cheryl or Aunt Mary Ellen or Joy. Or others.

A stampede of events crushed my pre-packaged faith, turning it into a bedraggled version that often left me babbling.

I shiver, thinking about the cold day in Boston, ten years before. It started when Rosario called from Spain to ask me if I knew of an American doctor who might be able to help her three-year-old nephew, Daniel. He had been born with a heart condition that his doctors in Spain left untreated. By the time he was three, Daniel turned gray and winded just from walking across the room.

Coincidentally, his condition was the same one that plagued the grandson of the pastor of a new church we'd been attending. A cardiovascular surgeon at Boston Children's Hospital had alleviated the baby's problems. *Was that a coincidence shepherded by God?* Surely it meant that we should contact that hospital. Carmen flew to Boston to meet with the surgical team and, to her comfort, learned that the chairman of the Department of Cardiovascular Surgery was from Madrid. Rosario and Magüi told me that they were also glad that the hospital was located in Boston because they knew an American girl named Daryl, who lived there. They were sure she would be willing to help. She agreed to pick them up at the airport and get them settled in the hospital for the procedure.

I took three-year-old Eric to preschool class and then called Daryl when all the plans were finalized. She said everything seemed under control. I'd been sick with a month-long case of pleurisy that zapped my energy and left me breathless and in pain at every cough and wheeze, stopping me, for at least once in my life, from "overreacting." I'd simply asked Daryl to call when they arrived.

The day Daniel and his parents were to arrive in the States was a cold January day in Cleveland. I imagined it wasn't much different in Boston. I was bringing a few logs into the family room to light a fire in the fireplace when the phone rang.

"Daniel had a heart attack on the way over," Daryl said, voice panicky. "He's flat-lining! Please, come to Boston! I can't handle this alone!"

Still coughing, I made arrangements for Jack and Mom to take care of Eric and flew off to Boston. My hands were shaking when I arrived by taxi at Boston Children's Hospital. Adolfo, Daniel's father, met me at the door. Daniel was still alive, but it was bad, very bad. I brought my Bible, thinking that its words could be more of a comfort than mine. Adolfo led me to the waiting room where Carmen tried to explain what had happened. It was a concert of Spanish and medical vocabularies I never wanted to learn. A machine was doing all of the work for their three-year-old son, work that his heart, lungs, liver, and kidneys were no longer doing. I leaned on the wall as Carmen told me about the heart attack Daniel had suffered on the airplane. I studied her face. Worried, white, and drained. Frantic.

"Can I see him?"

They nodded and led me past the nurses' station on what felt like a tightrope walk over the valley of death in the MICU, Medical Intensive Care Unit. I stared at Daniel, trying to hide my horror. He looked nothing like the child I'd seen eight months earlier at Rosario's wedding. His face was swollen beyond recognition, his skin shiny. I glanced at Adolfo and then Carmen. A tear traveled down her face.

Es mi culpa.

No, it's not your fault, I told her. It felt more like it was mine. The doctors said he wouldn't last twenty-four hours. I couldn't comprehend it. In a dream state, I paced and ran my fingers through my hair. I hadn't overreacted; I'd under-reacted! *Oh my God, why didn't I meet them in Madrid and escort them to the hospital? I could have prevented this!* My Susan-to-the-Rescue persona kicked into high gear.

Daryl met me in the waiting area. Her long brown hair not quite right, her blouse wrinkled as if she'd hurried from her house cloaked in a rescue persona of her own. She'd previously told me that she was a black belt in karate and as I bent down to greet her with a hug, I tried to imagine this small woman capable of such physical strength.

The hospital teemed with worried parents trying their best to stay strong for kids who needed all the prayer and positive energy they could muster. I thought about Eric and wished I could hold him. He was three days younger than Daniel. One father in particular caught my attention—a former Hell's Angel named Randy. He still looked the part.

"My twelve-year-old daughter is here for a liver transplant." He seemed confident, strong. "The Lord brought us this far. I feel confident she'll be okay."

"How long have you been here?" I asked, trying to make conversation, wishing I didn't have to chat about such things, but glad for someone who could relate to the panic I felt.

"Been here 'bout a week. Her surgery went well; now we jes gotta see if her body accepts it. So far, so good."

When I explained why I was there, he asked me if I wanted him to pray for Daniel. So, there we sat, in the lobby, this two-hundred-fifty-pound man in jeans and a biker vest, praying for a three-year-old from Spain.

Afterwards, he told me how he'd found Christ and turned his life around.

"I was on drugs, lost everything, my wife had just left me, I didn't have a job. I was desperate, sitting in my living room with a gun, spinning the chamber, thinking I needed to check out of planet Earth. I threw up one last God-if-you're-out-there prayer."

His manner was calm, not preachy, just telling me his story. "I sat there for a long time, ya know, jes thinkin' bout my life. How I'd screwed it up—gotten hooked on coke and pot. It didn't seem worth it to try any more. But then my doorbell rang. I couldn't imagine who it would be. Screw it, I thought and didn't get up. It rang again. Could it be my wife? Didn't she still have a key?"

For those moments, I was completely enthralled by his story. Somehow I forgot we were sitting amidst hundreds of sick people, with Daniel near the brink of death. I was sitting with my elbows on my knees, my ears tuned, eyes focused on his big, black leather boots, just waiting to hear what happened next. Thinking of him now, I realize how much I really get what he was saying then—that feeling that you just don't want to keep trying anymore.

"I went to the door to find a skinny guy standing there," he went on. "Looked like one of those clean-cut church guys I used to hate. He hemmed and hawed and then just came out with it. Told me that he had been driving by, and that God told him to stop at my house, knock on the door. He was sorry, didn't know why, but asked me if I needed help."

I got goose bumps as Randy wiped a tear from his eye.

"The guy prayed with me, told me that God loved me just as I was, said I needed to turn away from my old life and He'd give me a new one. Said there should be punishment for the way I'd been livin' but that Jesus paid for it all on the cross. Well, I'm not sure what happened, but something came over me as we prayed. I cried like a snot-nosed kid, and when it was over, we got up off of our knees and flushed all my drugs down the toilet."

Now we were both crying.

He gave me a big bear hug and said, "So now I'm here, alive and drug-free, happy knowing that no matter what I've done in the past, I can have a new life in Christ. Now it's my turn to pray with others, so I'm here for you, sister."

I went back to the MICU, and Carmen told me to call Daryl who had gone home for a change of clothes and wanted to know if I needed anything. When I let her know I didn't, she hesitated and then blurted.

"You know I can't become a Christian—I'm Jewish, and my family would disown me and..."

I was a bit taken aback by her comments. "Whoa, whoa. Who says you need to become a Christian?"

"Well I'm just saying that this is weird, and I can tell something is going on—some power or presence since you've been here, and, well, I dunno."

I pushed the phone closer to my ear and stood up. "Listen, all I've done is to call on the Holy Spirit—I'm not even clear on what or who that is—just that it's the presence of God on earth, maybe." I pulled on the black phone cord, twisting it around my fingers.

Daryl sighed and didn't say anything else, so I took another breath and continued, tapping my foot on the shiny sterile hospital floor and said, "In any case, I do think He's here. I also think He's sending people to be here with us. I think He sent you—because you've been incredible—for me and for Daniel's family." She sniffled a short cry. I did the same. "No one's asking you to convert. Just be here as you have been."

I didn't know if Daniel would be healed, but it did seem like some supernatural force was in play. We kept a vigil at his bedside for as long as the hospital staff would allow but were often sent to the waiting room. Walking around the large hospital complex was all I could do to calm my nervousness, and I always bumped into people from the MICU. We all needed to escape the *holdyourbreath* atmosphere of the place. "We're praying for little Daniel from Spain," they said. I remember thinking that we were connected in a dark beauty that enveloped our minds every waking moment.

When I returned to the unit, Adolfo asked me to read them the story of Daniel in The Lion's Den. I was surprised when they had told me earlier that they were not familiar with the story. I didn't have a Spanish Bible with me, so I had to translate after every few sentences.

"Okay, let's see...Daniel, Chapter 6:6 starts out with: 'So the administrators and princes went to the king and said, 'Long live King Darius!'"

"Darius?" Carmen asked. "His name was Darius?"

"Yes! But I had forgotten that!"

"That's the name of our Daniel's doctor!"

It gave me a chill as I continued to read the story of a man whose uncompromising faith provoked the king to send him to the lion's den, saying to Daniel, *"May your God, whom you worship continually, rescue you."* Alive the next morning, Daniel said, *"My God sent his angel to shut the lions' mouths."*

Surely the connected names of Daniel and Darius were a sign that God would send His angel and *our* Daniel would be saved.

After five days in MICU, the routine felt like a movie, sometimes in slow motion, other times so fast, I couldn't breathe from having to quickly translate grim news about Daniel's condition. On the fifth day, the doctors told us they were going to implant a stent in his coronary artery to try to open things up and improve blood flow. Daniel would be making history as one of the first pediatric coronary artery stent recipients ever. If the procedure went well, they told us, he would be transferred to the Cardiac Intensive Care Unit. I watched the activity as a staff of forty medical professionals prepared Daniel for the procedure. There was an air of anticipation as they wheeled him to the catherization lab. I held Carmen's hand, but we dared not talk.

Hours later, when Dr. Darius entered the room, I tried to read his face. Was that a smile?

"It was a huge success." He exhaled, wiped his brow, and smiled. "But he's not out of the woods yet. In time, we believe he has a good chance for a full recovery. He'll still need the surgery, but this should buy us about six months of time, allowing him to heal."

It was the news we were dying to hear.

Now that the worst had passed, I knew I needed to get home, but I hated to leave them. The nurses in the Cardiac Intensive Care Unit were less attentive and seemed less interested in little Daniel than those in the medical ICU. Something didn't feel right. Folding myself into the cab to head back to Logan International, Adolfo's warm brown eyes locked on mine.

"No te preocupes." Don't worry. *He* was trying to comfort *me*.

I felt as helpless as I feel now. In those six days, Carmen, Adolfo, Daryl, and I had an experience that bonded us for life. It was the kind of connection I imagine was forged by young soldiers in battle—people so blown away by what they'd experienced, they were forever changed and forever connected by the need to acknowledge something they'd never want to relive but couldn't escape. The rest of the world was ignorant of just how bad things could get, keeping on with their daily lives, oblivious to the torment we'd known.

The next morning back at home, I awoke early and immediately went to the phone to call Daryl. "He's stable, thank God," she told me. I grabbed my own little Eric and hugged him hard—relieved and grateful that Daniel seemed to be doing so well, glad my own boy had been spared the horrors of catastrophic health issues. I spent the rest of the day reading to him and watching the coverage of the Clinton inauguration, in between praying that Daniel would continue to improve.

At 6:00 A.M. the following day, the phone rang.

"Susan," Daryl screamed. "He's gone! He's gone! One of the doctors put a chest tube into him, and he had a heart attack and died! Oh my God!"

I couldn't believe what was happening. They were on the way to the crematorium. Guilt rushed through me like a hurricane. I had picked the hospital. I picked the doctor. I prayed for them, read the Bible, prayed some more. Gave them false hope.

God, why have you allowed this? I didn't know what to believe. If *this* was going to be the result, then a just and loving God should have allowed Daniel to die after the first heart attack. *How dare You lead us to believe he'd be healed?* I was sure it was God who'd gotten our hopes up, only to let them crash further to the ground. If God heard but didn't care, I didn't see the point in praying or reading the Bible. Were those moments—those precious, real moments when we felt a loving Presence—some kind of group hallucination?

I didn't understand why God was there for Randy, the Hell's Angel guy, in his hour of need, but not for us.

❧

After Daniel died, the only thing that got me out of bed was my own three-year-old, Eric. Nothing I had previously experienced compared with losing a child. Everything hurt. Everything was pointless. Who cared who won the Super Bowl or what some starlet wore to The Academy Awards ceremony? Carmen and Adolfo's *child* was dead!

Jack was as supportive as he could be, but I needed to talk about it almost nonstop. My friends stepped in and saved me. Both MJ, the former-cheerleader-turned-intellectual, and Julie, my former college roommate, patiently listened to me lament about my guilt and how I felt so betrayed by God for what happened to Daniel. Now they were both sounding boards for my grief. The three of us met at least once a week for dinner for what turned out to be deep philosophical, spiritual, and political conversations that would last for four or five hours at a time.

I told myself that we didn't invite Jodi very often because of her heavy drinking, which by then had proven to be a life-threatening problem. When I was honest with myself, though, I had to admit that our avoidance was mainly because of her openly gay lifestyle. Being around her made me uncomfortable, but I couldn't fully explain why.

Funny how we rail against what we hate in ourselves. How we hide and fake it. How I hate myself now! I'm forty-one and not at all who I thought I was. God isn't who I thought He was. I have no idea how to go on.

With suicides on both sides of my family, my DNA seems set for self-destruct. Aunt Nora didn't lose her sanity like Dad and Aunt Mary Ellen did, but I wonder if she battled it secretly, as I do now. Did she sometimes pick up the phone, as I do, to confess to a friend how close she was to packing it all in, only to lose her nerve and babble about some unimportant topic?

My sensitive, caring father couldn't stand to go on because he hadn't been able to stop his sister's suicide. I know the feeling; I haven't been able to stop loved ones from dying.

⚘

Carrie called three months after Daniel's death. She was probably the sweetest friend I've ever had. "Mind if I stop by?"

"Of course not. I'd love to see you!"

Carrie explained that she was going to the Cleveland Clinic for heart surgery the following day. The doctors were going to do a new procedure; a visiting cardiovascular surgeon from the UK planned to replace not only her malfunctioning heart valve, but also use her own pulmonary valve as the replacement, and then replace that with a synthetic valve.

"Why don't I know about this?"

"I didn't want to worry you. I know you went through a lot with your friends from Spain."

I worried that it was a mathematical impossibility to be equally safe if they were replacing two valves instead of one, and I tried to talk her out of agreeing to the procedure, but she assured me that they were such "nice" people who promised her all would go well. They sent flowers and quoted her statistics that she seemed to accept without question.

"Don't worry," she said, "I trust them. It'll turn out okay."

I hugged her in my driveway. "You know I'll be praying for you, right? Tell Gary to call me when you're out of surgery, 'kay?"

"Of course, don't worry! I'll be fine."

I stroked her hair and looked into her eyes. Time stopped, and we had a long conversation—her eyes and mine. She pulled away, and as we let go of one another, I was flooded with the feeling that I would never see her again.

Carrie got in her car and pulled away.

I sobbed and then turned to walk into my house to call Jack.

"Carrie is having heart surgery tomorrow. She just left here," I sobbed as soon as he picked up the phone. "They talked her into a new procedure, and I have a bad feeling about it."

"You're probably just overreacting." *Try not to worry, everything's going to be fine.* "But anyway, I'm sorry to hear she needs that, and I'll be praying for her."

The next day, Carrie's husband, Gary, called me to say that all had gone well with her surgery. The news came as both a relief and a surprise because I had felt so certain I would never see her again. Was that because of what we had been through with Daniel? I didn't know and chastised myself for expecting the worst.

That evening as I read a story to Eric, the phone rang.

"Susan, it's Gary."

"Gary! What's goin' on? How's she doin'?"

"Not well." He choked out a small cry. "She's had a massive heart attack."

"What?"

"They told me that the sutures on one of the valves didn't hold. Susan, she's on life support."

I couldn't speak. Once again, all I could do was pray.

I found out later that Carrie was placed on an ECMO machine, the same kind of life support that little Daniel had been on just months earlier. I didn't visit her at the hospital. I told myself that it was a time for just her family, but the truth was, I couldn't bear it. The thought of my sweet friend on that machine, bloated and dying, was more than I could take at that point.

The next day, her doctors told Gary that she needed a heart transplant. They desperately searched for a donor heart.

By then, Gary's spirit knew what mine had known all along. "They'll never find one big enough," he said.

Carrie died a few days later. She was forty-one. That very special number. I roared in pain over her loss and regretted not going to the hospital to see her. My grief turned to anger. How in the world could God take both Daniel and Carrie? They were two very loved and needed people, and the rest of us were left to face life without them. What good could possibly come from that? I was furious at God, and nothing could stop my growing anger.

I am so sick of trying to make God and people happy and having things turn out wrong—people dying around me. I can't change it. I can't trust the God I thought I knew.

Put prayers like quarters into the slot and pull the handle, get a miracle. I guess that's what I've been expecting. I'm kicking the machine now, trying to tip it over to get either the candy or my money back.

I am still a child.

Thirty-one

Houston, We Have a Problem

I FACE THE MOUNTAIN OF DIRTY laundry that still awaits me in the laundry room, a metaphor in fabric for what life has piled onto me. I pull a load of clean clothes from the dryer and hold Eric's and Allison's warm clothing to my face. Allison's green and white basketball uniform conjures hot Saturdays at the Y's gym and her eight-year-old frustration when well-intentioned parents shout, "Good job!" She knows it's one of many compliments without merit in a non-competitive league. "Why are they telling me 'good job'? *That* was terrible!" she'd say in exasperation. She was right.

Here's an old striped shirt from Target that Eric no longer wants to wear. At thirteen, he's starting to care about his wardrobe. I love these kids so much I can't even wrap my mind around the enormity of it. I always loved the honesty and innocence of children, but it wasn't until I had my own that I understood how crazy in love I could be with these little beings.

Little? How quickly the infant and the toddler turned into the third-grader and middle-schooler pacified by the TV upstairs. Nothing is more important to me than these two. I want what's best for them, but I'm not sure what that is. If I do it right, "checking out" might be the simplest and best solution all around.

A screech makes me jump, knock over a basket of clean clothes, and swear. Eric freezes in the doorway, a look of alarm on his face at my reaction to the un-oiled hinge.

"Sorry, I thought you were upstairs," I say.

He approaches me gently. "Mom. Aren't you going to drop us off at Miss Annette's? You have an appointment, right? Don't we have to leave…" He gives me the onceover, frowning with worry as he looks at my hair. "…like in half an hour?"

His eyes are soft. I brush back his hair. "Yeah, I know. Just trying to get everything done, sweetie."

Allie edges around the corner. I can see that she is watching me too. The looks on their faces say, *We've tiptoed across eggshells to make sure Mom isn't coming unglued.* They are handling me the way I used to handle my dad. *Shit.* I don't want to do this to them.

I smooth my hair, run a washcloth under cold water, and dab around my eyes. I smile. "Just give me a couple more minutes."

Whatever I do, I won't continue to let my worries and fears force my kids to live with an elephant in the living room. I can't subject them to the kind of forces that trampled my own childhood but could never be mentioned.

A mother's suicide might scar them terribly, of course, possibly worse than having a mother who is an abomination. It might establish a terrible precedent for them in the way that my suicidal family's ghastly solutions have for me. If I just bail out when life gets really hard, I might be enabling them to do the same. They might not have the strength to get past their own forty-one. A shudder spreads out from my spine.

And yet, how do I go on?

I heard a woman's voice, and it changed everything.

I'm exhausted; everywhere I turn I see unwelcome reminders. I can't even pass the black and white photo of Jack and the kids and me, all smiling, without deepening my despair because I remember what was going through my mind back then. Taken five years earlier, it captured the happiness I felt at knowing that I had found Charlotte, another human on the planet who loved me, who listened and understood, the deepest connection I'd ever known. At the time, it didn't feel incongruent with my marriage. It was separate, special and pure. I was happy being a mom, enjoying each day. Too bad that now it seems there was an expiration date on love—mine for Jack, hers for me.

Then I pass a floral painting of Dad's, another finger pointing at me. He signed his name in that funky Christian-Fish-Symbol way and then added "Phil 4:13." I don't need to look it up to know that it says, "I can do all things through Christ who strengthens me." Believing that had helped sustain me in the past. But what now? The faith I professed is now my tormentor.

I should have told the kids that I'd been growing uncomfortable with the Evangelical world for years. Instead, I kept taking them to church, hoping, I suppose, that something miraculous would happen. Things happened all right. At the Crossroads Southern Baptist Church, I was told I couldn't teach an adult Sunday school class because women can't teach men, according to scriptures in some of the writings of Paul—which scholars have since discredited. I didn't want my kids growing up with that mentality. Solid Christian foundations proved as elusive as the rainbow mist from the sun's rays hitting the sprinklers outside.

Other church members didn't seem to struggle with their faith the way I did. The worst incident had occurred back while we were still in Ohio, and Father Will instituted certain changes at church designed to promote "unity." Jack and I had viewed the new policies as coercion that required blind obedience—not a good trade-off. "My take is that the guy's in over his head, trying to lead this church," Jack said. I didn't disagree. We decided it was best to leave and asked him to our house one Saturday morning. After our conversation, we were confident that we had closed on good terms, agreeing to disagree. We still cared about the church and believed Father Will meant well but didn't understand us or the nature of our faith.

The following Sunday, we heard that Father Will used his sermon to denounce us along with another couple as agents of the "The Evil One."

The *Evil One?* As in *Satan, the Red Devil?* I couldn't believe it. We had spent nearly seven years of our lives as a part of the church "family" only to be identified as Satanic cohorts! It didn't help that there was no moral outrage about the whole thing. No one said, "Hey, wait a minute, we know them, they've been leading our youth groups and CRHP retreats. This isn't true!" Instead, like sheep, they said nothing. Only my dear Carrie had decided *enough was enough* and left with us. I told myself to swallow my bitterness, move on, and not look back, but it was a bruising jab in the face.

So one moment, the frame of our religion made our lives as comfortable as a Norman Rockwell scene, and the next, sent them up in smoke. The true nature of that particular frame would come years later. I read a blog entry from Father Will regarding the Episcopal Church's election of its first openly gay bishop, Gene Robinson. Father Will broke from the church in outrage, and wrote: "I don't ever say I've left the Episcopal Church. I just say the Episcopal Church has left me." A few clicks later, I found further information on the topic. This time it wasn't from Father Will, but from his former wife, a woman who started a coaching practice, in part, to assist people like her—people who'd discovered their spouses were gay. (Should I give Jack her number?) *Apparently, Father Will didn't mind that Bishop Robinson was gay, just that he was open about it!*

So is religion letting me down? Or am I letting it down?

Am I in this struggle alone? Who will stand by me now?

The black lace fan with red embroidery gracing my bookshelf, a present from my friends in Spain, reminds me of their warm circle and how important it is to me. I'm not sure about what they think about the topic, but risking the loss of their love and respect is almost too much to think about. Through the years, we've stayed close, visiting once or sometimes twice per year. They are family, people who have shown themselves able to handle whatever or whomever I am. But they might see me now as having changed too much. What if I become an abomination in their eyes too?

And here is the one Christmas decoration I leave out all year, one small Santa, bought just before I found out the terrifying prognosis for Eric before he was born. It stands for the kind of miracle Eric's birth represents and therefore reminds me to be joyful. Now, I often argue with it when I pass. Where was little Daniel's miracle? And Cheryl's and Carrie's? My dad should still be around for Christmases, I tell it. It never seems to feel guilty. It just keeps radiating joy. I let it. It also makes me feel guilty, though, as it grins over my own near-sightedness.

That same Christmas Eric was born, Jack and I got together with our gang of non-church friends for a celebration at a local restaurant. Near the middle of the long table of more than twenty people, we sat near MJ, Julie and her husband, and Jodi with her girlfriend, Annie, who wore black leather pants and a red shirt. Black leather wristbands with sharp silver metal studs completed her ensemble.

I immediately didn't like Annie and avoided most conversation with her, mingling with others before the meal was served. Carol and I compared pregnancy experiences—she was due at the same time. *So how are you feeling? No problems, really good, actually. You? Ready for it to be over.*

"I could never stand to be pregnant," spiky Annie said. Somehow she'd managed to hone in on my avoidance, as if eager to provoke something. My eyes narrowed, and Jodi quickly joined us. I wanted to run for the door.

Shortly after dessert, Jodi and Annie left, probably feeling my not-so-welcoming vibe. I picked up on a conversation that MJ was leading about gay rights. Her tone was insistent, but unlike me, she was always able to keep her composure and make her point without sounding contentious.

"Listen, I'm just curious how he can justify denying gay people their constitutional rights."

One of the husbands laughed. "What constitutional rights don't they get? They get the same thing we all do."

MJ sat up straight, lifted her long hair through her thumb and forefinger, and pulled it back behind her head, whereupon it fell forward again. Her voice got higher, the only indication she was upset. "Are you serious?"

I couldn't help but jump in. "You mean marriage and all?"

Chris stayed silent—lost interest, in fact.

"Well, that's part of it." MJ exhaled like she couldn't believe we could be so naïve. She made another attempt at controlling her hair, pushing it behind her ear. "There are other things too. The right to hold a job without fear of discrimination, the right to live where they want to live. The right to visit their partner in a hospital, receive the same tax benefits. Those kinds of things and more."

"But wait a minute," I said, "Jack and I just would *not*, for instance, be able to rent the first floor of our duplex to a gay couple. We don't agree with that *lifestyle*—it's against our religion."

MJ was incredulous. "So you wouldn't rent to two people who were in a loving relationship just because they were the same gender?"

I tried to make what I was saying sound not so bad. "Well, it's just that we don't want our soon-to-be born child to be exposed to that *lifestyle*."

"Is that fair?"

"Well, it's our house—"

"Yes, but you couldn't use race, for example, as a reason not to rent to someone."

"That's different. Race is genetic. Being gay is a set of behaviors."

"But it *is* genetic, Susan! Those 'behaviors' you mention are what people exhibit *because* they're gay." She lit a cigarette, exhaled the smoke, and looked in my eyes. "Have you ever wondered why you're so particularly uncomfortable with this? Why you seem so homophobic?"

Her comment flew over my head. I refused to see what she might be insinuating. I couldn't begin to go there. I hadn't even imagined a personal glimmer of possibility in a same-sex attraction.

Until Charlotte.

※

A voice, urgent but southern and soothing. "Y'all, this child has *got* to see a doctor!"

I will never forget her voice that day. I didn't know then that my world was about to change, but the honey in its tone registered somewhere deep in my soul. I heard a woman's voice, and my truest response turned me into an abomination in the sight of my family and other fellow Christians.

Jack and I were buying a home in Houston when the builder's receptionist told us that our blue-eyed boy of five years sat crying under one of the desks at the builder's office. Eric's chronic sinusitis would sometimes appear with little or no warning. Before I had time to come up with a plan to find a doctor, the receptionist, a woman I'd never met before, called her family doctor and scheduled an appointment.

Her name was Charlotte.

Her quick and compassionate action gave me one more reason to feel good about the house we had purchased. A few months later, I enrolled Eric in "Mother's Day Out," a fabulous, practically free, church baby-sitting service that was probably a desperate attempt to recruit new members. Whatever it was, I didn't care, so long as he was safe and happy and not telling me how bored he was. With Allison strapped in her car seat, I headed for the sales office to make design selections for our new house. Allison hated that seat. On the long drive from the temporary apartment in Houston, she would invariably find a way out. She had a Houdini-like ability to wiggle out of those straps and the stealth to do it without my notice. I'd look in the rearview mirror to change lanes and see her standing up, a big smile on her face and curly brown hair sticking up all over her precious head.

At the sales office, I thought of Charlotte's kindness. Hoping to thank her, I learned she'd been promoted and sent to another site nearby.

So, Allison, sweetie, let's go find Miss Charlotte.

With beads of sweat running down my back from the intense Houston heat and humidity, I pulled the blue and white stroller out of the trunk and opened the back door. I started to wrestle with the car seat strap in order to liberate my beautifully chubby baby girl.

She looked at me with glee in her green eyes. Freedom! I kissed her round cheek and marveled for the millionth time at how much love I could feel.

Once I folded her into the fabric of the stroller, I pushed her along toward the new models where I had been told I could find Charlotte. I felt under-dressed and out of place in the world of realtors, but I wanted to find her and congratulate her on her promotion. Charlotte seemed thrilled to see us. Her smiling brown eyes shined through her stylish eyeglass frames. She wore her dark brown hair short and perfectly coiffed. A blue and white floral print dress accentuated her long legs and busty figure, making me feel even more under-dressed, but still glad we'd stopped in. Even then I thought she was gorgeous, but I didn't allow myself to ponder what that might mean. After a few minutes of chitchat, we decided to meet for lunch the following week at a local homespun restaurant in a strip mall, like most of Houston's restaurants.

As we began to talk on that first of many lunches, I remember thinking that it felt somewhat like an interview. Charlotte tried to figure out who I really was as I gave careful answers to her pointed questions, flattered by her interest. The woman was *hearing* me, not just nodding and thinking of what she was going to say next.

When we finally got around to her turn, she said she was from Austin, twice divorced and re-married with three kids. Her past fascinated me. She'd been a hippie during the sixties, going ten years without shaving her legs or eating meat. Looking across the table at the well-accessorized suburban career woman eating chicken salad, I could hardly believe that this was the same person.

Charlotte told great stories about musical heroes like Janis Joplin, Willie Nelson, Bette Midler, Eric Clapton, and Carlos Santana. She'd met them and others during a time when she was part owner of a rock-n-roll emporium called The Armadillo World Headquarters. She was thirteen years older than my thirty-two years, but she certainly didn't look it.

At the end of our lunch, she asked, "So, was that good? Can we do it again sometime?"

"Of course. I really enjoyed it."

She offered to help me decorate my new house. I was glad because I didn't know how to integrate my somewhat traditional furniture into my somewhat contemporary home. Something told me that my new acquaintance with her eclectic tastes was well suited for the task. She swooped into a room and took a panoramic view of the entire space, her interior design radar properly calibrated. We made many excursions in search of items for my house and hers, each trip laden with deep conversations, delving into all kinds of issues, including her sixties-saturated adventures.

"One time, when I was high on LSD, I wanted to feel what flying felt like. So Mike and Jeff tied me onto the roof of the car, and I spread my arms and—"

"WHAT?" It was like watching a makeover show, looking at the "Before" and "After" pictures, trying to see what had happened in the process.

Charlotte became the tonic to the graciously unspoken assumptions of my ignorance. She challenged me with new examples and perspectives. She also soothed me with her gentle suggestions that I look beyond archetypes and labels and really see something authentic in myself. Our friendship and understanding grew as Charlotte began to unbury me with her stories and her questions.

One day, fairly early in our shopping forays—she was looking, I was spending—she blurted, "You know, I was raped. Yes, in my own home, with a knife pointed at my baby's head."

I could barely inhale before she continued, recounting what had occurred some twenty years before. She was home alone with her six-week-old baby asleep on her chest. Charlotte awoke to find an angry man in her room. Somehow she made it through it all, and when he was gone, called the police. Her mother called as the police arrived, and Charlotte answered it in a state of shock. "Momma, I've been raped." And her mother said, "What? No, you haven't, honey. Bye now."

That was it—all her mother ever said about it. I wondered if that had been as damaging as the rape itself, and Charlotte said that it had been.

Even though it was early in our relationship, I instinctively wanted to protect her from any future violence, and I cherished the ability we had to talk about anything—when people in our own families couldn't approach certain radioactive matters even if they were in a space suit.

Lunches, shopping sprees, years went by. Like removing layers of wallpaper to get to the original surface, I got past all facades and learned more and more of her story. She entrusted her past with me more than I did mine with her—mostly because she was more aware of how it had shaped her and what it all meant. I, on the other hand, was lonely and angry much of the time, hiding from something I couldn't see, pretending all was lovely.

My fundamental Christianity baffled her. I was a former Catholic attending the Southern Baptist Church, and she was a former Southern Baptist attending the Catholic Church. Whenever we talked about social, philosophical, or religious issues, I felt like I got such a new perspective on things. I often disagreed with her new angles and would have thought I'd prefer hard labor to sitting and listening to them, yet she had a way of making me ponder my most deeply held beliefs.

We talked about gay rights at times. Charlotte was for them, and I opposed them. It wasn't that I hated gay people, I said, I just hated what *they did.*

"Why do gay people bother you so much? Why are you so damn homophobic?" she asked.

Déjà vu. "*Me?* Why Jodi, my best friend from high school, is gay! Brian too! I fell in love with him." *Whadyamean I'm homophobic?*

Her raised eyebrows proclaimed *thou-protesteth-too-loudly.*

Charlotte didn't believe in "gay" and "straight." She believed in people loving people. She thought anyone could be attractive if you really *saw* them. She also said she thought we were moving toward a future where we wouldn't care about the gender of our partner as much as we care about how we feel about them.

After we had known each other for four years, it was becoming apparent that she was serious about those beliefs. I had just said good-bye and left her house to walk to my car, when she made the challenge that pretty much got the ball rolling.

"Do that again."

She had wanted to see me walk away again. A seductive come hither, go away—ironically marking the sweet beginning and fore-shadowing the cold ending of our relationship.

I was, of course, stunned and thought that I'd somehow misinterpreted her. But she crinkled her nose at me, and I blushed and reacted awkwardly. I felt wholly appreciated, noticed.

A few weeks later, I decided to show Charlotte something I had written about my faith, my struggle with my body image, and bulimia. I had spent so much of my life hating my body and hiding my secret addiction, but with her I felt safe enough to share my deepest fears. She read the piece and spoke softly, expressing sympathy, and she'd researched bulimia so she could understand it and know me better. Her caring attention amazed me, melted me, felt like balm on wounds. She wasn't afraid to address it; she didn't simply sweep it under the rug. She'd never contemptuously dismiss it as "spilling the beans."

She shared the difficulties of her history with me too, and her confidence honored me. We were driving through the rain one night in our carefully manicured master-planned community, and she told me that she suffered through four miscarriages. It took six pregnancies to produce two newborns over the course of four years. Her account of the babies moved me. She said that their passing had been more difficult to bear than the rape. Right before her first son was born, she had been assaulted, and it had transformed her naïve view of the world.

"But wait," I said, "before he was born? I thought it happened with the knife at his head."

"Oh it did, but six months into my pregnancy, I was driving to a party out in the country when a man motioned to me that I had a flat tire. Then he dragged me out of the car by my hair to the woods where he violated me." A pregnant woman.

She'd been raped twice. I wept that night, wishing I could get revenge on the bastards.

After her son was born, Charlotte wanted a life away from the music business, the drugs, and the late nights. With only ten dollars in her pocket, she bought a dress and a razor. Armed with the Yellow Pages, she looked up the most prominent businessman in Austin and arrived at his office at 10:00 A.M. With her baby tucked into his carrier and placed just outside the door of the office, she made her pitch to the secretary, telling her she'd be the company's number one producer if given the chance. The secretary politely declined to ring the man, and Charlotte thanked her and left. For the next three days, she repeated the process, in the same dress, at the same office with the same results. Finally, on the fifth day, the secretary relented, and Charlotte was allowed to make her prediction come true. This woman just blew me away.

⚜

She handed me a box, artfully wrapped, that first Christmas our families spent together.

Suddenly shy and hesitant, I peeled back the gold paper and lifted an ornate, round mirror. "I like it, I mean, you know I still need a lot for the walls of this house."

"You don't get it. Look in it. The present—it's *you*."

She had a way of healing me unlike anything I'd ever experienced, and before I knew what was going on, I realized that I was in love with her.

Thirty-two

The Sexless Soul

MY LOVE FOR CHARLOTTE BOTH frightened and excited me. How could I be attracted to her, as well as to men? It caught me completely off guard. I'd met friends of Jodi's—lesbians who wore plaid shirts and mullets. Surely I couldn't be one of them, *but I love her. I love her.*

In a great humility borne of the harsh judgments I used to hold, I now understand viscerally that my attraction to Charlotte grew out of so many things other than gender. The connection and comfort I felt with her made me happy. This feeling can't be forbidden, it just *is.* I knew in my heart I couldn't *not* love this woman. Maybe that sounds odd to most people, but should it? True relationships are not mostly about sex, and who we are is not mainly sexual.

As Marianne Williamson pointed out, "The soul has no sex—it has been poured into our body." How ironic that *religious* people— who supposedly care so much about the soul—are the very ones who most want to reduce human identity down to our sexuality.

❦

"Mom, remember we have to go to the hardware store for balsa wood." My eight-year-old jerks me back to reality. She knows she needs to keep me on top of things.

Five minutes later, Eric asks, "Mom, is *my* basketball uniform out of the dryer yet?"

I somehow had washed only Allison's in the first load. Both Allie and Eric spend time at the babysitter's even when I am not working because they are friends with her kids, a woman they politely call,

"Miss Annette." Her life revolves around kids, coaching, and carpooling. She's always had a the-more-the-merrier approach toward the kids in the neighborhood, especially on game days. She's been a godsend to our family.

It is now 12:30. At the most, I have fifteen minutes before I have to get out the door. I hurry to the laundry room and check the uniform. Still damp.

"Honey, check it again right before we leave. Have you seen my keys?"

My cell phone rings, and I recognize the phone number as Jodi's but let it go to voicemail. Too rushed. I'm glad that she's back in my life, though, after a four-year absence, owing to the fact that I couldn't tolerate her coming out as gay. (Go ahead, laugh.)

We first got back together when I was cautiously aware that the friendship I had cultivated with Charlotte was feeling like so much more. Jodi was planning to be in Houston and took a chance on calling me to ask if we could have dinner. I agreed and insisted she stay with us, knowing I had some apologizing to do, wishing I could make retroactive apologies for my narrow-mindedness all the way back to Uncle Art.

She said to meet her at The Galleria, which was about an hour from my house. I spent the drive thinking about what I would say to her.

"It's been a long time," I said, hugging her small frame.

"Yeah, too, too long." She smiled and cleared her throat.

We sat at the bar to wait for our table.

"Listen," I said, "before we say or do anything else, I need to tell you how sorry I am for making you feel bad all of these years. I wish I could take it back. I've really missed you."

"Don't worry. I'm just glad we're talking now. I know too that some of the distance between us has been a result of my drinking."

"Yeah, that's true, but a lot of it was because you're gay. And the ironic thing is that I have a story of my own to tell you." I cleared my throat, trying to think how I would begin.

Her already large brown eyes grew even bigger. Through drinks and dinner, we chatted. I revealed my feelings for Charlotte. She described her horrible relationship with spiky Annie who actually beat her a few times before Jodi could walk away. We talked about love versus obsession. I finally worked up the nerve to ask what she thought I should do and described some of the things that Charlotte had said to me and the clues she'd dropped.

"So, what d'ya think?" I asked. "Do you think she might feel the same way? Maybe that it's progressed to more than a friendship?'

Jodi grinned. "Does she have to hit you with a frying pan?"

❧

After my conversation with Jodi, it took me another two months to approach Charlotte about what was going on. I finally asked her to pick me up and take me somewhere, anywhere. By then I'd known her for *four* years.

"Where to?"

"Um... I uh... Anywhere, I don't care. I just need a private space where we can talk."

We listened to music in her car, and she drove along, patiently waiting for whatever it was I needed to say. She was like that. She didn't need to hear explanations. It was one of the things I loved about her. She had a way of making me feel calm and validated. Mostly though, it was that she knew me—really *knew* me and could figure out what was going on in my head long before I could.

I tried to think of some way to tell her how much I loved her, how I had fallen in love with my best friend and confidante, unwittingly at first and with no idea what to do with the feelings, but it was a truth that needed acknowledgment in words... or... music? I agonized for three days over and finally just let Bonnie Raitt do it for me.

Something in your eyes, makes me want to lose myself,
Makes me want to lose myself, in your arms.

She understood what I was trying to say. She felt it too, and was even matter-of-fact about it. That was the simple part, a statement of the obvious. There it was, just as it had been for some time, but now we had acknowledged it and made it breathe.

"Once you say something out loud, it's real," she said.

I was mostly just grateful to know that she felt as I did, and we both worried about where to go with it. Sometimes we pretended that it wasn't anything out of the ordinary, knowing inside that it was the most extraordinary of things. What would this knowledge do to the attraction? To us? She said it was Pandora's Box and that we'd have to see if our pure relationship could survive and change into something more, not less.

I didn't know what she meant then, but I do now.

※

The secrecy of our newly defined relationship became soil for my deceit, grounds for white lies, omissions, and broken promises that hurt Jack and the kids. *Running errands* usually meant I was hungry for Charlotte's presence and needed to follow her around as *she* ran to the dry cleaner, shoe store, and post office. Afterwards, we'd have a long lunch laden with champagne. I'd return home, starry-eyed and half there.

New Year's Eve that year stands out in my mind. My sister, Ann, accompanied us to Austin for the weekend. We returned to Houston with plans to celebrate the New Year at home, but since I hadn't seen Charlotte for three days, I was antsy. By ten that evening, the tension was more than I could bear. Ann understood Charlotte to be merely my best friend.

"Ann and I are going to pop over to Charlotte's for a quick drink," I told Jack, fully intending to return within an hour.

His eyes pleaded. "But it's late. You know how the kids like to celebrate the dropping of the ball."

"We'll be back, don't worry."

Ann and I scurried out the door before he could protest any more. Fifteen minutes later, Charlotte greeted us with a cheery "Happy New Year" and then poured us several glasses of champagne.

By the time we returned home, it was a new year. Although Eric had fallen asleep before eleven, Allie had been waiting.

"Honey, did you see the ball drop?" I asked as I tucked her in.

"Yes, but Mommy, where were you? Daddy and I were waiting."

"I'm sorry, baby, I lost track of time and—"

Jack flipped on the light in Allie's room.

"How could you? We were waiting! It's New Year's, for God's sake. Do you always have to go running over there?"

Rightfully enraged, he punched the wall and stormed off. A tear slid down Allie's cheek.

I hated myself for behaving this way, and I wish I could say it only happened once, but such encounters happened fairly often. I couldn't seem to stay away from the magic of Charlotte's attention, her caring, and her captivating presence. Even when I chose times that didn't interfere with my home life, I knew I was betraying Jack's love—such as it was. The weight of the guilt I felt was that of an elephant—a presence made of lies that I had created, the kind of mammoth I detested from my own childhood.

❧

Within six months, an array of physical symptoms plagued me. Exhausted all the time, I suffered headaches and pain that seared my hands and feet down to the bone. My legs tingled so severely they felt like they were buzzing; my jaw and face went numb. Bouts of diarrhea and urinary tract infections further zapped my strength. Mysterious rashes appeared and then disappeared suddenly.

Four months of testing at the Texas Medical Center left me without a clear diagnosis. My neurologist stuck needles into me to draw spinal fluid and tested my muscles against jolts of electricity. We awaited the results of the MRI. My rheumatologist looked me over and drew blood, which was then spun and analyzed. I waited for a call from his office and was surprised when instead I found a letter in my mailbox explaining I had a rare, stroke-causing disease called Anti-phospholipid Antibody Syndrome. I needed a blood thinner or I would risk life-threatening strokes. Further evaluation was needed to confirm the additional possibility of MS. I was scared and feeling vulnerable; fortunately, Jack was supportive as we awaited further news from the results of my MRI.

On the eleventh anniversary of my father's death, the doctor's office called me. The white markings on my MRI indicated probable Multiple Sclerosis. It was the news I was afraid of. I told Jack what the doctor had said, and he gave me a quick hug. I went to my room and picked up a photograph of Dad, touched his face.

"Daddy, I wish you were here to help me through this—I am so, so scared."

After sobbing into my pillow, I washed my face and staggered downstairs. Jack was sitting at the dining room table, head in his hands. My heart went out to him. *He's probably so worried about how he'll take care of the kids and me.*

I approached him quietly, thinking that he had been so kind throughout my ordeal with the doctors despite the fact that I hadn't been fair to him. Although I hadn't technically "cheated" by sleeping with Charlotte, I'd failed him all the same. So, as I approached, I wondered if maybe I should cut him some slack, find out if there was hope for us after all.

"Hon, what's wrong?"

He looked up at me, the face of disdain and anger I'd seen before but didn't expect in that moment.

"What's wrong? I'll tell you what's wrong. We have no fucking money, that's what's wrong."

I grabbed the side of the dining room chair to keep from falling over. I couldn't believe what I was hearing. He continued, his eyes bulging, beads of sweat forming on his forehead.

"We can't afford to continue to pay for private school for the kids."

I caught my breath long enough to choke out, "Well, I'm paying for the kids' school, remember? Don't worry, I'll handle it."

"You?" He looked at me, the ball and chain who'd ruined his life. "You'll never work again."

I couldn't breathe.

"I'm doing the taxes and trying to figure out what happened to my money."

There was Jack, going into the same gear as when I told him I had bulimia—the one that said *I've built a wall and don't want to deal with your problems.*

I pushed all the papers off the table with one backhand brush of my arm. "You're worried about our taxes when I've just been told I have MS?" I'd have walked away from him right then if I hadn't been so dependent. I leaned in closer, my glare, a tracking device honing in on his miserly soul. "Despite what you say, I will work again."

I stormed out of the house and went where I knew I was wanted and would find comfort: to Charlotte's.

"Honey, why don't you go and get a second opinion about all this?" Her Southern voice soothing, her hand on mine.

"It's taken months to get test results. I just don't know if I can afford to spend another three or four months going through more tests with different doctors. What if I have a massive stroke in the meantime?" It felt good to talk to someone who was listening.

"Well, you know, one of my clients went to the Mayo Clinic in Minnesota, and they gave her a diagnosis in less than a week."

That was all I needed to hear.

I called the department of vascular neurology and had an appointment for the following week. The only drawback was that the airfare was high on such short notice—$1,200. But I knew it was a small price to pay if I could get some answers quickly. When I told Jack, he was glad for me—right up to the point when I told him about the airfare.

"I think I'll just stay home and watch the kids."

The day before my trip, Charlotte hugged me and told me she wished she could go with me, but her fear of flying prevented it.

"Here, I got you something." She turned her head to the side and smiled at me with her eyes. I could feel her love as I accepted the gold and red gift bag that was the size of a grocery bag. Inside was a bottle of *Happy*, a red journal to record my thoughts on the trip, a fragrant, peace-inspiring candle, and a coffee-table book on the life and career of Hank Aaron. The woman really knew me. She couldn't accompany me to the Mayo Clinic, but desperately wanted to. I loved her for that and so much more.

Jack, on the other hand, could have accompanied me but wouldn't have, even if our marriage had been thriving.

Alone, I still faced diagnoses of multiple diseases that would at some point in the near future label me as unemployable and leave me to degenerate into an invalid, dependent on others for my care and a burden to my children. I prayed, of course, and I contacted my mother in Cleveland and arranged to meet her and her husband, Dan, in Rochester, Minnesota. I needed *somebody* to hug me when I got the news.

Mom and Dan kept mostly to themselves once we arrived at the hotel by the clinic. We shared breakfast before I went to the hospital, but they said they wouldn't be accompanying me for my first appointment. We'd catch up later.

Later? After I'd gone into shock and fainted from the catastrophic diagnosis I feared?

Knees trembling, I faced the barrage alone. Initial tests quickly revealed that the Texas doctors had made grossly incorrect interpretations of their tests, and I had neither Anti-phospholipid Antibody Syndrome nor MS. The doctor promised to get to the bottom of it all with a new round of extensive tests, at once filling me with hope, yet still terrifying me.

Shortly after receiving the initial good news, I got my hug, and then Mom and Dan took off. Their departure shocked me because they'd been with me for less than thirty minutes, and I still didn't know what was actually wrong with me. For all I knew, it could be worse than the Texas diagnosis. For three days, I felt utterly abandoned to my fears.

I had been the good daughter, the good wife, and yet what was the payoff for all that responsible behavior? Loneliness. It really just came down to me. I couldn't rely on others. So, the hell with them. As disheartening as this was, it was also—in that mysterious way of life's emotional journeys—my first baby step toward independence and liberation. I didn't have to live out a role any longer. I would find a new job back in corporate America so I could get my own benefits and start saving for the eventuality of divorce. I could support the kids. I felt a new surge of strength and purpose.

Fibromyalgia. That's what my tests revealed. I would have to learn to manage it, but I could live a reasonably normal life. I was grateful and hugely relieved. My mother called, crying, apologizing, wanting to come back and tour the Minneapolis Mall of America with me. I just wanted to get back to the kids, and to Charlotte. I marveled at how remarkably out-of-sync my mom and I were. Her stop-and-start dance typified our relationship. A one and a two and six-seven-and-eight—no rhythm, a cadence neither of us could predict. Dr. Looney, my therapist, called it her come-hither/go-away approach.

He was the only other person I could talk to about my love for Charlotte and the demise of my marriage. He challenged me to tell Jack the truth, but that was way too scary. I'd heard of people losing their kids over the issue, especially in Texas, and there was no way I would risk that. I still cared for Jack, but I didn't trust him or believe that he could ever understand me. So, I straddled both worlds: one foot in therapy, seeking the last dregs of love and hope in the bottom of our glass to save the marriage and spare my children the pain of a divorce, and one foot in a new world where there was love and understanding, but no commitment. Charlotte and I held hands, occasionally sharing kisses that sometimes turned passionate. Then there were those mystifying other times where what we had together felt like a road toward something more to me, but an obligation to her. She was distancing herself from me, and the more I sensed it, the more I pursued her. The more I pursued her, the harder she pulled away.

As time went on, my relationship with Charlotte felt like a re-run of my college relationship with Brian. Dr. Looney asked if it was like the come-hither/go-away relationship I had with my mother. Ugh. I hated the thought of any connection between my relationship with Charlotte and the one with my mother. I wanted to be an integrated person who made love to someone with whom I had a strong emotional connection. It's what turned me away from Jack and toward Charlotte.

Despite my feelings, and maybe because of them, Charlotte and I started having a communication breakdown. She said something about "the bubble bursting." I was in a constant search for a way to re-spark our relationship. Panicked and desperate one Friday, I drove my new convertible to her house. She opened the door, looked at me with a blank stare, and turned around without a word. *Was she mad at me? Was something wrong with her kids? Did she have a bad day?*

"Hi. You okay?" I followed her to the kitchen.

"I'm fine." Her voice dripped with disdain.

"So, um, I bought a new car—well, it's not a new car—but it's new to me. A convertible. Wanna go for a ride?"

Blank stare. "I don't think so." Her ice-coated words cut through me.

By then I felt like an emotional junky, so spun around I couldn't tell what was real and what wasn't, couldn't read her anymore. I was riding a bike on a bumpy trail down a hill, trying my best to avoid a big crash. Now, not only did she resist most of my attempts at affection, she appeared not to like me anymore. From "exciting" to "intolerable" in eighteen months.

I was crazy with grief.

⚜

A year of trying to re-ignite our relationship has produced little more than episodes of bad temper and drama. It's like I'm going through two divorces at the same time. I glance at my watch and realize I'm running late for my meeting with Jack. Now I have to face him, extricate myself from a toxic marriage, maintain enough cordiality to honor the many blessings we've had together, keep custody of the kids, and provide the right parental balance—given the destruction of their source of stability, the stalwart Christian family.

Part Five

Just As I Am

Thirty-three

Pachyderms

LATE AS USUAL, I WEAVE through stop-and-go traffic of weekend shoppers and soccer moms, tires screeching a bit as I make the turn into the Starbucks parking lot. Through the dirty windshield, I glimpse a tall man's head turning as it rises above those around him, seated near the door. No doubt Jack has been there awhile, arrived early. He's heard my tires and is saying "Finally!" to himself. Carefully planning what to say and how to say it, I nervously circle the parking lot before finding a spot. Halfway to the entrance, I drop my keys, bend down, and then watch in horror as my cell phone slips out of my pocket, skids across the asphalt and under another car. *Great. Perfect.*

I stumble inside, avoiding Jack's eyes. "Sorry I'm late," I mutter.

"No problem, I knew you would be; it's only seven minutes...," he smiles, nodding toward the parked cars outside, "...and then maybe another three or four if you count the parking lot." He offers me a chair.

I sit with my back to the window instead. "The glare, ya know?" I squeeze by him, the scent of his cologne mixing with the roasting coffee. My insides percolate like Java beans in boiling water. He's wearing designer jeans, a black knit shirt, loafers. He looks at me with the same ice blue eyes and handsome features that once attracted me so powerfully and that appear now in my children's faces.

"Can I get you a coffee?" he asks.

One more cup and I'm over the edge. "I'm fine, thanks. I drank a pot full this morning."

A gray-haired woman pushing a toddler in a stroller tries to maneuver her way through the door. Jack jumps up. "Let me get that for you." He opens the door with a smile for the grateful grandma.

As he sits back down, I feel worse, wishing he was a total jerk so I could divorce him without guilt. His eyes search mine, but I look the other way, focusing on in-store advertising that promises expertly blended beverages that will "delight me." *Right.* The only thing that can delight me right now is getting out of here.

Jack thanks me for meeting him. I reply as if it were the breeziest of things, hiding my shaking hands under the table. While Billie Holiday croons above the soft murmur of pleasant conversations, I wonder how long we can add to the good vibe of the place.

"Listen, I wasn't able to get the tax stuff together yet."

Jack shifts his weight and clears his throat, hiding his irritation, I can tell. "Oh, okay, well don't worry. Think you'll have it soon?"

I feign confidence despite the fact that I'm embarrassed and overwhelmed with the spinning plates in the juggling act of my life. "I'll get it to you next week at the latest."

"If you need any help getting the information together, let me know."

"No, I've got it covered. So, how's work?"

"The usual. How're the kids? I'm planning to pick them up for dinner tomorrow."

"Good." I stare at the dirt-darkened grout of the tile floor; the baby on the far side of the room starts to cry. A few more *that's-good-how-nice* exchanges, and I'm wondering when we can get to the point and get this over with. Jack takes a sip of his Venti, Two-Splenda Caramel Macchiato. Neither of us wants to start the chess match. A young couple sitting on the chocolate-brown velveteen couch to my left hugs each other and giggles. *Were we ever that happy?*

"Did you have the kids clean their rooms this morning?" he asks.

"Is that really important right now?"

"Well, you know, I'm just trying to figure out what's going on over there."

"Fine but—"

"And I tried calling Eric on his cell phone today, but he didn't pick up." A vein in Jack's forehead starts to bulge.

"You want to know what's going on? The usual. The day-to-day things that need to be done—school work, clean up, meals, that sort of thing. Conversations about their days, their friends, and their homework. As for the phone, he told me that he couldn't find his charger, so probably his battery is dead."

"That's sort of irresponsible, don't you think?"

"Maybe, but I may have misplaced it while I was cleaning. I'm sure it'll turn up soon. In the meantime, just call me if you want to chat with him."

He brushes his jaw line with his knuckles, possibly trying to think of some new line of reasoning that will underscore my incompetence and reduce me to dependency on him. "Are you taking the kids to church tomorrow?"

He thinks he has me on this point. I wish I could comment on the way political ideology has overshadowed mercy, forgiveness, and love in my old churches and how I'd rather not worship with people who think I'm an abomination, thanks just the same. I long to point out how disgusting it is to clap along to Las Vegas-style theatrics on behalf of my soul's simple longing to connect with Jesus. But it's a minefield I don't need right now. "No, I'm not."

"Susan," his gaze is an attempted mind-probe, "can you have dinner later?"

"Jack, I'm not looking for reconciliation. It's too late for that."

He exhales loudly, and then leans in, eyes flashing. "Damn it! Why are you doing this to me? To the kids? Is your *lifestyle* really that much better now that I'm out of the house?"

Lifestyle. All I can do is stare at him. Jill Scott scats in the background. My heart races. *He knows about Charlotte.*

He smells my fear and uses it. "You're crazy, you know that? Look at you! You're stressed; you sure don't look happy to me. What's wrong with you? You can't even—"

"What's wrong with *me*? Have you forgotten all the insults? All the arguments? Beer in my lap? I'm not saying it's all your fault—just that I'm not happy, and you aren't either. This hasn't worked for a long time, and you know it."

"Oh my God, you always cling to ancient history and your little grudges. You're unbelievable. Know this: I'm never going to give you a divorce."

The couple on the couch looks over at us. *I wish the music were louder.*

"Lower your voice! Look, this is a no-fault state; I don't need your approval. Besides, the kids—"

"The kids need discipline. They need a two-parent home and you—"

"Jack, stop it."

"No! They need to go to church. You better think about what you're up to—the consequences of what you're doing. I know more than you think I do, and I won't stand for it!"

So. More cold beer in my lap. He'll play every card he has to take the kids away from me.

Part of me wants to say, "Fine, whatever. I'll be leaving a last request that you try to be a better father—along with a footnote as to what to do with my body." At least, that's what I expect to feel. Deep down, a truer part of me whispers, "Take him on."

I will not leave my kids with this man as their only parent, especially now that his anger against me is so often aimed at them. They will not make important choices in life based on avoiding his anger. They will not grow up in a home filled with elephants like I did, not daring to speak of the great pachyderms of weird family behavior and its underlying forces. They will not squeeze themselves into emotional contortions to dodge the monstrosities of rigid, hateful, and irrational fundamentalist dogmas masquerading as Truth. I won't let them.

I walk out without another word.

I hardly trust myself to drive. I want to just sit in the over-warm car and grip the hot steering wheel to keep from shaking. But I don't want Jack to see me. If I show up at the kids' games, he might be there. My brain is a tossed salad. Toss me up into the clouds, see where I land—or not. I drive north for thirty minutes to Lake Conroe, thinking that I can't imagine how to summon the strength for the fight ahead.

On the road along the shoreline, I pull over, roll down the window, and breathe in the cool lake air, freshened by recent rain. *God, oh, God, how beautiful.* Tall southern pines sway, their balsam scent filling the woods. Children skip stones, and water sloshes as a motor boat passes by, heading away from the boat dock toward the northern end of the lake some five miles away. I drive on and soon reach a bend in the road that skirts a bank maybe ten feet above water level. I could speed up and just keep going, right over the edge. I picture it, can almost hear the splash, feel the cool water at first buoyant, then sucking the car down, filling the interior as I sink. This thought shuts off the spate of memories, self-accusation, fear, the scenarios based on fear, and the sound of Jack's voice, still fresh in my ears. I so want to be done with this shit.

Without speeding, I find a place to park near the bank, overlooking a deep section of the lake. Why waste a good car? Tears run down my cheeks. The old ducts must be pumping the last of the salt water in my reservoirs. I climb out of the car. I'm picturing my two darlings. And then Jack raising the kids without me, controlling every mundane thing in their life, their personal grooming, their homework, their posture. And meal times...

Leaning against a headlight, I barely notice a rowboat floating along in the distance. What I'm seeing instead is an evening a few months earlier. After my ninety-minute commute and picking the kids up at the sitter's, I'd hurried to make dinner, as usual.

Jack walked through the door, and Allie ran to greet him. I was relieved that he looked glad to be home. We sat down to dinner, the kids antsy, chuckling and chatting about Pokémon cards and episodes of *SpongeBob SquarePants*. Jack soon seemed bored. His apparent good mood had evaporated into dissatisfaction with the kids' behavior. He started in with the order in which food groups should be consumed.

"Eric, slow down on the potatoes, eat your pork chop. Allison, what are you doing? Sit up straight, don't forget to eat your corn."

I tried to steer things in a more positive direction. "What happened at school today, Eric?"

"Miss Bethel let us watch *Shiloh* in English today, but I liked the—"

"Eric, sit up! Speaking of school, have you started on your homework? What about the science project?"

"Jack, let him finish."

"Well, I'm trying to make sure he's on top of his studies."

"He is." I nodded at Eric. "Go on, honey."

"I liked the book better than the movie."

"That's usually how it goes." Had his father's lack of interest bothered him? I couldn't tell. "Allie, what's new with you at school?"

"We learned more about Christopher Columbus today."

"Remember when we saw his tomb in Spain?"

"Yeah, I tol' the teacher about that." My second-grader stood, found her backpack, and returned with a paper. "Okay, here are the three things I learned about Christopher Columbus for Miss Johnson's class: Number one, he made the Indians into slaves. Number two, he brought diseases to the New World, and number three, he died a poor man."

Stone silence until Eric laughed. I joined in, but Jack was a grump. (Had I done that to him or had he always been that way?)

"What do they teach you in that school?" Jack asked.

"Honey, didn't you learn any good things about Christopher Columbus?" I asked.

Eric answered for her as he so often does, "Dad, Mom, don't you see? She's not impressed by the discovery because she feels bad for the Indians. Right, Allie?"

My little girl looked at her brother with a why-is-he-the-only-one-who-gets-it look as she sat back down to the dinner table. My Allie typically ignored what impressed most people, and in her simple, little emperor's-new-clothes way, often told a bigger truth.

"You're awesome, sweetie." I squeezed her arm.

Jack just shook his head. "What kind of PC bullshit do they teach at Barbara Bush Elementary School?" he asked me later. "Don't indulge her so much. That child needs a firm grip to guide her." I disagreed. I preferred to give curious puppies a long leash.

❦

Thinking back on the first sign of my pregnancy with Allison reminded me that it was a time of crushing disillusionment with Jack. This was especially true since it was nearly two months after little Daniel's death in 1993, and I was still in grief.

"I'm late," I said, exiting our downstairs bathroom. After what we went through with Eric and all of the recent hospital drama, I was having a hard time. "I just really don't think I can bear the thought of another pregnancy."

Jack looked up from the newspaper. "But don't you think it would be fun to have another baby?"

I leaned on the kitchen counter. An airplane flying overhead was so loud I had to wait for a few moments before responding.

"You know I love babies, but I'm afraid, Jack." I waited for him to say something comforting.

If only his angels had whispered to him, *Psst! Here's what you say: sweetheart, I know that what we went through during Eric's birth was so traumatic that it might seem like we just can't go through it again, but we held onto each other and to our faith, and things came out fine, and I know we can do it again.* Jack would have been dumfounded a moment, but then he might have said just that. But Jack was not in contact with such angels and, in this case, had no natural instinct to be simply loving and empathetic.

His narrowed eyes conveyed disgust. "I wish you would have told me that before we got married."

That was Jack. He tended to launch preemptive strikes when something threatened his expectations. Power. Control. Counter-threat. Those were his main resources. So often, he seemed like a great guy with so much potential for happiness, and then—*Boom*. An emotional grenade would hit. One such statement could make all the goodness in him seem like an illusion.

The night I went into labor with Allison started with knifing pain followed by successive pains every minute. Apparently, she was anxious to arrive. Earlier that day, I'd told the doctor I thought the baby would be here soon. "No, I think you have a few more weeks to go," he'd said. So much for his professional opinion. I slowly made my way up the stairs, stopping midway up when another pain hit. Jack was asleep on the bed, the TV blaring.

"Jack, wake up—I'm in labor."

He grunted and rolled over. I repeated the news and watched him rub his eyes and yawn.

"What? No, no you're not."

"What do you mean?" Another pain hit me. I wanted to hit *him*. "Get up!"

Finally convinced *this was it,* he called his parents. We waited for them to arrive to watch Eric, and then we headed to the hospital. At the hospital, Jack told the admitting nurse I didn't need a private room. I stared him down and told her I most certainly did. He wasn't yet ready to give in.

"She's in a lot of pain and doesn't know what's best," he said. "She doesn't nee—"

I pounded my fist against his leg and demanded a private room. Afterwards, I told Dr. Chapman I wasn't looking for a beautiful experience, just a healthy baby and a way to get it over with as soon as possible. I wanted to "order" the C-section, because the pain came after the birth, when I could be certain the baby was okay. That seemed better than having pain while I was still worried about the baby's health. C-sections were controlled and familiar. The doctors though, encouraged me to have a vaginal birth, and I relented. The next morning, I kissed the head of a perfect baby girl and said a long prayer of thanks for the blessed difference between Allison's birth and the trauma of Eric's. Despite my fears, all was well. My sweet baby girl was here.

Three months after Allison's birth, Jack was offered a job in Houston, and we jumped at the chance to live in a warm climate for a few years. Our house sold quickly, so the kids and I joined Jack in Houston within a few weeks, moving into an apartment near his office. We planned to house-hunt together on the weekend, but Jack encouraged me to visit a particularly attractive and reasonably priced neighborhood he'd found earlier. When I called for directions, it was Charlotte who answered the phone.

❦

The sun sparkles on the lake, and I find I've wandered away from my car. Despite the warm rays, the shadows of the pines chill me as I pass through them. I am so locked into my dramas that I'm nearly oblivious to the tranquility around me. At least my ruminations have diverted me from walking ever deeper into the expanse of liquid blue. Yet, I think I'm still hoping to hear Jesus say, "It's okay, my child; come Home, if you want."

Thirty-four

Uncle Art

LOVE AT FIRST SOUND. SOMETHING inside me—call it my True
Nature, was repressed so far down, it was about to explode. I hadn't
even seen Charlotte, and yet she somehow spoke to that authentic
self lost inside me, her voice a mysterious life-line. By slow degrees,
I entered an emotional free-fall. I grew increasingly dissatisfied with
Jack's inability to be a loving partner. I wanted more love and honesty for my kids. At the same time, I started hating this inconvenient
True Nature of mine for its selfishness and weirdness. And I hated
accommodating the false Me as well. Madness, exhilaration, frustration, hope. Hot, cold. Come here. Go away. Sunlight and shade.

The dark shadows of the pines have lengthened, and the late
afternoon rays shine into my eyes. Joggers approach from one of the
lakeside communities up ahead, so I bend down to tie my shoe, not
wanting them to see the tear streaks or the bleakness in my face. One
of the Southern voices shares the honey-quality of Charlotte's, yet it
doesn't evoke a response in me the way her one sentence did five years
ago. After they pass, I head back to my car, struck by Charlotte's
voice and its strange cupid-arrow effect on me. I had kept this secret
from my friends for several years until Jodi came back into my life.
We sat on my patio and grilled steaks, and as usual, we analyzed and
re-analyzed both of our relationships.

"From the moment I heard her voice, I was done. I can't explain
why, but it was as if we already knew each other." This was well after
Jodi's does-she-have-to-hit-you-with-a-pan speech. "Not sure where

this is going to lead, but I love the way she makes me feel, and it's the truest thing I know."

Jodi smiled. "Yeah, it's good to be in love. Bad when it doesn't last or is polluted by booze." Her expression turned dark. "I thought I was in love with Annie, even after she started hitting me so hard I thought she'd kill me." She swigged her iced tea. "I hated myself so much, I didn't think I deserved any better."

"Oh, Jodi, I'm so sorry. Now you know you do, right?" I felt a little bit hypocritical asking this, because I understood it so well, the self-hatred that flares up, the accusing inner voices.

She'd looked away, as if in thought. "Yeah, I do know it. But sometimes it takes me awhile."

"I can't believe I wasn't there for you."

"It's okay; you're here for me now."

I regretted that I'd had to fall for a woman before I was able to understand and respect Jodi, but at least I'd made amends. And I'd also had a long, healing talk with Brian, my old crush from Miami who had considered the priesthood. He'd come to Houston for a visit. Sitting at a Mexican restaurant, I felt happy just being able to chat with him like old times. People often mistake him for being Hispanic or Arabic, but if they tried his made-from-scratch spaghetti sauce or watched him roll homemade gnocchi, they'd realize he was Italian-American through and through. I watched his soft brown eyes that evening as he told me a story I hadn't heard before.

He glanced over the menu. "Remember Jennifer? The girl I was dating when you and I first met?"

I leaned in. "How could I forget her? Her eyes flashed hatred every time we talked."

"Well, she was smart—she knew how I felt about you." He chuckled.

"I know, I know, you loved me. What can I say?" I smiled, remembering the rough texture of the beard he'd grown in college.

He smiled, stirred his margarita, and continued. "She lived a few doors down from my parents' house. While we were in junior and senior high, I went to her house all the time. We'd play Monopoly or Scrabble, and her whole family joined in." His eyes were tearing up.

I reached across the table and touched his hand as he continued.

"Her parents loved me, always said they wished they had a son just like me. It was nice. Didn't see them for a long time, ya know? I went out to South Dakota and worked at the Indian School. After that, I moved to Chicago and "came out." I guess the word spread fast to our small town back in Ohio." Brian tensed, his expression dour. "I was visiting my parents and thought I'd stop by and visit Jennifer's too. I was kinda nervous, but mainly in the way you are when you haven't seen someone for a long time. I rang their door and—"

"Tell me they were glad to see you," I interrupted.

"Not quite. Jen's dad answered the door with a look of hatred I'll never forget." Silence. Brian collected himself. "Then he pointed a shotgun at me and said, '*Faggot, get off my property.*'" A tear traveled down Brian's strong and sweet face.

I couldn't breathe.

"It hurts when people hate you for who you are, you know? But I tell ya, the alternative is worse."

"What's that?" I whispered, barely audible over the restaurant noise.

"When you hate yourself."

I nodded, too overwhelmed to speak. I knew exactly what he was talking about.

A devilish gleam appeared in his eyes. "Can I ask you something? Do you always do the hard thing? The thing that isn't you?"

"What d'ya mean?" I struggled to focus on the question instead of the image of a gun pointing in Brian's face.

His dark eyes bore into mine. "I mean, look, it's not a criticism, I think I've done a lot of that too. We met at Miami, remember? Wanna tell me it was a fit for either of us?"

I leaned back and sipped my beer. "No."

"Right, and then there's the little fact that you live in a master-planned community in *Texas*."

"Well, uh, yeah—"

"And *now*, you're attending the Southern Baptist Church? You? The one who does such a good job *submitting* to your husband?" Brian chuckled.

I was getting slightly irritated. "Yeah, really, but I don't think I always do the hard thing. My kids are easy. My marriage hasn't been easy lately. And yeah, where I live makes me crazy sometimes. And, well, the church wasn't hard *at first,* but now... You wanna hear something else? Now I'm in love with my best friend!"

His eyes widened. "Is your best friend a man?"

"Naw, that would be too easy."

He raised one of his incredibly perfect eyebrows and laughed.

"I know, I know. Can you ever forgive me for all my lecturing?"

"I already have."

Both Brian and Jodi would be furious with me if I took the easy way out now, but at least I no longer have to atone for judging them. I guess I've been building my case to Jesus. *See, Lord, Brian and Jodi were gracious enough to forgive me. Will you forgive me too? Can I come to You now?* Then I remembered one person to whom I didn't apologize.

❧

Jack, the kids, and I spent Christmas of 1993 at Aunt Nora's house. It would be the last family get-together before our move from Cleveland to Houston. During dinner, I put six-week-old Allison down for a nap and caught the tail end of a conversation between my cousins about Uncle Art.

"Yes, he's very sick—it's starting to affect his brain," my cousin Rick said between bites of ham and scalloped potatoes.

My cousin Karen looked concerned and put her fork down. "Does he have friends in Philadelphia who are helping him?"

"Yeah, he's still in Philly. Has a friend taking care of him, a woman who he's known for a long time—might be a neighbor or something."

"Can we visit him?" I interrupted.

"Other than Rick, he doesn't want to see anyone from the family."

A pang of guilt hit hard, and I stopped feeding Allison. By then, we all knew Uncle Art had AIDS, the unspoken disease of his unspoken orientation. He was dying without his family. The goodwill-toward-men idea of Christmas dissolved for me in that moment.

Within an hour, the phone rang. Aunt Nora's face changed as she heard Art's voice, her tall frame shrinking at the reminder of his existence.

She didn't say anything for a while, and I can only imagine what Art was saying on the other end—probably confronting her about why he was an outcast in his own family. We all avoided looking at each other as we strained to eavesdrop. "Art, you need to repent—we want you to be with us all in heaven." That must have been hard for him to believe, because we didn't seem to want him around here on earth. Had it taken him all of his forty-seven years to decide *not* to accommodate his family's discomfort with who he was? Had he finally decided that for too long he had dodged and weaved, carefully choosing even his pronouns to hide the existence of the people he loved?

Did he challenge Nora over the way his own blood kin had *shushed* him when he wanted or needed to share his real hopes and disappointments? Surely our lack of interest told him that we thought his life had somehow been less than ours, that we regarded it as shameful, insignificant, and sinful.

All I know is that her response hit him with a barrage of condemnation, complete with the ever-popular abomination card.

I felt sick inside as I turned to walk out of the kitchen. The phone slammed down hard, and Aunt Nora started to cry. Within six months, AIDS took Art. Now that I'm trying to face the truth about myself, I realize I'll never have the chance for healing and reconciliation with Dad's half-brother.

❧

I stop walking and face the lake. I'm so deeply sorry, Uncle Art. There are so many things I'd do over. But now, do I have to live out your same agony? Must I be an abomination in the sight of my family and others?

If it weren't for the children playing in the distance, I might scream *no* until my vocal cords ripped apart.

I can't stand it. I hate this vision of my future.

Jesus, surely you don't see me as an abomination? Your arms are open. You want me with you, don't you? Now?

No reply.

Maybe the idea of Jesus welcoming me with open arms is pure self-delusion—a particularly wretched form of lying?

I collapse, sobbing on a bed of pine needles. I just want to be loved. I don't really want to die, but I need love. Just as I am. I want to be loved *for* who I am. I want to express love. I want love to be what defines my relationships. I want a life full of love. I choose *love*! Why is that so damn hard?

The evening sun approaches the horizon, and I am spent. And terribly thirsty. I head back to the car. Walking beneath the tall pines, I'm grateful for their calming presence and take in their scent. The woods and the lake are more spiritually satisfying than church. I wish I could camp here and sleep in the arms of nature, where everything is so much simpler.

Ducks wintering at the lake fly into the inlet ahead, trusting its shelter for the night. Crows are calling to each other. I feel soothed and something more. The words to an old John Denver song come to me. "*I talk to God and listen to the casual reply...*" I may be starting to get what he meant. I was conditioned to expect a burning bush or a prophetic revelation, but maybe that's just naïve. Since church dogma is so tidy, I had unconsciously believed Nature and Truth were tied up in its neat, trim package as well. I believed it was the only clarification of our relationship to Whoever or Whatever sent us here. But those narrow dogmas are far too small.

Careful to avoid scaring the ducks, I bend down and wash my hands in the icy lake. I splash away the tear streaks, loving the sting of the cold water on my face—a get-your-act-together baptism.

Driving back south on the interstate to pick up the kids, I pass billboard after billboard that advertises everything from friendly churches and new neighborhoods to vasectomy reversals, the tall ugly signs a stark contrast to the lovely southern pines I'd just seen. I leave the lake with the realization that I have to find a way to break the chain of shame and suicide in my family. If I don't, I'll be a combination of my uncle, my aunts, *and* my father. Worse yet, my kids will be left to inherit the same.

All these years, I thought I hungered for righteousness, but I think it was actually authentic love, starting with a love of self, for which I was starving, along with a hunger for a Truth that didn't punish me for asking questions. Somehow I've been eating at a big fat banquet of misconceptions, swallowing them for years, digesting them as self-hatred, and then spewing forth in episodes of literal and emotional bulimia.

I'm gonna figure out a way to take responsibility and stop doing that. *My God!*

This new understanding hits me, an epiphany as personally powerful as Paul's road trip to Tarsus. A car honks behind me, and I see that the light has changed at the bottom of the off-ramp. I drive on.

One day I'll explain it to Jack and to everyone, starting with the kids. For now, after my own pep talk, I'll have a sit-down with Jesus. Tell Him that I won't take my life, but instead, do my best to live it as honestly as I can. It'll be a conversation wrapped in the hope that all these years I've been railing against a poorly conceived, vengeful, patriarchal Jehovah and the repackaged God of twentieth-century American marketing. Not the real One.

Thirty-five

The Healing Garden

NINE MONTHS AFTER MY ALMOST suicide year, I find myself in Los Angeles with an attractive woman I'm dating who has a kind heart, an easy laugh, and an inquisitive nature. Leslie has convinced me to attend something called a *Fearless Living* seminar. I'm wary, thinking it might be a New Age flight to the lunatic fringe, but I decide to go, thinking that living without fear sounds like a good goal. What strikes me most are not the tips and techniques but the stirring stories of the other twenty participants. I guess I should have expected people who'd been traumatized to be attracted to this sort of thing. Still, I had no idea how inspiring it would be to spend a weekend hearing so many stories of survival from those who want to thrive beyond their bad experiences.

The trainers, Grace and Rosie, set the stage with inspiring stories of their own, allowing themselves to be vulnerable and open while keeping us in a comfort zone of love and laughter. After the seminar, I hired them both as "life coaches" to help me maneuver through my new focus on personal responsibility and more honest living. "Have I known you in another life?" I ask Grace. "Oh that's right, I don't believe in reincarnation."

"I do," she says, not unexpectedly. I laugh often with Grace on the phone and am surprised that healing, though difficult, makes me feel so incredibly lighthearted.

Eight months later, Leslie, whom I've grown to love deeply, and I are at a local spa, unaware that I'm about to meet yet another person who will help me.

"I hope I get a female massage therapist," I tell her after we've signed in. I didn't feel comfortable with a man seeing my cellulite and making some sort of evaluation. The first therapist who comes to the door is as a big guy, about 6'3". He shuffles some papers, looks up, and calls her name. I feel relief. Then a young African-American woman enters the waiting room and looks at the chart.

"Susan?"

"That's me," I say. She's too young to understand cellulite or wrinkles.

"Hi, I'm DaRhonda." We shake hands. Her warm eyes immediately make me feel that things are going to be fine. DaRhonda shows me to the room and leaves, allowing me privacy as I disrobe and slide in under the white sheets of the massage table.

DaRhonda returns and plays a CD of nature sounds, lights some candles, and asks, "Do you have any health concerns I should know about?"

Forty-seven complaints come to mind, but I simply mention the fibromyalgia that precludes deep tissue massage. We talk about what I might do to feel better. She starts working on the knots in my back and neck.

"Do you mind if I ask you a question?"

I try to get comfortable on the table. "Go ahead."

"Normally I don't dive in with clients like this, but, well…can you tell me about your book?"

"My book? What do you mean?"

"You're writing a book, yes?"

"Well, um, yes, I am. How'd you know?"

She pauses, then says matter-of-factly, "I heard it when I shook your hand."

"What?"

"Well, yeah, that's really the only way for me to describe it."

I'm frowning, but not from the magic her hands are working on my knotty muscles. "Did you *hear* anything else about me?"

"Well, yes, but first tell me about your book."

"Okay. Well, it's an historical novel set in Civil War Spain. I studied there during college and passionately loved the country and the people. Over the years, people have told me about their civil war experiences, and I based my fictional characters on the stories I heard. I'm writing about it because I think what happened there in the thirties is a picture of what's happening in the world today."

"So, it's about Spain?"

"Well, it's *set* in Spain."

DaRhonda the massage therapist/savant was silent, and then she took a breath and suddenly she got way more animated.

"Momma, that ain't the book."

"Excuse me?" I said, shocked to hear her demeanor and accent change so suddenly. "What did you say?"

DaRhonda continued in her more animated tone. "I said that's not the book you're supposed to write—at least not the first one."

"Okay, you're freaking me out. What are you talking about?"

"Well, I heard that you're going to tell *your* story."

She finishes her massage, and I ungracefully lift myself off of the massage table, clutching the white sheet to make sure nothing falls out. *Who is this person?*

DaRhonda proceeds to tell me that she knows I've gone through a painful divorce, and that I'd fallen in love with my best friend several years earlier. She knows I've been struggling to accept myself as a gay woman, and she's hearing that God has something in mind for me.

How can she possibly know this? I live forty-five minutes away and don't know anyone who lives in the city except Leslie. DaRhonda doesn't know either of us; she couldn't have even seen us together. How can she know that my divorce feels right for me but has been grueling? She knows that I have children whom I adore and need to protect, an ex-husband I don't want to hurt, and a Church that tells me I'm an abomination of the worst kind. Has someone slipped her the *Cliff Notes* version of my life? This is all overwhelming, but I can't seem to tell her to back off. Do the spa people know she talks like this to their clients? I look into her eyes to see if I can discern any cynicism, but instead, I'm even more on her wavelength.

"How old are you?" I ask. "Because you seem like five hundred, but look about twenty-five!"

She laughs. "I'm thirty."

"How do you know all of this about me? Are you, like, Yoda or something? What religion are you?"

"I'm a Christian. Actually, this is my last day here. I've been working on my master's degree in psychology and also have a consulting business. Puttin' it all together, ya know? Seein' what He has in store for me as I claim a victory, knowin' I'm more than a conqueror in Christ, Jesus."

Whoo boy. I'm not sure what to think of DaRhonda's *gifts*, or even if I trust her yet. People have done stupid things on the advice of psychics and religious savants, but what harm can come from writing a book? I wonder how this surreal experience has come out of a simple day at the spa. I'm especially taken by the fact that although she has an intuitive gift, she is using a vocabulary I recognize from my Evangelical roots.

"Okay, well I want to hear more about your business. What's your last name?"

A split second before she answers, I hear it in my head and say it with her.

"Williams," we say in stereo.

Holy Moses! How did I know this? "This is freaking me out."

DaRhonda suggests we meet for lunch, and I agree, setting in motion our weekly calls. On one of our phone calls, she urges me to re-connect with God. "God has so much for you, and He wants you to receive it, but you don't have time, can't get there, are too ashamed or fearful about everything. Listen, God is saying, It's time to *show up.*"

As if I hadn't been trying. I put the call on speakerphone and pour myself a Diet Coke, reminding myself not to let my frustration over her inane advice come through as defensiveness. "Okay, I have no idea where you think I should go or what you think I should do to *show up*! Do you mean I should pray?"

DaRhonda giggles. "I mean you should *listen*."

"Well, how the hell do I do that?" I yell at the receiver.

She guffaws. "You know this, but you're fighting it."

I grab the phone and fumble for the button to get it off *speaker*. "Just tell me, will you?"

"I'll give you a break since you're on vacation. Look, what you need to do is set aside time to just get *still* and *listen* to what God is saying. Some people might call it meditation, others prayer, and maybe it's both."

Another sigh. "DaRhonda, I have a hard time praying right now— pretty hard when all the people you went to church with think that you're now damned to hell. I mean, what am I supposed to say?"

"Why do you think we know each other?"

"I needed someone short to bug me?"

Laughter. She thinks we were brought together for a reason and that God has a plan for me. "I don't understand it. I'm not gonna make a judgment about your lifestyle, but..."

"Lifestyle, huh? I hate that word. I don't have a lifestyle, other than being a working mother in the suburbs."

"Okay, sorry, but what I'm trying to get you to see here is that God is the Unending Source Who wants you to take your place, wants you to have peace." DaRhonda convinces me to get up at 5:30 A.M. to have a conversation with God.

The alarm goes off the next morning. I consider skipping the session, but when it comes to blowing off God, it's pretty hard to come up with a story you can get away with. After I struggle out of bed, I stumble the ten paces to my family room couch. *Should I kneel?*

No, I think I will just sit and maybe lean forward a bit, with my elbow on my knee and my hand under my chin like Rodin's *Thinker*. I soon realize that this is not the proper posture, but my real problem is that I can't stop thinking. I've never been formally diagnosed with attention deficit disorder, but it would come as a surprise to no one if I had been.

Dear God,
    I'm here, like DaRhonda said I should be.

Wait, what day is it? Oh no, I forgot to finish my status report for work. Oh, wait, I was praying. Sorry, God. Okay, see? What am I doing?

I decide to picture myself on a rowboat. Rosario once told me that Jesus came to her in a dream and sat in a rowboat. Look, God, here I am on the boat. I'm here to listen to what you have to say to me. I'm going to try to keep my mind from flitting all over the place. Not sure it's possible, but I am trying. Please reveal yourself to me. I really want to know what you want from me. Honestly, I've been avoiding talking to you because it's scary to think that maybe now you hate me.

Nothing happens, but then again, I feel good for my efforts. I also didn't get struck dead by an angry God throwing lightning rods.

※

DaRhonda joins Grace and Rosie as part of my crack team of experts who encourage me to take steps toward a life that is more mine—more *me*. She finds a writer's conference about which she'd heard good things and persuades me to attend. In October, I head to California for the *La Jolla Writer's Conference*. "Baby steps, Susan, baby steps."

While crossing the street in front of my La Jolla hotel, I nearly pass out. It's not surprising. For years, my heart has chugged and slowed and now it's beyond the point that I can ignore. When I return to Houston, a famous cardiologist orders a host of tests administered by an alarmed technician. The results: my heart is stopping for *eight to ten seconds* at a time. "What would you do if you had these results?" I ask the technician.

"See that door? I'd *run* for a pacemaker."

The next morning, my cardiologist is equally alarmed and schedules a pacemaker implantation surgery for the following day, which happens to be Election Day 2004. I feel that this heart problem stems from my bulimia, but there has been so little research into this area that no one can say for sure. Home and a bit rattled by the news, I need a diversion. I hop on our clunky gray tandem and start pedaling as fast as the beast can travel. It feels good to get my heart pumping; sitting for long periods of time is the dangerous thing. I breathe in the cool November air and feel grateful for everything. Trees, bike trails, my awesome Allie and Eric—and the invention of *pacemakers*.

The following morning, I'm wheeled in for my titanium ticker. When I awake from the anesthesia, I find that my home state of Ohio puts Bush back in the White House for another term. Pundits chalk it up to Republican scare tactics related to gay marriage. (That's right, the real threat to America and American marriages is not spousal abuse, financial and parenting pressures, miscommunication, or even divorce, but same-gendered people wanting to get married.)

The next day, Eric and Allison hug me when I come through the door, arm in a sling, election-day dismay on my face. "Mom, come see what I made you," Allie says and leads me to the kitchen to see a sign on the fridge decorated with a picture of cowboy hat with a red circle and slash: "No Cowboys for President—Get Well Soon." I laugh and my stitches hurt, but I don't care.

As we slide into the holidays, I easily recover from my surgery, even after receiving a call from the doctor's office telling me I had a brain tumor. Never mind, I didn't and I don't.

Late one night, I'm determined to heal not just my body, but also my spirit. I sit in my study and make a list of all of the things Jack did right during our sixteen years of marriage. It's longer than I would have created even just the year before. Holidays seem like the time to reconnect, and the next day Charlotte and I meet for dinner and a gift exchange. We keep up with each other every few months, trying our hardest to resurrect at least the remains of a basic friendship, never really getting there. She hands me a small box, beautifully wrapped. How can I be seeing what I'm seeing? I remove a silver angel engraved with a quote from Helen Keller:

> What we have once enjoyed we can never lose....All that we love deeply becomes a part of us.

Nodding and smiling at her shining eyes, I hand her a present. She gasps when she opens it to find *the very same angel*.

I have the strangest feeling that finally, at age forty-three, I'm growing up.

❧

My hands. They remind me of my dad's as I fidget with my scarf, then my jacket. I smooth my pants down three and four times, my nerves kicking in. Dad did that too. Déjà vu. I've rented a space at the famed *Rice Hotel* for the first showing of the Alex Daniyel Gallery.

DaRhonda helped me come up with the gallery name. Alex, meaning *Defender of Mankind* and Daniyel, *God is my judge.* I thought I'd use it for both my art business and as a pen name because DaRhonda said, "Susan Parker couldn't write this book. You have grown into a new person and so need a new name." She was right at the time, but after years of writing and re-writing, what I find is that I didn't need a new name or a new me, I just needed to get back to the true me.

It's spring. New beginnings and all that. DaRhonda and I had continued to speak by phone nearly every week. She convinced me to take the plunge and organize an art show downtown. I'm constantly amazed that DaRhonda doesn't judge me, admits she doesn't understand everything about God—thank goodness—herself, or me, and doesn't need to in order to believe that God wants to use me for good. At least, it's a different take than most Evangelicals seem to have.

Jodi and my sister, Ann, have flown in; they've worked all day to help Leslie and me set things up. Before I greet the guests, I remove a light blue artist's apron from my canvas bag. I think about the last time I saw Dad wearing it. He had been working on a landscape oil, excited about the progress he'd made. Walking to the entrance, I drape his paint-stained apron over an easel: "Thanks, Daddy, for sharing your love of art with me. I think you're going to like the show we've put on."

Thirty-six

Yoda's Dream

EIGHT WEEKS AFTER THE ART show, the kids and I fly to Cleveland
for a visit. They are happily baking cookies with my ex-mother in-law
when I slip out for a walk. I'm getting better at my quiet times with
the Creator. I drive my dinky, white Korean rental car to a nearby
park that is a section of Cleveland's 20,000-acre Emerald Necklace.
Ten minutes later, I park the car under a canopy of trees and feel
an immediate rush of peace. I locate a winding path among soaring
deciduous trees, whose roots cling to the black earth despite the blus-
ter of wind, the weight of many snows, and the freeze and crack of
ice. These trees stand strong, calmly watching over whatever comes
their way. Stable, serene, composed.

I hike for an hour, soaking in the tranquility, and then cross a
softball field to get back to my car. I grab my water bottle and granola
bar and head for a shady table on the other side of the field, bringing
Anne Lamott to share the mini-picnic with me.

I settle in to read her words, picking up where I'd left off the night
before, and come to a passage near the end of the book stressing the
importance of determining how to spend the one unique and precious life I've been given. Lamott affirms that I must let go of the
illusion of control to explore my true spiritual identity. This woman
knows me.

> ... [you] can close your eyes and feel the divine spark concen-
> trated in you, like a little Dr. Seuss firefly.

Yep, she's talking to me right here under these trees, encouraging my quiet response to nature. I love it that she's okay with not being able to fully explain the spiritual. I watch a small brown squirrel eye me suspiciously as he hides an acorn in the dirt and then scurries for the safety of a tall oak. The sky overhead is clear. A powerful sense of well-being fills me, and I think of the hot evenings when Dad, Ann, and I caught fireflies at Gramma's house so many years ago.

Reading on, I enjoy Lamott's image of the firefly God-spark flaring up inside when it encounters something the soul knows to be true, the way a tourist experiences grateful relief upon hearing her native tongue spoken on a journey through a strange land. My firefly spark glows inside me with Lamott's reminder that what really matters in life is loving freely and being loved, remembering moments of beauty—simple non-original messages, but deeply satisfying.

I breathe in that calm, quiet moment of comfort. Deep inside, I feel that is a manifestation of a small voice of assurance that gives me the sense that I'm not alone.

I'm grateful to DaRhonda. Although an Evangelical and completely straight, she is part of the quiet chorus. She said God told her I needed to get up off the floor and *stand*. If that were true, then *this* God also knows that it is unfair and unjust to reduce me—and others like me—down to nothing more than definitions of our sexuality.

Maybe I can't silence every self-righteous Evangelical or discredit the Levitical texts once and for all. Maybe I can't explain very much about this God of subtleties and mercy who somehow uses lakes, tall trees, music, and the voices of children to make me feel loved. Maybe it's bizarre that a diminutive massage therapist has reconnected me to the Creator. None of this will stop the flow of love around me now. I am determined to follow God as honestly as I can perceive Him and be something more than the angry, depressed person I used to be. I will defy the hundreds of millions of religious people on the planet who consider me an abomination. I will find the courage to speak with dignity, yet ask relentlessly: *How dare you be so cruel? How dare you invoke the Creator as part of your hatred and cruelty? How dare you assume God's role as my judge?*

Maybe instead of slogging around in the deep end of my misery, I will stride confidently on solid ground through an honorable, meaningful, loving life.

❦

I'd been going to Spain every year since 1983—the diet, the generous hospitality, the relaxed pace, the country's lifestyle and people all better for me than any resort or health spa.

Hablas muy bien, they tell me every year. Every year I remind them that part of the reason I speak the language as well as I do is because they repeat themselves so often, making it so much easier to learn. They laugh and nod, and then repeat what I just said, making me laugh. The kids and I always revel in the sun and sea and a culture that revolves around food and family with late night dinners and strolls along crowded city streets until two or three in the morning.

This year, I finally have the chance to return the favor in my home in Houston and am hosting the son of Carmen and Adolfo, Fito— little Daniel's big brother. I've seen him and his parents every year since Daniel's death thirteen years earlier. Our friendship was born in the most difficult of circumstances and cultivated through the years with a deep connection ingrained with laughter and understanding. Over the years, I've watched Fito grow up to be the handsome and charming twenty-two year-old now sitting in front of me at a Houston Starbucks.

"Susan, when my brother died I was only nine, but the sadness in our family was nearly unbearable."

"Oh, I know. It was just so awful." Even now, my words seem horribly inadequate.

"I loved my little brother so much. It was lonely. My parents, so depressed."

I watch his big brown eyes tear up, and remember the way little Daniel looked in the ICU.

"Your annual visits brought light to our household—more than you know."

My turn with the waterworks. His words soothe in the way that touching a wound, even to apply a balm, is painful. I brush away a tear, reminded of how much I love this boy and his whole extended family. "The love of your parents and others in Sevilla helped me get through so many difficult times. Originally, I thought I went to Spain for adventure, and I found it—but what I realize now is that I went there to find a branch of my family."

Fito reaches over and touches my hand, and I can't stop the tears sliding down my face. I haven't yet told him about my new "lifestyle." This terrifies me, but I must be loved now for my whole self and not a play-acted role of a straight person.

I cower, staring into the depths of my coffee cup. "I'm afraid to lose that, you know?"

"Susan, you cannot lose that. We *are* a family."

I take in a deep breath. "Do you know that Leslie is my girlfriend?"

Fito brushes the tear on my cheek and lifts my chin, reminding me of how demonstrative my Spanish "relatives" are. His brown eyes fixate on mine. "Of course, Susan."

More tears. My challenge now is to keep from weeping any more. I break the profound eye contact and drain the last dregs of my coffee.

"Is this what you're worried about? She seems like a lovely person, just like you."

More drama at Starbucks. I hug this sweet, gorgeous young man whom I love like a son.

❦

I am on a business trip; my job as a sales person and recruiter takes me on the road. This week I'm checked into an AmeriSuites hotel near DFW airport. I spend the evening on my computer, following up on paperwork and client correspondence. Early the next morning, the hotel's wake-up call shocks me into consciousness. I plan to finish my appointments early so I can begin the four-hour drive back home after lunch. There is no room service, and the stale doughnuts and coffee in the lobby don't interest me. What time is it again? Seven-forty-something. I bump my knee on the corner of the desk and curse, as I check my calendar. There by the 8:00 A.M. slot: *call with DaRhonda*. Ugh. I'm in no mood to talk about my life right now.

I stand up and try to stretch my aching back, then shuffle over to the counter where the tiny, plastic coffee maker is. I turn on the faucet to fill the carafe. My mind wanders and the water overflows. *I'm tired and just want to go home!* I open the gold and green packet of coffee and breathe in the strong smell. I check outside my door for a newspaper and then remember the no-frills location. Dressed, coffee ready, I am seated and uninterested when my cell phone rings.

"Wassup, momma?"

"Hey, Yoda, what's goin' on?"

"Well, I'm fine. Looking forward to the weekend. Why don't we get started? But first—where are you?"

"I'm in Dallas on business in my hotel room."

"Oh, okay, well what are we talkin' about today?"

DaRhonda has this way of pretending that I am actually in charge of the conversation/session. Still, I play along, because frankly, I'm not in the mood for any of it. Not analyzing my mother, not talking about why I haven't talked to my kids about Leslie yet, and certainly not things that happened in my childhood.

"Maybe we could talk about nothing. How 'bout that?"

"Naw, c'mon now, you know that won't do, so let me tell you about a dream I had last night that was odd."

I'm surprised to find that DaRhonda sounds nervous; I can always tell because she does the same thing that MJ does: she laughs and the pitch of her voice changes.

"Well, I had this dream that you were in this large gray bathroom, with all of these people who were lying around on the floor because they were in some kind of trouble. You walked around and reached down and helped them up, one by one and walked them out into the sunshine and into a beautiful field that appeared."

I sit up straight. "You dreamt this last night?"

"Yes. The field was peaceful and beautiful, and it kept gettin' more and more beautiful, but rather than stay out there, you kept goin' back in the bathroom and picking people up off the floor. Does that mean anything to you?"

I blink several dozen times. "Yeah. It does."

"Well, why don't you tell me how it makes sense, because it didn't make any sense at all to me. I told my husband, Anthony, about it. I said, 'Anthony, how am I gonna ask her 'bout some bathroom?' He said I should just tell you like I'm tellin' you, but, ya know, I'm nervous because I thought you'd think I was crazy."

"Well, I mean, it makes sense to me because, well, when I was eleven my Dad tried killing himself."

"How come I don't know about this?"

"I dunno—we never got there, I guess—I don't think about it anymore."

"So, tell me what happened then."

"Well, he took an overdose in the bathroom. My mom was screaming, and I ran upstairs with her and saw him lying on the bathroom floor in his underwear. She was really upset and was yelling at him and crying and asking him what he had done. We could see the bottle of pills that was empty. She told me that she was going to call the ambulance, and that he needed to be kept moving. I'm feeling stressed out just thinking about it—can you tell?" I have to take a deep breath, and another.

"Yes. Tell me what happened next."

"Well, my mom went to call the ambulance, and I reached down and picked him up off of the floor—or else, wait, I think she helped me get him off the floor, and then she went to call an ambulance. Then I walked him down the short hall to their bedroom and kept him moving the best I could."

"Was he totally out of it?"

"Mostly, although I remember that I begged him not to die. I told him I wouldn't trade all of my baseball cards for him, that I loved him...I dunno, just sort of begging him to keep fighting and reminding him that I loved him and needed him."

"Then what?"

"Well, I got tired—or he did, don't remember which—but we walked over to the bed, and I sat him down, making sure not to allow him to lie down."

"And?"

"And then, I pulled him up to a standing position again and walked him around some more. The emergency squad came in sometime after that, and they talked about pumping his stomach. One of them ushered me out of the room. I remember then that my friend's mom, Mrs. Bowen, came over and walked me down to her house. It was raining and there was a crowd gathered, I guess because of the siren and all."

"So, who does that?"

"Excuse me?"

"Who reaches down and picks up a suicidal and grown man off of the floor? Who does that?"

"I dunno, I mean, my mom might have told me to do it and might even have helped me get him off the floor. I can't remember. All I know is that I was left to walk him around the room until help arrived."

"Exactly! So, how long do you think it took your mother to call the ambulance?"

"I dunno, although I do remember she ran back downstairs. *Hmmm...* I wonder why she did that since there was a phone in her bedroom."

"Go on."

"Well, I don't know, although I was in there with my dad long enough to babble about a lot of things—my coins, baseball cards, all kinds of I'll-do-anything-just-hang-on things."

"Who else was in the house with you that day?"

"My little sister and my grandmother."

"Your grandmother—your dad's mom?"

"Yes."

"Why didn't she help walk him around the room?"

"I don't know—I never thought about it—just like I never thought about why my mom took so long and never came back upstairs to spell me off."

A pause.

"How old is Allison?"

"Eleven." I am lying on the bed now, exhausted from the memory of it all.

DaRhonda's really getting excited now. "That's about same age you were when this happened, right?"

"Yeah."

"So, again I ask you—*Who does that?* Honey, can you for one instant imagine Allison walking her daddy around the room like that?"

"No."

"So the answer is, '*no one* does that!' Can you see how *big* this is? I don't know anyone who would have the strength to reach down and pick that man off of the floor—whether or not it was your idea or your momma's."

"Okay."

"So, now let's go back to my dream—this is amazing. Do you see it now? You have been spending your whole life since that day—goin' in the crummy bathroom, pickin' people up off the floor! And it didn't matter whether it was your idea or your mother's—you did it, and I don't know any eleven-year-olds that could do that."

"I guess I never really spent much time thinking about it. I guess that's why I haven't told you about it before."

"Well, you need to think about it because there are lessons here: first, that you are very strong; you have a purpose, but you can't get to it if you're tryin' to save everybody. That's not how it was meant to be. You're meant to be out in that beautiful field in the sunshine!"

DaRhonda goes on and on, a preacher on fire. Somehow it sinks in.

I put the phone down, my hands shaking. I feel like I've just awakened from a dream, my foggy head trying to make sense of it all. My cell phone rings, but I ignore it and get up and walk to the window. Pushing aside the vinyl-lined drapery and looking out over the drab, flat, and treeless scenery, it hits me:

I've been trying to pick people up off of the floor ever since my eleventh birthday.

I may have helped some, but the problem was I was stuck in that egocentric, child-like view that I could save people, that it was *up to me* to save them. Not even *Susan-to-the-Rescue* could change the fact that sometimes people die. Relationships end. I'd been living to resuscitate lives and improve circumstances while extinguishing my own, maybe even to *compensate* for extinguishing my own priorities. Not only did it not work, it sometimes made things worse and left me angry, depressed, and disillusioned. I'd failed at my task. I'd failed God.

How it boosted my damaged ego to envision myself as God's special agent. How it devastated me to know I wasn't. And now, how liberating.

This strange role has been my choice, and I am finally realizing that I will not only let it go, I will also accept responsibility for it. With DaRhonda's help and that of my friends, I'm also gently forgiving myself.

Even now, Susan-to-the-Rescue would love to save the world from itself, save gay people from the narrow-minded judgment and hate the Evangelicals have inflicted on them, rescue Christianity from all forms of power-mongering and ignorance. Yet all I have to offer are my small truths, written and sent with love.

⁂

Nearly six years after my suicidal meltdown, I'm wearing a "Life is Good" T-shirt. My heart is still ticking, thanks to my pacemaker. My fibromyalgia is mostly in check, and I've even started working out on a regular basis with Manny, my fun-loving seventy-four- year-old personal trainer who likes to spout off on his Fox-News-Induced politics while I pump iron.

Despite the divorce, my kids are happy and healthy and have a better relationship with their father, who lives nearby and stops by often. Jack and I first "talked" about the rest of the truth about our marriage breakup via e-mail. (Some things never change). I asked for his forgiveness for not being forthright, for the big part I played in the failure of our marriage. Mostly, he has granted it.

Eric enjoys a full academic scholarship in a nearby university, and Allie excels in art. She's also a budding comedian who keeps me laughing, while I keep providing her material.

We don't live with an elephant in the living room anymore. The kids know who I am dating. My mother continues on with a smile and an amazingly good attitude despite all the difficulties she's faced in her life. I know she prays for my *deliverance* and behind my back tells people I'm too busy with the kids for dating or a relationship. To my face, she refuses to acknowledge any female romantic interest in my life, but is otherwise loving and kind until she experiences moments of fear and frustration and calls me "sick"—something I'm trying to overlook, knowing it's all part of her journey through the fear created by great masses of Evangelicals and politicians ranting in God's name.

While it's not easy to give up the privileges that heterosexuals enjoy and join a maligned minority, it's been worth it. I know people look at me differently when they understand I identify with the LGBT community, but it's a consequence I manage to accept. To get here, I had to lose something, had to disassemble the old me to find the real one. I had to deconstruct old beliefs rooted in the history of both sides of my family, a history steeped in shame, fear, and hiding. Some might say that our clan was crazy, but maybe we were just depressed because we were constructing lives that were not really ours. We needed to reclaim ourselves from institutions that discourage its members from thinking for themselves, owning their own feelings, and being unique.

I've tried to help my kids maneuver through the religious and cultural complex too. Now that Eric is in college, he no longer needs my help. Allie worries. She's heard homophobic comments; knows a girl at her high school who is taunted because she "has two mothers." For her sake, we don't put out any Rainbow Pride flags, but we also don't hide. It's a process, a balancing act. I won't sit small, quietly apologetic, on a shelf so as not to disturb others, carefully choosing my pronouns or hiding pictures of loved ones to avoid inquiry. I won't get in anyone's face, but neither will I accept the kind of judgment that says I'm deceived, wrong, sick, or damned for being myself and loving whom I love.

Much of what I thought was Christianity was really a cultural construct benefiting pastors and televangelists. I became more a follower of an American marketing-inspired lifestyle than a disciple of the profound love that Jesus of Nazareth had in mind. God is so much bigger than my old orthodoxies.

As human beings, we are so much more than sheep. While I can appreciate the imagery of the Good Shepherd, I don't believe Jesus intended for us to be two-legged members of the genus *Ovis*, blindly following any self-proclaimed "Godly" shepherd and bleating *Amens* to blind hatred. I've thrown off my fleece along with my fear. I defy the Evangelical herd in favor of a world of personal faith less certain but more authentic.

DaRhonda always reminds me that God said to *stand*. So, here I am, sometimes shaky and often burdened with the doubts I find preferable to a dogmatic certainty that destroyed the faith of my youth and nearly destroyed me. Here I stand, no longer intimidated by deceitful messages that whisper and scream in both subtle and obvious attempts to invalidate, taint, and damn. I've moved beyond the falsehoods of those who have the arrogance to claim to speak for God and I've stepped into *my place* here, in this, *my* life.

God has entrusted me with this story I call mine. While it hasn't been an easy road, neither has it been the hardest. I am grateful. I have dignity.

As in my old King-of-the-Mountain days, I stand with pride, but this time, it is locked so powerfully inside that no one can take it from me again. I define who I am in the humbling light of an honesty born from my journey so far.